ane 22 Wed.

# THE REFERENCE S...

## Volu...

## Volume XII. $6

## Volume XI. $6

THE  REFERENCE  SHELF

Vol. 16                                                    No. 7

# RECONSTITUTING THE LEAGUE OF NATIONS

COMPILED BY
JULIA E. JOHNSEN

THE  H.  W.  WILSON  COMPANY
NEW YORK                                              1943

# PREFACE

Among the many plans proposed for the establishment of an international or world postwar order, that of a reconstituted or revitalized League of Nations is generally accorded a foremost place. The League of Nations has the distinctive status of an already existing concern. Temporarily in eclipse by reason of world conditions, it retains, nevertheless, an appreciable background of properties, working organization, expert personnel, and an experience in world affairs covering more than two decades. It represents an established precedent and far-reaching loyalties; and it commands a substantial sentiment for its retention both here and throughout the rest of the world.

Among observers best fitted to evaluate the League there is little question as to the impressive record it has made in its technical, humanitarian and other nonpolitical activities. More controversial, however, are the political aspects of the League's life. Here there is an admitted series of both failures and successes. Outstanding is its acknowledged inadequacy in the events leading up to the present great world tragedy. That a plethora of new plans are now being discussed in which the League's existence is dismissed with perhaps a brief account of its deficiencies, calls attention to the great desirability at this time of a more widespread understanding of its intrinsic values and constructive possibilities.

Today, in considering such an understanding, we may well join other commentators in asking: Has the League failed or have we failed? Is the League structure defective or have we failed to make use of it or to use it rightly? Were we ready in the past to understand and undertake world responsibilities? And if we are more ready today might we not reasonably ask whether the League would not be as successful as any other plan, if reconstituted with the same painstaking concern as is proposed for a new international organism?

There appear to be varying opinions as to what may be assumed by a "reconstituted" League. On the one hand there is discussion of a revived League with "no essential change in its purpose, structure, or function," and on the other the differences between a reformed League and a completely new international organization are minimal in that the latter would without doubt embody any lessons which experience with the League has made clear. Between these views appear a variety of suggestions, among others, a reformed or a new Covenant, provisions for executive or world military powers, structural changes embodying any principles needed to establish world security and welfare, and its retention as a nucleus upon which almost any structure of collaboration among nations can be built.

Prior to the establishment of the League of Nations in 1919, throughout the debates over our adherence to it, and over the years of its subsequent operation, much discussion has grown up around it. Such material is widely available, and today interest in the League's immediate present and future, in line with a postwar plan, is paramount. This book has endeavored to present up-to-date discussions, with such background as seems essential, for and against the League as a continuing factor in our international life. In making a relative division it is perhaps important to realize that discussion of alternative forms of organization or of principles to be embodied does not necessarily imply an adverse attitude by an author to a reconstituted League. Where international modes of thought prevail the advocacy of a plan preferred or under immediate review may not of itself constitute the rejection of another.

For the convenience of debaters and others wishing comparative discussions the bibliography has been grouped into general, affirmative and negative sections. Alternative forms of postwar world organization have been covered amply in several preceding numbers of the *Reference Shelf* and are here given sparingly except for the more recent references. The reader is referred to the earlier books for such discussions as may seem called for.

The compiler acknowledges the many courtesies that have facilitated the preparation of this book, with special thanks to authors and publishers for copyright permissions, and to the Woodrow Wilson Memorial Library which gave access to various materials not available elsewhere.

JULIA E. JOHNSEN

October 5, 1943

# CONTENTS

# GENERAL DISCUSSION

## THE COMING REVIVAL OF THE
## LEAGUE OF NATIONS [1]

As the perplexed peoples of the world go through a new bath of blood and a fresh orgy of suffering, they find themselves in the broken-hearted world predicted by Woodrow Wilson if they rejected the League of Nations. The plain people everywhere, muddled, suffering, taxed to death, are asking what is wrong with the world. What can be done to set humanity on a better course after these terrible wars are over?

Twenty-odd years ago a minority group in the United States Senate defeated Wilson, yes, but they also defeated the American people and dealt a telling blow to democracy by recording a triumph of minority rule in the powerful Foreign Relations Committee of the Senate and sabotaging the only constructive plans to save democracy and the world, viz., the League of Nations and the World Court. The American boys who died on Flanders Field were betrayed; their last sacrifices came to naught. Their supreme gift for democracy and for a warless world was thrown into a political and personal wrangle and dumped into the discard—at least, up to the present time. But we may yet be able to build something to pay for their sacrifices; we shall have a second chance to set our course along the pathway of genuine international cooperation.

Before a builder can construct a building, before an engineer can erect a Golden Gate Bridge, he must have a blueprint. It is so with great social advances. Somebody must map out the ideological blueprint. This has been done for us by some of the great men of the past. Dante, Crucé, Grotius, Penn, Kant, Bolivar, and many others have told us that the prospects for world peace would be greatly increased if we had (1) some

[1] By J. Eugene Harley, Professor of Political Science, University of Southern California; President of the League of Nations Association, Southern California Branch. *World Affairs Interpreter.* 12:235-46. October 1941.

form of a league or association of civilized nations for the purpose of settling political, economic, and racial problems, and (2) some form of world court or world tribunal to settle legal disputes. As to these points there is practical unanimity among the great minds that have been addressed to the problems involved. There is a third point as to which the war-peace doctors tend to agree: there must be some form of force (economic, military, or both) to check the aggressor. Even the peace-loving Quaker, William Penn, proposed (1694) that the force of all the states in his league should be "united as one strength" against the peacebreaker.

With the close of the Napoleonic wars a first step—pitifully inadequate—was taken in the name of peace, viz., the Holy Alliance. But the three monarchs of Russia, Prussia, and Austria turned the piously stated objectives away from their meaning and in practice used the "Holy" Alliance to uphold the doctrine of legitimate monarchial succession and to squelch the "menace of democracy." What a remarkable parallel (or contrast) if we now think of the struggle of the "democratic" countries to preserve their way of life and their very existence.

Simon Bolivar inspired the Panama Conference of 1826, which later led to the Pan American Union (1889). In 1823 President Monroe gave us the Monroe Doctrine, which with its protection of the political independence and territorial integrity of American nations is almost identical with the world-wide guarantees envisaged by Article X of the Covenant of the League of Nations.

During the second half of the nineteenth century helpful international organizations were founded, such as the International Red Cross, the Universal Postal Union, the Union of Weights and Measures, and the Telegraph Union. In 1899 the First Hague Peace Conference gave us the Permanent Court of Arbitration, and rules of arbitration were set out in the Convention for the Pacific Settlement of International Disputes. The Second Hague Conference (1907) improved upon the methods for peaceful settlement begun in 1899. Then came World War I with its tremendous costs and its awakening influences which led to the League of Nations (1919), the World Court (1921), the International Labor Organization (1919), the Washington Naval Limitation Conference (1921), Locarno treaties (1925), the Kellogg-Briand Pact (1928), the London Naval Conference (1930), and—believe it or not—the World Disarmament Conference at Geneva (1932). World peace efforts were—for the first time—*officialized*. Instead of being merely the dreams of closet philosophers and writers, world peace was brought to the fore and put in the "What to do today" basket on the desks of prime ministers, kings, secretaries of state, and diplomats. Moreover, the people the world over became increasingly concerned about war and peace. It seemed as if we were definitely on the pathway toward a new day in genuine international cooperation. But came the—*Interlude of Retrogression.*

With the Japanese attack at Mukden in 1931 there began the dark *interlude of retrogression* in the hopeful march of official international cooperation. Then came Ethiopia, Austria, Czechoslovakia, the present debacle in Europe, Asia, and the whole world; gloomy, uncertain, sacrificial days of deterioration in international relations are now unhappily upon us. Our forty years' effort (1899-1939) to build the delicate structure of international cooperation bogged down in the quagmire of isolationism, politics, excessive national selfishness, ignorance, and general lack of understanding of the values of continuous international cooperation. We sought security in isolation and the discredited balance of power system. We lacked the spiritual power to back up and sustain our official machinery, of which there was plenty. But when the bloody war storms are once over and we have our second chance—*What of the future?*

There should be few thoughtful Americans who would sustain longer the isolationists who, perhaps unwittingly, have brought so much suffering to the world. Nor does the balance of power system (the alliance system) offer the way out. The balance of power system failed miserably in 1914-1918, and again after Munich (which really amounted to a sidetracking of the League and collective security for a sort of balance of power).

We know that nations will continue to have disputes. The only question before us is how these disputes are to be settled, by *rationality* or *by brute force;* by *courts* and *conferences* or *by big Berthas, bullets,* and *bayonets.* The high-water mark of progress toward substituting rationality for force came with the League of Nations and the World Court, both of which we allowed to be sabotaged by a handful of narrow-minded, isolationist Senators. The failure of the United States to back up the League and the Court served to discourage friends of these great agencies of peace in Europe. Instead of a League of Nations, there was a League of *some* nations. The League was not allowed to become the great agency hoped for by President Wilson, to rectify and to correct the sore spots and undesirable conditions that inevitably crept into the Versailles Treaty and other postwar treaties. But even so, it did splendid work; it attracted fifty-eight sovereign states of the world to its membership, and its $8,000,000 magnificent palace stands on the banks of Lake Geneva beckoning the peoples of the world to send men and women, once more, to fill its thinly manned offices, and to revitalize the great work of international cooperation, forever symbolized by such a worthy structure. In every stone and office of this building lives the spirit of an illustrious President of the United States—Woodrow Wilson—whom the City of Geneva has honored as the "Founder of the League of Nations."

Though kicked about, snubbed, unappreciated, inadequately backed, the League of Nations still functions; it still has nearly fifty members; it is only temporarily eclipsed by the forces of war, isolation, and ignorance. The League has made notable contributions to the welfare of the peoples of the world in the fields of public health (standardization of medical formulas, Singapore Health Station, nutrition, housing), regulating opium traffic, checking white slave traffic, research studies, publication of 200 volumes of treaties, forum for discussion, and in standing as a great beacon light to symbolize world cooperation for peace and prosperity.

We now have a timely opportunity to plump attention upon some fundamental truths centering around the great advantages that will come to us all by

1. Substituting courts and conferences for brute force in the settlement of international disputes;

2. Replacing fear and coercion with cooperation and federation;

3. Stressing the failure of isolation and the balance of power system—two miserable failures in twenty-five years—and the promise of collective security;

4. Participating in a world-wide educational program emphasizing the above-stated objectives and leading to the possibility of a real welfare economy (better educational facilities, old-age pensions, better homes, etc.), rather than military economy (excessive armaments, backbreaking defense taxes, mutual fear, etc.).

There are now many encouraging evidences of renewed interest in a revitalized, adequate League of Nations. A most notable endorsement of a revived League was made by the Honorable Sumner Welles, then Acting Secretary of State, on the occasion of the laying of the cornerstone of the new wing of the Norwegian Legation in Washington, July 22, 1941. Among other things, Mr. Welles said:

> At the end of the last war, a great President of the United States gave his life in the struggle to further the realization of the splendid vision which he had held up to the eyes of suffering humanity—the vision of an ordered world governed by law.

Welles stated that the League of Nations had been weakened "because of the blind selfishness of men here in the United States, as well as in other parts of the world," because of "political and commercial ambitions," and because of too rigid an insistence upon the *status quo* rather than utilizing the League for "peaceful and equitable adjustments" as "its chief spokesman had intended." Such adjustments must be permitted in the peace organization of the future. The Acting Secretary laid down as further essentials for a durable peace the abolition of offensive armaments and the limitation and reduction of defensive armaments and "some rigid form of international supervision and control" of armaments. He saw no lasting peace unless it "established fully and adequately the natural rights of all peoples to equal economic enjoyment for so long as any one people or any one government possesses a monopoly over natural resources or raw materials which are needed by all peoples, there can be no basis for a world order based on justice and peace." Mr. Welles sounded a call to peoples of good will

> . . . once more [to] strive to realize the great ideal of an association of nations through which the freedom, the happiness and the security of peoples may be achieved.
> That word, security, represents the end upon which the hearts of men and women everywhere today are set.

Speaking to the Veterans of Foreign Wars, June 27, 1941, Governor Olson of California urged that the United States should assume the leadership in uniting the free peoples of the earth to stop banditry. He asserted that he could not help feeling that "if a real league of nations had been established after the first great war we would not now be facing world catastrophe."

A notable manifestation of interest in the establishment of a strong world organization for peace was revealed by the special resolution of the legislature of the state of North Carolina (March 13, 1941), which called upon the President of the United States to call an international conference "to formulate a Constitution for the Federation of the World."

> Unnoticed and unheralded by even the shrewdest political observers over the past months, public opinion in the United States has undergone a marked reversal on the question of American membership in a league of nations.

Dr. Gallup put to a selected list in *Who's Who* the question "Would you like to see the United States join a league of nations after this war is over?" The result showed: Yes, 61 per cent; No, 23 per cent; Undecided, 16 per cent. It should be noted, however, that the Gallup poll of a general cross section of the voters does not show such a high percentage in favor of a league but does indicate a favorable majority.

The New Education Fellowship, headed by Dr. William H. Kilpatrick of Columbia University, has recently revealed its elaborate program for world reconstruction. The eighth point states that

> The well-being of every society springs from a brotherhood of nations. As are the duties of man to man, so are the duties of societies to one another. And this is the only basis for a durable peace.

Dr. Walter van Kirk, secretary of the department of international justice and good will of the Federal Council of Churches, told the members of the Institute of Human Relations, at Williamstown, Massachusetts, August 26, 1941, that "a lasting postwar world peace will be achieved only through a reconstituted League of Nations and an end to American isolationism."

Dr. William E. Rappard, a brilliant Swiss educator and international relations expert, sees international federalism as infinitely promising, as "the only happy outcome to the tragic chaos into which the anarchy of national sovereignties has plunged our contemporary civilization." He refers to the early experiences of the American colonies and the Swiss cantons with their systems of "popular" representation and "state" representation, and declares that by a "combination of these two systems in a bicameral régime" they have found happiness and prosperity.

Future international organization for peace must be flexible enough to provide for "peaceful change" of boundaries and for a fair economic deal to all. There must be adaptability to meet the legitimate trade, financial and economic needs of *all nations*. It should be recognized once for all that no people can be expected to be sweet spirited and peace minded on empty stomachs and without jobs.

The peoples of the world are gradually seeing the light. As the truth is being revealed to them, they will demand and sustain a progressive strengthening of world organization to stop aggression, to promote their economic welfare, to guarantee their peace and security, and to bring them that immense spiritual satisfaction that will come with the participation in the delicate task of building a new world worthy of men and women created in the image of Almighty God—men, women, and children who are entitled to a better deal than that offered to them by a handful of misguided, war-crazed, self-seeking, pseudo leaders, whose hollow and false promises will fade away in the realization of the superb work of genuine Christian cooperation for peace and reconstruction. The cold, calculating superselfishness and domination of the military dictators will melt away in the sunlight of God's truth as it leads men everywhere to set their minds and their hearts to the difficult but magnificent task of world reconstruction.

## LEAGUE OF NATIONS AGENCIES [2]

The general structure of the League, as it emerged from the peace treaties following World War I, is described in its constitution, the Covenant of the League of Nations. Under this Covenant, the League acts through two policymaking bodies —the Assembly and the Council—aided by a permanent Secretariat and a network of expert advisory committees and special agencies. The League setup also includes the International Labor Office and the Permanent Court of International Justice, as well as the Permanent Central Opium Board. In addition, the League of Nations takes a directing part in the activities of various other international agencies, such as the International Institute for Intellectual Cooperation which, although largely independent financially, work under its auspices.

The Assembly is made up of government delegates representing member states, and meets once a year as well as in extraordinary sessions. The Council consists of representatives of some fifteen countries—in many cases the Foreign Ministers; the great powers have a permanent seat, while other members are elected by the Assembly for three-year terms. The Council, which in peacetime held regular sessions three times a year, as well as extraordinary sessions (over 100 in 20 years), directs the multiple activities of the League.

The Secretariat is the permanent administrative organ of the League and constitutes, in fact, an international civil service. In compliance with Article 7 of the Covenant, it is located at Geneva, the official seat of the League. Its main functions are to prepare the work of the Assembly, the Council, and the numerous committees and conferences of the League; to undertake such research or executive work as the Assembly or Council may decide; and to handle the mass of detail connected with

[2] From "Geneva Institutions in Wartime," by Ernest S. Hediger, Research Associate, Foreign Policy Association. *Foreign Policy Reports*. 19:39. May 1, 1943.

the League's far-flung activities. It is at present divided into three main departments, dealing respectively with economic, financial and transit questions; social and humanitarian problems (health, drug traffic, child welfare, social work, refugees, intellectual collaboration); and legal and administrative questions (registration of international treaties, protection of minorities, mandates, slavery).

## LEAGUE REFORMS ATTEMPTED AND ADOPTED
### 1920-1935 [3]

The question of the reform of the League of Nations and of the revision of its Covenant is as old as the League itself. As early as some five months before the first session of the League Assembly draft amendments and additions to the Covenant had been put forward. But these proposals and many of those made subsequently, however important they may have been, contemplated only detailed changes in the various articles of the Covenant in accordance with experience and actual practice and the lessons resulting from the different crises in the life of the League. The system of the Covenant itself was to remain intact and its main principles were always considered as well founded and right.

On the other hand the greatest and gravest crises in the first fifteen years of the League, namely, the sanctions experiment against Italy, preceded by the withdrawal of Japan and Germany in 1935, raised the question of the necessity of a fundamental change in the League's structure and the soundness of the principles on which it was based.

Before the official proposals which were made at that time, and their discussion by the organs of the League, from 1936 to 1939, are examined in detail, the changes attempted and adopted previously must be recorded briefly. In this connection not only should proposals which resulted from the procedure

[3] Reprinted from *League Reform, an Analysis of Official Proposals and Discussions, 1936-1939*, by S. Engel (Geneva Studies, Vol. XI, nos. 3-4, August 1940), by permission of International Documents Service, Columbia University Press, on behalf of Geneva Research Centre.

provided by Article 26 of the Covenant be taken into consideration, but also such measures which, although they did not
constitute formal amendments to the Covenant, aimed at improving or developing it, namely, resolutions of interpretation and
supplementary agreements.

*The First Session of the Assembly* (1920). Some five months
before the first session of the Assembly took place in 1920,
the Scandinavian Governments, which, like others, had not
been admitted to full collaboration when the Covenant was
drawn up in Paris, submitted "draft amendments and additions
to the Covenant." These proposals concerned the meetings
of the Assembly (Article 3), the election of the temporary
members of the Council (Article 4), the institution of commissions of arbitration and conciliation and of obligatory jurisdiction (Article 12, 13) and the authorization by the Council
of Member States to maintain intercourse with a covenant-
breaking state (Article 16). During the Assembly meetings
the Portuguese delegate likewise presented amendments regarding the appointment of the non-permanent members of the
Council (Article 4) and obligatory arbitration (Articles 12, 13).
In addition to this, the Argentine representative urged amendments with a view to admitting to the League all sovereign
states, including the small states, the latter however without
the right of voting. Colombia's delegate announced the submission of a proposal to change the unanimity rule (Article 5),
while the Canadian Government advocated the suppression of
Article 10 stipulating respect and protection for the territorial
integrity and existing political independence of League Members.
On the report of Mr. Balfour (United Kingdom) who emphasized the short experience of the League and pointed out that
changing the Covenant would be changing the Treaty of
Versailles, the Assembly decided not to consider immediately
the proposed amendments. It invited the Council to appoint a
committee to study the proposals presented together with any
which might be submitted within a period to be fixed by the
Council.

The Assembly, on the motion of the Netherlands Government, further requested the Council to entrust the examination

of the scope of Article 18 on the registration of treaties to a special committee which should prepare all relevant proposals.

The third committee to be appointed by the Council was the International Blockade Commission which was to consider the application of Article 16 of the Covenant. The conclusions of that Committee as well as those of the two others were to be placed before the Assembly at its second session. For the interval the Assembly adopted a resolution providing for a series of measures which should be taken "to render as effective as possible the Economic Weapon of the League under Article 16."

Finally the Assembly declared its approval of the Statute of the Permanent Court of International Justice and of the Optional Clause annexed to it providing for the compulsory jurisdiction of the Court, under certain conditions, and thus made a far-reaching contribution to the development of Articles 12 and 13 of the Covenant.

*The Three Committees* (1921). The Committees set up by the Council at the request of the Assembly met during 1921. The Committee on the Registration of Treaties proposed an almost new Article 18 which was again redrafted by the First Committee of the 1921 Assembly. "Desiring to profit by experience gained over a longer period," the Assembly, in 1922, postponed *sine die* further consideration of the suggested amendments.

The International Blockade Commission discussed the proposals relating to Article 16 and concluded that the application of this provision necessitated its amendment on "the procedure to be followed in respect of unanimity within the Council when it has to take decisions for the employment of the Economic Weapon" and on "the exemptions to be granted in specific cases." On the proposal of its First and Third Committees, the Assembly, at its second session in 1921, adopted important resolutions and amendments relating to Article 16. According to the latter the "nationality" principle of paragraph 1 was to be replaced by that of "residence" and the Council should be competent to give an opinion whether or not a breach of the Covenant had taken place, to recommend to the League Members the date for application of the economic pressure, and to postpone, under certain conditions, for particular Members, the coming into force of any of the contemplated measures for a specified period. The resolutions and amendments were, so long as the latter had not been put into force according to Article 26 of the Covenant, to constitute "rules for guidance which the Assembly recommends as a provisional measure, to the Council and to the Members of the League in connection with the application of Article 16."

The Committee on Amendments, at its first two sessions, dealt with the above-mentioned draft amendments; further, with Dutch proposals to mention expressly in paragraph 2 of Article 5 the Rules of Procedure of the Council and the Assembly and to replace the method of expenditure allocation provided in paragraph 5 of Article 6 by a new one to be adopted by the Assembly itself, and finally, with proposals submitted by the Governments of Czechoslovakia and China relating to "agreements and conferences of a limited nature" to be mentioned in Article 21. On the agenda of the third session of the Committee figured, *inter alia*, amendments to Articles 12, 13 and 15 necessitated by the establishment of the Permanent Court of International Justice, the methods of amending the Covenant, and a French proposal to enlarge the powers of the Military Commission provided for by Article 9.

*The 1921 Amendments.* The discussion of the two reports of the Amendments Committee resulted in the adoption by the 1921 Assembly of a number of draft amendments. One provided for insertion of a new paragraph between the second and third paragraphs of Article 4 according to which "the Assembly shall fix by a two-thirds majority the rules dealing with the election of the non-permanent members of the Council." Another aimed at replacing the last paragraph of Article 6 by the following: "The expenses of the League shall be borne by the Members of the League in the proportion decided by the Assembly." A third provided for addition of a new paragraph to Article 6 and a new annex to the Covenant, both relating to a provisional allocation of the League's expenses. A fourth for insertion into Article 12, 13 and 15 of references to the decisions of the Permanent Court of International Justice, in view of the establishment of that organ. Still others contemplated a new drafting of Article 26, specifying a three-fourths majority for the voting of amendments by the Assembly, the relevant date for the establishment of that majority in so far as the ratifying members of the Council were concerned, and the periods allowed for the deposition of the instruments of ratification and the notification of any refusal by a League Member to accept the amendment. These and the above-mentioned revisions of Article 16 were the only amendments voted by the Assembly; all the remaining proposals, including that of M. Alvarez (Chile) for the "complete revision of the Covenant," were not accepted.

Finally, the Assembly expressed its approval of the procedure of conciliation as urged by the Scandinavian Governments. The special committee set up at its request by the Council recommended the formation of Conciliation Commissions by "freely concluded" conventions and submitted a body of rules for conciliation proceedings. These proposals were, in the main, adopted by the Assembly at its third session and Articles 12 and 15 of the Covenant were thus supplemented.

At the same Assembly (1922), Canada, which in 1921 had been unable to obtain the suppression of Article 10 of the Covenant, proposed an amendment according to which the Council, in advising upon the means for the fulfillment of this provision, should "take into account the political and geographical circumstances of each State" and should not be competent to oblige any Member to engage in any act of war. Neither this amendment nor an "interpretative resolution" drafted along these lines was adopted.

*The Draft Treaty of Mutual Assistance* (1923) *and the Geneva Protocol* (1924). The draft Treaty of Mutual Assistance was the fruit of long labors undertaken by the Temporary Mixed Commission for the Reduction of Armaments. It was regarded as a "prolongation" of the Covenant and might have necessitated amendments to the latter had it been accepted.

The same is true for the next important attempt at developing the system of the Covenant, the Geneva Protocol for the

Pacific Settlement of International Disputes of 1924. According to Article 1 of that Protocol, the signatory states were to make every effort to secure the amendment of the Covenant along the lines of the Protocol, and the Assembly requested the Council to appoint a committee for the drafting of those amendments. Such a "harmonization" of the Covenant with the Geneva Protocol, if effected, would have required far-reaching alterations in the provisions of the former regarding the reduction of armaments, the pacific settlement of disputes, and sanctions.

*The Locarno Treaties and the Draft Model Treaties.* After and owing to the failure of the Geneva Protocol the Locarno Treaties were concluded. They were regarded as an application of the principles of the Protocol on regional lines. They were approved by the Council and the Assembly and on this basis model treaties relating to security and the pacific settlement of disputes were drawn up (in 1928).

*The 1926 Crisis.* The League crisis in 1926 which arose in connection with the creation of a permanent Council membership for Germany, passed without any amendment to the Covenant. The Committee on the Composition of the Council set up on this occasion was charged by the Council to "bear in mind the various proposals on the subject which have been previously discussed by the Council or the Assembly." It did not, however, propose the modification of Article 4 of the Covenant, but adopted draft regulations on the number and the election of the non-permanent members of the Council.

*The Interpretations of Article 11.* While an official interpretation of the Preamble and of Articles 3 and 4 of the Covenant proposed in 1926 by the United Kingdom delegation could not be secured, this was possible with regard to Article 11. Following the memorandum by the Belgian jurist de Brouckère, a Council Committee, on March 15, 1927, approved a report on that article which was adopted by the Assembly and the Council as a "valuable guide" for the future. It was supplemented by a Council resolution of June 7, 1928, on the measures to be taken in the intervals between sessions of the Council and by a memorandum on Articles 10, 11 and 16, drafted by the Dutch jurist Rutgers, the conclusions of which were recommended to the Council by the Assembly and adopted by the latter.

*The General Act and the Briand-Kellogg Pact* (1928). In the same year 1928 two further very important contributions to the development of the Covenant were made. There was the adoption by the Assembly of the General Act for the Pacific Settlement of International Disputes to which twenty-three League Members have acceded. It provided a complete system for the pacific settlement of international disputes and thus supplemented Articles 12 to 15 of the Covenant.

By the Briand-Kellogg Pact the parties "condemn recourse to war for the solution of international controversies, and renounce it as an instrument of national policy," whereas the Members of the League, according to the Preamble of the Covenant, agreed only to "the acceptance of (certain) obligations not to resort to war." The "harmonization" of the Covenant with the Paris Pact had already been proposed at the 1928 Assembly but was decided upon only at the following session. The Committee of Eleven set up by the Council for that purpose confined itself to the draft amendments which it considered to be strictly necessary. It proposed the modification of the Preamble and of Articles 12 (paragraph 1), 13 (paragraph 4) and 15 (paragraphs 6 and 7) of the Covenant. With the exception of those relating to Article 15, paragraphs 6 and 7*bis*, these proposals were in the main accepted by the First Committee of the 1930 Assembly. The latter transmitted the drafts of the two Committees to the Member States for their observations. As many Members made the ratification of the proposed extension of their obligations "conditional on the entry into force of the Convention for the Reduction of Armaments" and, as the Disarmament Conference failed, the question of bringing the Covenant into harmony with the Pact of Paris remained unsettled.

*The Plan for European Union* (1929). M. Briand's Plan of 1929 for European Union and a Chinese proposal of the same year to consider "the best methods to make effective Article 19 of the Covenant" met with no more success. The former

initiative to secure the "close cooperation between the Governments of Europe . . . for the preservation of peace . . . within
the framework of the League" led to the institution of a
Commission of Enquiry which met in 1931 and has since
remained, in fact, adjourned.

*The Draft Conventions of 1930 and 1931.*   On the other
hand the Assembly, in 1930 and 1931, approved two draft
conventions relating to Articles 11 and 16 of the Covenant.   In
the case of their entry into force they would have constituted,
for the parties thereto, important improvements of these provisions.   The one is the Convention of 1930 on Financial
Assistance which provides for the operation of guarantees to be
granted to a state victim of aggression or threatened with war.
The other is the General Convention of 1931 to improve the
means of preventing war.   According to it the Council may
decide upon military and nonmilitary conservatory measures
without counting the votes of the parties to the conflict for the
purpose of unanimity.   Again the failure of the Disarmament
Conference prevented the two Conventions from coming into
force.

*Disarmament and Security.*   Other attempts at developing
the Covenant or facilitating its application were made in connection with the disarmament question.   Because of the close
relationship between disarmament and security they concerned
principally Article 16 of the Covenant.   Thus the French
Government, in a memorandum submitted to the Disarmament
Conference on February 5, 1932, proposed to place civil aviation
and bombing aircraft as well as certain land and naval forces
at the disposal of the League and to create an international
police force in order to prevent and repress war and to bring
immediate assistance to any victim of aggression.   On November
14, 1932, it suggested, furthermore, that the parties to the
Briand-Kellogg Pact should concert together in the event of a
breach or threat of breach of this Pact.   Similarly, the draft
Disarmament Convention proposed by the United Kingdom
on March 16, 1933, referred to special regional agreements
between certain of the contracting parties, while the Soviet and
Belgian delegations submitted proposals  concerning the defini-

tion of the aggressor and the establishment of the fact of aggression. On this basis the Committee on Security Questions of the Disarmament Conference drew up a European Security Pact and three Acts on the Definition of the Aggressor and on the Establishment of Facts Constituting Aggression. The main objects of the European Pact were to "prevent states from resorting to war, with or without declaration" and to "increase the efficacy of the mutual assistance obligations (established by other treaties)" in the draft Disarmament Convention of September 22, 1933. The first part of that Convention deals with the above-mentioned possibility of consultation in the event of a breach or threat of breach of the Paris Pact.

*The Argentine Anti-War Treaty of 1933.* Outside the framework of the League, but largely in response to the Assembly resolution of September 26, 1928, the Anti-War Treaty of Non-Aggression and Conciliation of October 10, 1933, was signed. It was characterized as an "effort to adapt the special spirit and traditions of South America to the conceptions of Geneva." The Council complied with the proposal of the Argentine Government to place the Treaty before the Committee set up to bring the Covenant into harmony with the Pact of Paris.

*The Four Power Pact.* Similarly, outside the framework of the League but related to its disarmament efforts, another initiative was undertaken which may have exercised a great influence on the evolution of the League, namely Mussolini's Four Power Pact of March 18, 1933. Article 2 of the Italian draft stressed the principle of the revision of the Peace Treaties which should be applied within the framework of the League, while Article 1 and 4 provided for the close cooperation of the four powers (France, Germany, Great Britain and Italy) in all political and nonpolitical questions. This might have resulted in the creation of a super council or a "directory of the Great Powers laying down the law for the smaller nations." Thus a fundamental alteration of the League's structure, which is based on the principle of the equality of states, would have been brought about.

*The Fascist Grand Council Resolution and its Repercussions.*
After Germany's withdrawal from the Disarmament Conference
and her notice of secession from the League in 1933, the main
ideas of the Four Power Pact were again put forward by Italy.
Apparently this was meant when, on December 5, 1933, the
Fascist Grand Council passed a resolution to the effect that "the
continued collaboration of Italy with the League of Nations
shall be conditional upon a radical reform of the League in its
constitution, organization, and objectives within the shortest
possible time."

Among the various reactions evoked by this challenge only
two need be mentioned here: (1) The reply given by the
highest League official, the Secretary-General, and (2) the only
governmental statement made at that time by a League Member,
the Dutch memorandum of January 13, 1934.

In his speech before the House of Commons of December
11, 1933, M. Avenol, after dealing with the criticisms levelled
at the League, argued that "the sources of its (the League's)
life must be preserved pure and intact." He showed "how
many things are possible by a process of development within
the limits of the Covenant" which "in its general structure . . .
represents the minimum number of obligations without which
no League and no effective international cooperation could
exist." He concluded that "it is essential to realize that the
alternative before the world is not a choice between the League
and some better system of international relations, but between
the League and complete anarchy."

In its memorandum on the reform of the League of Nations,
the Netherlands Government stated likewise that it saw "no
necessity for modifying the Covenant, which in its opinion
offers ample possibility of achieving the League's objects, provided that the Members are actuated by a spirit of collaboration."
It was of opinion that the criticisms of the League "owe their
origin very largely to preoccupations which cannot be met by
any modification of the Covenant." It would protest against
any proposal calculated to infringe the principle of the legal
eqaulity of Members. The unanimity rule was not the cause
of the League's lack of success in several respects; nor should

the alleged drawbacks of the connection between the League and the Peace Treaties be overestimated.

*The Committee for the Organisation of Collective Security.* While thereafter official discussion on the question of League reform came to a halt for the time being, Germany's rearmament, in 1935, led to a new effort in that direction, as had done her notice of withdrawal in 1933. As a result of an appeal to the League by the French Government, the Council, on April 17, 1935, appointed a committee of thirteen members to propose, for cases of unilateral repudiation of international obligations, "measures to render the League Covenant more effective in the organization of collective security" (a title which now suggests the terms of reference of the Committee of Twenty-eight set up in 1936). In that Committee the French delegation suggested the conclusion of general or regional agreements on the measures to be taken "in the event of a breach, duly recorded by the Council, of an undertaking of concern to international security and the maintenance of peace in Europe." Without discussing the French proposal in detail, the Committee at its first session, held in May 1935, set up two sub-committees to consider the legal and the economic and financial problems involved in the Council resolution of April 17. The Legal Sub-Committee which met in June 1935, held that the Council might in the above-mentioned case recommend, under Article 11 of the Covenant, "economic and financial measures . . . calculated to contribute to the maintenance of peace" and, under Article 13 of the Covenant, the same measures "calculated to ensure effect being given to the award or decision." In the absence of any special undertaking to that effect, there would be no legal obligation to comply with such a recommendation. As to the question "whether the negative vote of the delinquent state could prevent the Council from taking the necessary decisions," the Sub-Committee was unable to reach unanimity. The Economic and Financial Sub-Committee, which met in July 1935, had as its task to discover the measures which, though "less comprehensive than those prescribed under Article 16 of the Covenant" would nevertheless induce the treaty-repudiating state to modify its course of action. The Sub-Committee considered the withholding of certain supplies as a preventive measure in such a case, namely "(1) arms, ammunition and implements of war; (2) 'key products' required for the manufacture of armaments . . . ; and (3) other products required for . . . warlike preparations (but also) widely employed in industry." It submitted further observations on the interruption of exports from, and financial pressure upon, the repudiating state, on the legislative and administrative means for the application of the proposed measures, on the regional arrangements necessary to produce the requisite effect and finally on the relations of the contemplated measures to commercial treaties and navigation and transit conventions. At its second session in July 1935, the Committee of Thirteen took note of the reports of the two Sub-Committees. Its president submitted a draft report to the Council which was, however, neither adopted nor discussed. Instead the Committee charged its president to designate competent experts to investigate the question of the key products necessary for the manufacture of arms and to finish their work by November 30, 1935. The development of the Italo-Ethiopian dispute, however, prevented the experts from meeting and the contemplated third session of the Committee was never held. On the other hand the study and report of the Economic and Financial Sub-Committee was particularly useful to the Committee of Coordination of the sanctions applied against Italy.

We may now sum up the results of the period from 1920 to 1935. As regards the revision of the Covenant, formal amendments to the Preamble, to Articles 1, 3 to 6, 9, 10, 12, 13, 15, 16, 18, 21, 26 and to the Annex of the Covenant were presented. The Assembly however adopted only those relating to Articles 4, 6, 12, 13, 15, 16, 26 and to the Annex, and only the amendments to Articles 4, 6 (paragraph 5), 12, 13 and 15 came into force. The reform of the League as distinct from the revision of the Covenant was attempted either by interpretative resolutions or by supplementary agreements. Of the first, only the interpretations of Articles 10, 11 and 16 were adopted by the Council and/or the Assembly. As for the second, we recall as the most important contributions the establishment of the

Permanent Court of International Justice, the Optional Clause, the General Act of 1928, the Briand-Kellogg Pact and the Argentine Anti-War Treaty of 1933, while, unfortunately, the Geneva Protocol of 1924, the draft Conventions of 1930 and 1931 and the efforts of the Disarmament Conference failed.

## THE COVENANT OF THE LEAGUE OF NATIONS AS A PACT OF PEACE [4]

The Covenant of the League of Nations represents the most ambitious attempt which has ever been made to provide for the maintenance of peace. This is not merely because its provisions have at one time or another been accepted by sixty-two states of the world; it is also because their substance is such as to call for the abandonment of many ideas which have prevailed in the past, and because they are supported by the existence of flesh-and-blood human agencies which are established to realize its purposes.

The preamble of the Covenant states in dual form the aims of the states which have agreed to its terms. It says that the League of Nations is created "to promote international coopera-tion and to achieve international peace and security." Histori-cally, however, the first of these aims was really incidental to the second; international cooperation was to be promoted because of its bearing on the maintenance of international peace. Popu-lar opinion has always placed a similar emphasis on the objects of the League, and I think it is not improper to say that the principal purpose of the Covenant is to proscribe war.

In the atmosphere of Paris in 1919, the creation of the League of Nations seemed "essential to the maintenance of the world settlement" which the Allied and Associated nations were "met to establish." If President Wilson wished to inaugurate a "continuous superintendence of the peace of the world," he was disposed to entrust this responsibility to the nations which were represented at Paris and which had so recently conceived them-

[4] By Manley O. Hudson, Bemis Professor of International Law, Harvard University. Condensation of an article in the *Southern Review*. 1:120-38. July 1935, prior to the author's election as judge of the Permanent Court of International Justice.

selves to be defending a general interest in the struggle with their enemies. Perhaps it was inevitable that any plans for the future which could be adopted in 1919 should have been linked with an attempt to perpetuate the settlements embodied in the treaties of peace. Only a world in the grip of a maelstrom could have been so bold as to seek the departures which the Covenant represents, and such a world was bound to attempt at the same time solution of its more immediate problems. The incorporation of the Covenant in the treaties of peace now seems to have been the only practical way by which such a large number of states could be brought to agree upon its terms.

In spite of its limitations, I think it must be said that the League of Nations has achieved a surprising success as an agency for promoting international cooperation. All of the expectations of its founders have not been realized, perhaps. Yet what has been accomplished has been truly remarkable. For the first time in the history of the world, effective and continuous attention has been given to the legislative needs of world society. With the Council of the League of Nations at hand, meeting at frequent and regular intervals, international conferences possessing legislative functions have been assembled much more easily than before, preparation for their work has proceeded much more efficiently, and decisions taken by them have been executed with more expedition. The result today is that in a large number of collective, multipartite treaties the frontiers of international law have been advanced into new ground, and states are cooperating in the protection of their common interests on a scale hardly dreamed of when this century dawned. If all of this cooperation is not to be put down to the credit of the League of Nations, much of it has been inaugurated within the framework of the Covenant, and the mere existence of the League has inspired a new confidence in the efficacy of conscious effort directed toward an intelligent approach to the problems of our world community.

In the field of administration, also, the record of the League shows a big improvement over the preexisting situation. Most of the so-called international offices or bureaus created before 1914 were under the supervision of some one government, and neither the recruitment of their personnel nor the methods of their functioning justified the description of them as international. This may be seen in such a useful organization as the International Bureau of the Permanent Court of Arbitration at The Hague, the personnel of which has always consisted entirely of Netherlands nationals, and the expenses of which are met in the first instance by the Netherlands Government with a later reinbursement by the various "Contracting states." The various international bureaus at Berne are similarly controlled by the Swiss Government. When an International Ice Patrol was set up in the North Atlantic, following the Titanic disaster, its entire management was entrusted to the Government of the United States, though the expense is ultimately borne by various governments. The Director of the Pan American Union at Washington has always been a national of the United States. In some cases, notably in that of the International Institute of Agriculture at Rome, serious difficulties have arisen because of this national complexion of international bodies. On the whole, we may say that prior to the establishment of the League of Nations, little advance had been made in the creation and maintenance of truly international bodies. Patterns were lacking for their organization, and standards did not exist for international administration.

The progress in this field at Geneva has been on strictly international lines. Numerous standing committees and a permanent secretariat have been created, and new administrative standards have been set. It is unnecessary to enumerate the many committees now existing at Geneva.

This extension of interstate cooperation has been possible chiefly because of the existence of the Assembly and the Council of the League of Nations. Some prototypes of the Assembly existed before the war, but the Council is a brand new type of agency. The Universal Postal Union, for example, has long had a series of conferences meeting at regular intervals—its most recent conference met at Cairo in 1934; and other series of conferences which still meet date from the nineteenth century. When an attempt was made to establish a series of more general "peace conferences" meeting at The Hague, however, serious difficulties were encountered. Though the Covenant did not require annual sessions of the Assembly of the League of Nations, it did envisage meetings "at stated intervals," and the convening of the Assembly in September of each year has now become a fixture on the international calendar. In fifteen years, eighteen sessions of the Assembly have been held. The Council, on the other hand, meets more frequently, and in the same period it has held eighty-five sessions. It was the eighty-sixth session of the Council which was held in Geneva a few weeks ago [1935].

One cannot lay too much stress upon the importance of this element of continuity in the effort of the League "to promote international cooperation." It means not merely that continuous attention is being given to the world's current problems, but also that a failure upon any given occasion does not spell complete defeat for all time to come. Of course it is inevitable that there will be failures. Time after time at Geneva hopes have been dashed and efforts have been abandoned; yet the threads can always be taken up at some later time. A thoughtful observer will attach more importance to the existence of the Assembly and the Council and to their inculcation of the habit of conference than to their success or failure in dealing with any particular subject.

Our principal concern is with the Covenant as an instrument for the proscription of war, however, and I have dealt with the League's record in promoting cooperation only as an introduction to this subject. The Covenant nowhere contains a general proscription of war. It does not profess to "outlaw" all war. It does not proclaim any moral condemnation. It does not embody any ukase concerning the maintenance of peace. Instead, it enunciates one great general principle, it provides a set of definite commitments based on this principle, it lays down specific interdictions, and it confers upon agencies in being a general authority.

The general principle which the Convenant enunciates constitutes its greatest innovation. It is a flat repudiation of conceptions which had dominated three centuries of international relations. Ever since the seventeenth century, an idea had prevailed in international law that if two states wished to go to war, it was their own affair. Other states were free to enter the war for any reasons which were to them sufficient, but unless they chose this course, they were to assume the attitude of neutrals. In course of time, an elaborate system of law grew up, establishing the rights which neutrals might assert against belligerents and prescribing the duties which they owed to belligerents so long as they remained neutrals. Spasmodically, collective efforts were made by the more powerful states in Europe to restrain other states from going to war or to prevent war as between themselves, but the Concert of Europe was never a factor to be relied upon with confident assurance; and despite such efforts, in the large it is true to say that prior to 1919 states were free to resort to force at any time and for any reasons. There was no orderly procedure to be exhausted before an appeal to force.

In line with changes which have occurred in the world, the Members of the League of Nations made a solemn declaration that a war anywhere affects people everywhere. The words of Article 11 of the Covenant are that "any war or threat of war, whether immediately affecting any of the members of the League or not, is hereby declared a matter of concern to the whole League." This holds out as the basic principle of twentieth century international relations a conception of the *World's peace,* not unlike the conception of the *King's peace* which was made the basis of national unity in England some seven hundred years ago. It is the conception of the world's peace which has dominated so much of our striving during these postwar years. It is the world's peace which transportation and communication have made the paramount interest of a world society. It is the world's peace which a new twentieth century international law must be constructed to safeguard. It is the world's peace which present-day effort would place above the unbridled freedom of states to plunge into war as they please.

Article 11 constitutes, therefore, the heart of the Covenant. Of course, the Article is not to be construed to declare that all peoples have or feel that they have an equal concern in all wars, or that they have the same concern in any war that may occur. Some limitations may exist, of course, on the way in which a particular state may be expected to express its concern in a particular war. Yet it is immensely significant that in Article 11 we have a wholly new approach to the problems of war and peace, and it does not require much imagination to see the thoroughgoing reforms which would have to be made in international law if it were adopted as the controlling factor of each state's national policy.

Yet the Covenant has not stopped short with the enunciation. It proceeds to make certain provisions which are designed to encourage conduct in accordance with the principle enunciated. It provides methods for the pacific settlement of disputes, it creates obligations to refrain from going to war under certain circumstances, and it outlines measures which may be taken if these obligations should be violated.

Perhaps it is not generally realized that the Covenant does not establish any global system for dealing with international disputes. It is concerned chiefly with disputes which are "likely to lead to a rupture" (Fr., *susceptible d'entrainer une rupture*). Arbitration and judicial settlement are held out as appropriate means for the settlement of other disputes, but no obligation is created with respect to them. For disputes "likely to lead to a rupture," the obligation is precise, and the commitment of Members of the League is quite definite. If they are not submitted to arbitration or judicial settlement, they must be submitted to the Council, in order that it may endeavor to effect a settlement, and this failing, in order that it may make a report for the guidance of the parties, of other Members of the League, and of a general world opinion. The parties to the dispute are not bound to carry out the recommendations made in such a report, but its existence may serve as a barrier to hostilities against a party which does not comply with those recommendations. These provisions of the Covenant are now supplemented by other arrangements to which many of the Members of the League are parties: by the "optional clause" of the Statute of the Permanent Court of International Justice which is now binding upon forty-one states; by the

Geneva General Act of 1928 to which twenty-two states are now parties in whole or in part; and by several hundreds of bipartite treaties which represent a great advance over the treaties concluded before the League was established. As a matter of fact, two hundred and forty-four bipartite treaties of pacific settlement had been registered with the Secretariat of the League of Nations on March 1, 1935, and were in force on that date. The legal system of pacific settlement resting upon or inspired by the Covenant may not be altogether adequate, but it is in some measure complete and it may be strong enough to afford escape from war where a will to peace exists.

It is this collective system of pacific settlement upon which the Covenant's proscription of war rests. Let me repeat that the framers of the Covenant did not draft a general fulmination against war. They were not bold enough to attempt to outline a method of preventing all wars. They thought first of introducing order. In a field where almost complete anarchy had previously reigned, they devised an orderly system by which effort should be made to settle any dispute that might arise "likely to lead to rupture." Yet they realized that in some cases the settlement might be sought in vain. Within very cautious limits, they proceeded to say that war was proscribed; beyond these limits, Members of the League are left "the right to take such action as they shall consider necessary for the maintenance of right and justice," which is a euphemistic way of saying that they are free to fight as they please.

The dispositions in the Covenant proscribing war may be briefly stated. First of all, it is provided in Article 12 that if a dispute arises which is likely to lead to a rupture, the parties will in no case resort to war until three months after an award by arbitrators or a judicial decision or a report by the Council with reference to that dispute. Then there is a provision that after a dispute likely to lead to a rupture has been submitted to arbitration or judicial settlement under Article 13, either by the Permanent Court of International Justice or by any other tribunal, "the Members of the League agree that they will carry out in good faith any award or decision that may be rendered and that they will not resort to war against a Member of the League which complies therewith." When a dispute has been submitted to the Council and when the members of that body (other than the representatives of the parties to the dispute) have unanimously agreed to a report on it, "the Members of the League agree that they will not go to war with any party which complies with the recommendations of the report." A report may be adopted by a majority of the Council, but without the same legal consequences. Even if an arbitral award or a judicial decision or a report by the Council or Assembly is not complied with by either party, there is the obligation in Article 12 for both of the parties to refrain from resort to war for a period of three months after it is rendered.

By Article 4 of the Covenant, the Council is empowered to deal "with any matter within the sphere of action of the League or affecting the peace of the world." It is a very general mandate, the apparent effect of which is greatly reduced by the requirement of unanimity for any action to be taken. As any Member of the League whose interests are "specifically affected" is entitled to representation on the Council (Article 4, paragraph 5), unanimity limits the mandate with reference to disputes to a role of conciliation. This is similarly true of the mandate of the Council under Article 10 to "advise" upon the preservation of states' integrity and independence, and of its general mandate under Article 11 to take cognizance on its own motion of "any war or threat of war," and to "take any action that may be deemed wise and effectual to safeguard the peace of nations." Yet the fact that such general responsibility rests on the Council is important, and it may enable efforts to maintain peace to be continued even after the exhaustion of the methods of pacific settlement for which the Covenant provides.

The sanctions of the Covenant present very different problems. As they are embodied in Article 16, the only sanction which applies to a violation of any of its covenants by a Member is that of expulsion from the League, which may be effected by a unanimous vote of the Council, exclusive of the representative of the Member affected. This sanction has never been applied, and its nature is such that its application must be made only rarely. More important are the sanctions which are intended to apply to any "resort to war" by a Member in disregard of its obligations with respect to pacific settlement. The expression "resort to war" is not one which reveals its application automatically; in recent years, its meaning has exercised many lawyers. It ought to be clear that the term as used in the Covenant should not be restricted to the limits of a judicial term of art. Yet the vagueness of the term leaves room for uncertainty as to the answer to be given to many questions.

Who is to say when the various conditions have been fulfilled which will call for the application of sanctions? Who is to say when a Member of the League has resorted to war "in disregard of its covenants under Articles 12, 13 or 15"? To what extent is a Member of the League bound by a decision to this effect by any authority other than its own government? Must a Member of the League await such a decision? Uncertainties continue to prevail as to these questions, and they have not been banished by the excellent reports prepared by M. de Brouckère (Belgium) in 1926 and by M. Rutgers (Netherlands) in 1928. It was truly said by M. Rutgers that "if ever the question of the application of Article 16 arose, the decision of the different countries would not depend on interpretations, however authoritative, or on the deductions of lawyers; the great question would be whether the principle of Article 16 was or was not a living reality."

Once it has been determined that a Member of the League has resorted to war in disregard of its covenants under Article 12, 13 or 15, it is stipulated in Article 16 that a very serious consequence will follow; such Member "shall *ipso facto* be deemed to have committed an act of war against all other Members of the League." This does not mean that all other Members must immediately regard themselves as at war, i. e., in a state of war, with the defaulter; they are merely to treat the latter's action as a basis for the imposition of penalties which Article 16 then proceeds to prescribe. "Act of war" is an unhappy expression in the Covenant in this connection. It tends to create an impression that any coercive action against a covenant-breaking state constitutes a waging of war in the historic sense of the term, an impression which was evident in the drafting of the abortive Proctocol of Geneva of 1924; but such coercion, if it is approved by the Council and undertaken in the assertion of the general interest in world peace, ought to be viewed as policing, and as such it would have little in common with war as it has been known in the past.

As to the nature of the sanctions for which Article 16 provides, there is more definiteness. Perhaps this criticism is to be made that there is too much definiteness on this point; it reflects too accurately the aims of the Allied powers which in 1919 were still fresh in the minds of the men who drafted the Covenant. The Members of the League undertake "immediately to subject it [the covenant-breaking state] to the severance of all trade or financial relations, [to] the prohibition of all intercourse between their nationals and the nationals of the covenant-breaking state, and [to] the prevention of all financial, commercial or personal intercourse between the nationals of the covenant-breaking state and the nationals of any other state." This is the enforcement of peace with a vengeance. It envisages not merely economic blockade, but also complete isolation. The very nature of the obligation would seem to presuppose cooperation between the various Members of a well-nigh universal League. Even if the obligation of a Member does not become operative until it has determined for itself that the prohibited resort to war has occurred, the obligation cannot be preformed effectively in any part of the world without common action by numerous states.

Sanctions might conceivably be brought into play without the use of force against the covenant-breaking state. That contingency is expressly envisaged, however, in a provision that the Council shall "recommend" to the various states the military contribution they should make "to the armed forces to be used to protect [Fr., *faire respecter*] the covenants of the League." It is not military action by any state in its own interests which the Covenant allows; that would be war. It is only the use of the armed forces of one or more states on behalf of the community of nations and as recommended by the Council which is approved; and that is certainly not war of the kind which we have known in the past.

Article 16 is not left to operate merely *in terrorem.* It is definite, it is onerous, and it is imperative. As M. de Brouckère put it in 1926,

> Article 16 deals with a contingency to be dreaded. It lays down terrible measures for the extreme case in which the pacific endeavors of the League finally fail before the criminal determination of a state resolved on war.

Moreover, complete performance of its obligations may impinge upon the interests of states which are not bound by the Covenant, and which Article 17 may fail to bring under its aegis.

Precisely because of the severity of Article 16, certain things have happened, to which I can refer but briefly. There has been a tendency to give it an interpretation which will take account of the hesitance of certain states with respect to this general commitment. When the Locarno agreements were being negotiated in 1925, certain states replying to a request by Germany for an interpretation of Article 16 stated that in their view

> each state Member of the League is bound to cooperate loyally and effectively in support of the Covenant and in resistance to any act of aggression to an extent which is compatible with its military situation and [which] takes its geographical position into account.

This interpretation tends to deprive the obligations stipulated in Article 16 of some of their general applicability.

In view of the difficulties of applying Article 16, a persistent activity has been carried on at Geneva with a view to saying when a state is to be branded as an aggressor." That term is not employed in the systematic part of the Covenant (it is employed in Article 10), but it has been employed quite generally in discussions of the application of Article 16. Many people seem to think that no useful definition of aggression can

be devised; yet any contemplation of action to be taken as a
sanction of peace after preventive measures have been exhausted
must rest upon the conception.

In practice, the Covenant's system for the proscription of war
has not, as a whole, been tested.  Disputes in large number,
some sixty or more, have come before the Council, and two of
them have been referred to the Assembly.  In many instances,
the system has worked admirably.  The Council has either been
able to encourage a direct settlement by the parties, or with
the aid of  the Permanent Court of International Justice or
of some *ad hoc* committee it has succeeded in devising a
*modus vivendi* which, after delay in some cases, the parties
could accept.  In some of the earlier disputes over frontiers,
the assistance of the Council proved most valuable.  In a few
instances, the record of the Council is even triumphant.  In
a dispute between  Bulgaria and Greece in 1925, the functioning
of the Council was an instant success.  In the Leticia dispute
between Colombia and Peru, two years ago, an orderly settlement was reached in a situation rife with talk of war.  In
the more recent difficulty between Hungary  and Yugoslavia over
the alleged harboring of terrorists, the Council's action was
prompt and decisive.

Nor can one say, even in cases of its failure to maintain
or restore peace that the collective system has broken down.
In the Manchurian difficulty, seventeen long months of patient
effort, in which neither China nor Japan refused its participation,
preceded the adoption of the Assembly's report of February
24, 1933; and if the recommendations of that report were not
carried out, if Japan was at no time completely restrained
from pushing on with hostile operations, the result was a
mobilization of an informed world opinion on a scale never
before known in human history.

In none of the cases which have arisen to date, has there
been an attempt to bring Article 16 of the Covenant into play.
Indeed, there has been no very serious contemplation of the
employment of all the sanctions in any case.  At one time
when the Council was dealing with the Vilna dispute it was
planned to assemble an international force to go to Vilna; to

assure the orderly conduct of the plebiscite in the Saar, armed forces sent by Great Britain, Italy, the Netherlands and Sweden were on hand at the Council's request, but with the consent of interested governments. Yet no Member of the League has ever been called upon to carry out the extreme measures which Article 16 outlines.

The severity of Article 16 has had the consequence of encouraging an extreme reluctance on the part of the Members and the organs of the League to declare the existence of the conditions which would call for the application of its sanctions.

In view of this analysis and history, what are we to say of the Covenant as an instrument for the proscription of war?

The strength of the Covenant lies first in the fact that it does not attempt a general condemnation of war. On the other hand, it does not stop with an incantation of peace. It lays down a very useful general principle that the world's peace is the concern of all peoples. It creates a basis for cooperation by various states to make peace a viable condition. It provides a systematic procedure for dealing with international disputes. On a background of cooperation and pacific settlement, it forbids recourse to war in definitely but cautiously defined cases. It envisages the possibility that such recourse, though illegal, may occur, and it prescribes sanctions, by no means automatic, which should be taken against a covenant breaker to protect the general interest in the world peace.

The weakness of the Covenant lies first in the fact that powerful states have not accepted its provisions, or having accepted them have sought freedom from their restraints. Its "gaps" have not contributed to this result, but gaps do exist. Its system may be too general, but some of its provisions are too particular. If the whole scheme of sanctions is practicable, that fact is yet to be demonstrated, and its sanctions are too easily identified in the public mind with "pledges to wage war."

Revision of the Covenant is now being much debated, chiefly among people in states which have done least to make its provisions work. Few definite improvements have been suggested in this debate; while some changes have been proposed which are very questionable. If the Covenant had to be written for the first time in the world of today, there would be little hope of producing an instrument as good, or as likely to command a world-wide support. The advance which the Covenant represents can only be appreciated when it is compared with what went before and with what has followed since it was launched.

## AN APPRAISAL OF THE LEAGUE OF NATIONS [5]

The League of Nations may be regarded as an episode in a continuing evolution toward international, and eventual world, government. This movement, whose roots lie deep in the past, has not yet reached its culmination. The growth in the nineteenth century of international law and legislation, of international administrative agencies, and the scores of private international organizations, were all portents of a closer world integration which was bound to become more organized in the twentieth century.

Through World War I this movement was precipitated into the first League of Nations. In its technical aspects, the League was already long overdue; politically, however, it was born prematurely, or more accurately, it was projected into a world psychologically and politically unready to receive it.

Political evolution in recent decades had been hard pressed to keep pace with technical advances. This uneven development created a tension in international life which proved to be incapable of peaceful adjustment. In the present conflict this tension has again reached the breaking point. But seen in perspective it can hardly be doubted that it will have the effect of hastening the tempo of political evolution toward further integration. The great uncertainty, however, is whether this impulse will be directed toward free federation or toward rigid domination in regional or world-wide areas.

The experience of the League in its first phase will doubtless be of value to those who may be engaged in projecting new blueprints of world organization following the conflicts now in

[5] By Benjamin Gerig, Associate Professor of Government, Haverford College; Commissioner General, League of Nations, at New York World's Fair, 1939-1940. Paper presented to the Commission to Study the Organization of Peace. *International Conciliation*. 369:303-16. April 1941.

progress in Europe and the Far East. But whether the unit in the new organization will be the fully sovereign or modified nation state, and, if the latter, what the number and nature of those nation states will be, will have a very great bearing as to the amount of material from the existing League which can be built into the new and—unless the course of evolution is set in reverse—the more highly integrated structures which must be created.

For, it cannot be too often repeated, there was very little integration in the League of 1920-40. It was a loose association of states whose seat or meeting place was at Geneva, but whose sovereign powers were retained largely intact in their respective capitals. These states, whose numbers varied from year to year, acted together according to a set of principles which were outlined in the Covenant in a manner generally more ambiguous than precise. And if the lawyers attempted to make the obligations precise the governments still retained the power to render them inoperative by the unanimity rule.

Thus the League in practice became an expression of the maximum international cooperation that was possible at any given time. This varied both with the subject matter under discussion, and with the governments of the day which states happened to have in office. For, broadly speaking, the people and the various governments of nearly all states may be classified under two categories—those who support international cooperation, and those who do not. It is this fact which makes the classification of states as "members and nonmembers of the League" of somewhat dubious value. Indeed, as everyone knows, certain states members were at times represented by governments whose policies were not only more noncooperative but actually more destructive of League principles than were those of nonmembers.

In making an appraisal of the League, it should also be remembered that twenty years is but a brief episode in the longer time perspectives by which the history of political evolution must be measured. It is much too short on which to base any final or dogmatic assertions as to the success or failure of this effort to develop the rule of law and the principle of cooperation in international affairs.

In this perspective, what may be learned from the League's less successful experiences which may point the way toward the necessary improvements? First, consider this experience as introduced by a few historical paragraphs.

At the end of World War I, Europe was left in unstable equilibrium. America did not win that war. But America undoubtedly decided which side would win. She also influenced the terms of the armistice which terminated the war just short of a knock-out victory. That armistice was to be the prelude to an organized peace, a peace which assumed that a fundamental settlement existed and that necessary minor adjustments could, from time to time, be effected by the League of Nations and the World Court.

If it had been possible then to move quickly into some sort of organization of Europe with easier commercial relations, the new frontiers would not have become so important, and an exaggerated political and economic nationalism would probably have been held within reasonable bounds. Had the defeated nations been quickly brought into the new European and world organization, stabilization at a new psychological and economic level might have been achieved, especially if those who won the war had cooperated to win the peace. Irresponsibility, however, was mistaken for normality, and the collective effort which won the war was soon dissipated in the ensuing peace. It thus became increasingly difficult if not impossible to give effect to the principle of collective action, that is, action in favor both of stability and of change.

One possibility short of collective action through the League of Nations was for nonmembers like the United States to consult with League members, and, in case of agreement, independently arrived at, as to the aggressor, to undertake not to interfere with the restraining efforts of League members. Such obligations seemed inherent in the Pact of Paris. Moreover, a considerable body of opinion began to feel that the states which did not wish to discourage aggression should at least not prevent others, who were explicitly bound by treaties, from doing so. Two efforts in this direction—one at the London Naval Conference in March, 1930, the other by Ambassador Norman Davis at the Disarmament Conference in May, 1933—failed to materialize, with results which were apparent in the Manchurian and Ethiopian cases. [This lack of effective cooperation may now be briefly considered under the following subheadings: Universality, Sovereignty, Neutrality, Security, Armaments, and Peaceful Change.]

*1. Universality.* Nearly every appraisal of the League of Nations made in the past twenty years points out that the first and principal handicap was the failure to achieve a universal or near-universal membership. It was, therefore, only a truncated League lacking the basic elements necessary to give effect to the two principles of *stability* and *change* which alone could avert recurrent war. It required, it was held, a great power like the United States, disinterested and detached from Europe's internal differences, to press certain states to make concessions, and others to modify their demands, if the new situation which her participation in the war helped to create, was not to revert to the condition of an armed truce and eventually to renewed hostilities. Her absence, it will hardly be denied, seriously weakened the guaranty function of the League, for the other leading sea power, Great Britain, was unwilling to assume this added responsibility and perhaps run afoul of the now equally great United States navy in doing so.

This fateful decision of the United States, which deprived the League from the beginning of a very great moral and material influence, was accompanied by an equally fatal decision in Paris in 1919 which kept Germany and the Soviet Union out of League membership and on probation till 1926 and 1934 respectively. This deliberate separation of the "sheep from the goats" was further reflected in the wording of the Covenant—designed to be the permanent charter or constitution of the new international order—which contained repeated references to "the Allied and Associated Powers." The psychological effects of these decisions doubtless went very far in poisoning the atmosphere in which the infant League was intended to grow and prosper. The constitutional effects were equally great since it prevented the systematic coordination of various international bureaus and world services in the League framework as was intended under Article 24.

Membership alone, of course, was not enough. To be effective it had to be coupled with wholehearted cooperation. And the history of the League shows that in some cases nonmembers, like the United States for example, cooperated more helpfully and effectively than did certain of the formal members. This was particularly true as regards the League's technical (as distinct from its political) activities where near-universality was achieved during the period 1926 to 1934 in the fields of health, social welfare, economic questions, and disarmament, with varying degrees of resulting success and failure. Cooperation, however, did not prove to be an adequate substitute for the assumption of corporate responsibility. And failure to agree on major political questions, like disarmament and security, together with the League's condemnation of specific acts of aggression, led to the succesive withdrawal of Germany, Japan, and Italy from the League, including, finally, withdrawal from its technical activities as well. Later still, the Soviet Union was expelled for her aggression on Finland.

This development led to an apprehension on the part of many remaining members of the League, notably Chile, Switzerland, and the Scandinavian countries, lest the League become a bloc or an alliance directed against a too-powerful group of nonmember states. They argued that the sanctions obligations of the Covenant had become too onerous in a League which no longer bound the majority of the Great Powers. Prolonged discussions consequently took place in the period 1936 to 1939 as to reforms which should be made in the Covenant (as if that instrument were to blame for the difficulties). These discussions, which mainly turned on the question of universality, resulted in a deadlock as to whether it was better to have a League without universality or universality without League principles. A proposal by Lord Cranborne, looking toward a *via media* between a coercive and a noncoercive League, by leaving it to be decided in each case *ad hoc* as to how much coercion should be applied, and who should apply it, was received with interest but not acted upon. The double paradox still remains "that in a coercive League universality may be essential but impossible of realization, while in a noncoercive League it may be easy of realization but cease to be essential."

One important subsidiary result, however, emerged in 1939 from these discussions; namely, the creation of an autonomous Economic and Social Organization to be managed by a Central Committee of thirty experts not all of whom must be nationals of states members of the League. Thus it is hoped to give a more independent status to the principal technical organizations of the League which have been working so successfully in the fields of health, transit, and social questions and with equal energy but less success in economic and financial relations, and in all of which the United States has for many years cooperated. It is also hoped that this will permit the greatest possible degree of universality to be maintained during these difficult times in the technical field.

Two conclusions may be drawn from this experience. First, that no great progress can be made on so-called technical international questions until there is a more fundamental settlement of the main political issues now dividing the principal nations of the world; and, second, that no great progress can be expected in either the political or technical fields unless near-universal cooperation is supplemented by a willingness to assume a greater degree of corporate responsibility through modification of national sovereignty.

*2. Sovereignty.* Doubtless one reason why a larger degree of universal unity was not realized by the League was the general reluctance of all states to abridge their sovereignty. This was, and continues to be, the principal obstacle to effective world organization. The framers of the Covenant probably realized this as well as anyone. But being practical men who faced realities they did not argue with reference to untenable analogies of the Swiss, British or American Unions as they might have done. Instead they introduced into the League's constitution as many elements of a corporate character as was possible without setting up a super-state on the ruins of its sovereign members. For example, in admitting and expelling members without unanimous consent, establishing a permanent secretariat, appointing certain committees by majority vote, limiting freedom of members to make war, providing for collective action in restraint of aggression, and in amending the Covenant against the will of a minority, the League founders went a long way in subordinating national independence to the collective will. At the same time, by admitting the right of secession, expressly refraining from domestic interference, by recommending instead of imposing most of its decisions, and by maintaining the general practice of the unanimous vote, the national sovereignties of member states were substantially safeguarded.

The League of Nations thus is clearly a corporate entity which is something more than the mere sum of its members in permanent conference, but something less than an international government or even a confederation of states.

The crux of most criticism directed against the League falls into two categories; First, it went too far; second, it didn't go far enough. In the latter category today are those who advocate federal union on the ground that the League not only failed in practice but was bound to fail because it was unsound in principle through its retention of the sovereign nation-state unit. Without admitting this point or even discussing it here, it might be asked how states can be made to agree to sacrifice *all* their independence when they have shown themselves unwilling in many cases to give up even the modest amount necessary to make the League work. Anyway, national sovereignty in the international sphere corresponds to individual liberty in the domestic sphere, and while both must be greatly abridged in modern society they will not readily be sacrificed altogether. The next step ahead is to bring them gradually under control and demand only such sacrifices as seem natural and inevitable.

Then what has the experience of the League to suggest in this connection? First, it has been shown that nations are as yet unwilling to take automatic universal commitments for the maintenance of peace and the restraining of the aggressor. The Covenant laid it down that war anywhere is the concern of *all* members. Experience has shown, however, that while war anywhere is of *moral* concern it may not be immediately of *equal material* concern to all nations. Without further developing this point it would seem that the logical conclusion to be drawn is that regional or continental systems of mutual assistance with more immediate and far reaching commitments should be set up on the basis of graded responsibilities as among the members of the different regional groupings. These would, of course, be supplemented by universal consultation in case of war or threat of war in order to determine the aggressor, all states agreeing at least not to help the aggressor nation, and perhaps rendering various degrees of assistance to the victim as was the case with Finland. Such systems would not replace the League but be complementary to it and operate under its aegis. This reform has been widely promoted and has received the support *inter alia* of the Baltic and Scandinavian countries. If federalism is ever to develop it would seem to proceed more naturally on such geographic and economic foundations than in any other conceivable way.

A second modification of sovereignty which experience has proved necessary is in the application of the unanimity rule. As is well known, the sovereignty of states members of the League was safeguarded by requiring, with the rarest exceptions, that no state could be committed to a course of action without its express consent. So absurdly far, however, was this practice carried that even under Article 11, which was designed to permit early preventive measures to be taken in case of threat of war, the threatening state has been able by its vote to hold up all pacific action, while proceeding apace with its preparations for or even its actual attack. It was hardly intended by the framers of the Covenant that the Council, which should be able to intervene effectively at an early stage, and which in later stages should be able to place every obstacle in the path of aggression, was to have its action made subject to the vote of the attacking state. To do so is to deprive the preventive measures of Article 11 of all real efficacy.

Proposals for moving in the opposite direction were in recent years initiated by a number of states, notably Norway, Sweden, Switzerland, France, Denmark, Latvia, Finland, Peru, and others who called attention to the need for remedying this defect.

Some have indeed been ready further to modify the unanimity
rule as regards action under Articles 10 and 16 relating to
sanctions.  It seems clear that any reorganization must go farther
than does the present League in abridging sovereignty.

3. *Neutrality.*  One of the most difficult problems which
harassed the peace-keeping and war-restraining efforts of the
League was the retention of neutrality both by nonmember and
member states.  It seems obvious, though it is not everywhere
admitted, that the principles of neutrality and collective responsibility are incompatible.  If the Covenant had been universally
supported no neutrality would have been permissible before
the maximum nine-month period had elapsed for attempting
peaceful settlement under Article 12.  After that members might
have been neutral though not necessarily impartial.  But if war
was resorted to in spite of this delay, no neutrality was permissible; instead, the immediate severance of trade and other
relations was required.

In practice, however, this neat arrangement never worked
out.  A special exception was first made when Switzerland was
permitted largely to retain her traditional neutrality though
agreeing to cooperate in economic measures against a Covenant-
breaking state.  Later, it was seen that certain Latin-American
states, members of the League and parties to the Pact of Paris,
freely entered into neutrality treaties despite their obligations
under the Covenant.  Later still, after the failure of sanctions
against Italy and the withdrawal of more great powers from the
League, certain of the Scandinavian powers announced that the
new situation required them to return to their previous position
of neutrality.

This development was perhaps most largely due to the uncertainty which was felt by members of the League concerning
the position which might be taken by the United States if coercive measures were applied to covenant-breaking states.  It was
obvious that the resources as well as the naval power of this
nonmember state were so great that no effective economic or
perhaps even naval measures could be taken without her assent.
And although in the Manchurian and Ethiopian cases attempts
were made to avoid possible conflict with the United States

these experiences did little to reassure those states who would have had to bear the brunt of imposing a blockade. In fact the doubtful position of the United States has been cited as the reason why Great Britain would not accept the Geneva Protocol of 1924, that the London Naval Conference of 1930 had no more success, and that the effort to harmonize the Covenant with the Pact, failed.

And while the United States has temporarily modified her previous policy of neutral rights, the effect has been to encourage aggression by enlarging the zone for belligerent action and by discouraging repressive measures.

Under these conditions it was unlikely that any greater progress toward the maintenance of world order could be expected.

4. *Security.* The League's experience in attempting to apply the principle of collective security in the form of sanctions to restrain (not punish) the aggressor would seem to support the following generalizations which can only be stated and not elaborated. First, it is probably true that the sanctions provisions of the Covenant were largely responsible for the League's lack of universality. Second, had the sanctions provision been abandoned the League would perhaps have suffered an equal loss qualitatively if not quantitatively. Third, all nations will independently apply a form of sanctions in certain conditions under the guise of self-defense. Fourth, no universal sanctions system will at present receive uniform, equal, and immediate support from all states, hence, fifth, regional or continental forms of security and mutual assistance have been formed or adumbrated. Sixth, economic sanctions alone may not be fully effective against the threat of war, unless backed by international police measures. Seventh, the Italian case showed that economic sanctions though effective could hardly succeed after it was announced that no sanctions would be resorted to which were really inconvenient to the aggressor, and that in no case would military sanctions be undertaken. Eighth, any system of collective security cannot receive universal support which is not properly balanced with a system providing for peaceful change. Ninth, peaceful change cannot be carried out except under conditions of order and secur-

ity, hence, tenth, the principle of third party judgment must be accepted fully and unreservedly in order that measures of security and change may be proceeded with simultaneously without threat and counterthreat from the parties immediately concerned. Finally, when such economic and social policies are adopted by the whole community of nations as will make frontiers less important and obviate any arguments based on military self-sufficiency, the need for applying sanctions will greatly diminish. Moreover, ways may be found to apply coercive measures not against a state as such but against the government of the day which violates its legal obligations and proceeds on an aggressive policy without the full approval of all citizens.

5. *Peaceful Change.* In the postwar period, a great many changes and adjustments were made outside the League, relating to the military, and financial chapters of the Treaty of Versailles. Most of these, however, were made too late to produce the best psychological results. Moreover, the condonation of illegal territorial changes resulted in the worst feelings and suspicions culminating finally in the resumption of war.

The procedure for peaceful change, adumbrated in Article 19 of the Covenant, though invoked in three instances, was allowed to remain inoperative with the resulting charge that the Covenant remained in complete unbalance. It should be remembered however, that changes were constantly being effected through the League's ordinary procedure, including inquiry by the Council, and improved methods of conference and treaty making.

But had certain apparently legitimate changes been made earlier there is no proof that they would have sufficed to appease the aggrieved state whose ambitions went far beyond what any third party tribunal could have considered just. It now seems apparent that the Treaty of Versailles was the pretext rather than the cause for the breakdown of peace whose real causes lay far deeper and are much anterior to this overmuch maligned instrument which, in comparison to the Treaties of Bucharest or Brest Litovsk, was really quite generous.

But the lesson should now be learned that in a dynamic society there will be change—if not peaceable, then forcible.

6. *Armaments.* In addition to the efforts made in the direction of security and change, another approach was tried

through the problem of armaments. Here, the governments tried both the direct and the indirect methods, and in all the years of its work no other subject has occupied so much of the League's time and documentary space.

The principal question was, and continues to be: Are arms the principal cause of war or is the existence of war the principal cause of arms? Those who held the first view urged the direct approach of straight reduction of armaments, quantitatively and qualitatively, believing that international conflicts and war would thus be diminished if not eliminated. Some partiality was shown for this method both by the United States and Great Britain.

Others, however, held that armaments are merely an instrument supporting and reflecting the nation's foreign policy which, if aggressive, must be met by force of arms applied either nationally or collectively. Hence provision must be made for security either on a national or collective basis. States which were partial to this view included France and the Little Entente.

Others held that armaments had to be retained or increased until such time as a just settlement was achieved and meanwhile no support could be given to collective security. The defeated powers in the last war were partial to this view.

Was it to be disarmament, security, and revision—or security, revision, and disarmament—or revision, disarmament, and security? This deadlock has never been resolved and further progress must now await the outcome of the present war.

A similar inconclusive discussion resulted from the effort to classify war implements as defensive and offensive regardless of who were in possession of them.

But the years spent in examining the armaments problem were not all wasted. Not only was every aspect of the problem thoroughly considered but several useful draft agreements were elaborated which, the political situation permitting, could quickly be put into effect, notably as regards: Private Manufacture and Trade in Arms, Publicity of Arms Expenditures, International Inspection and Control of Armaments, and Draft Instruments relating to Arbitration, Security, and the Determination of Aggression.

7. *The Technical League.* As indicated before, near-universality was achieved in the League's technical activities pertaining to health, economics, and social and communications questions. And many solid achievements stand to its credit. Millions of people throughout the world enjoy greater safeguards from diseases and find life more secure, with living standards improved, as a result of these efforts.

Perhaps the least successful of these agencies was the League's Economic Organization. But as it could only recommend and not enjoin, and as the tide toward economic nationalism crept higher and higher, it could only point out the inevitable result of these policies which indeed it never failed to do. Delegates came to Geneva decrying the economic trend but went home feeling themselves compelled to adopt policies of national self-protection.

These economic policies result from war or the threat of war. Until war is eliminated through more effective world organization there is little hope for more rational economic policies based on the general welfare. When there is a basic political settlement, experience would indicate that the technical activities of this or any other League will present few insurmountable difficulties. Machinery for such technical cooperation is now almost universally admitted to be essential.

8. *Location.* The League of Nations in these twenty years has enjoyed the hospitality of the Swiss Republic on whose soil, by invitation, it has established its headquarters. The Swiss are a great and courageous people, but because of their location they are also obliged to be prudent. For centuries they have managed to exist peacefully on a spot swept with the fiercest cross currents of political tension. It is basic in their foreign policy never to incur the simultaneous animosity of any two of their three great power neighbors.

With the breakdown of European peace, Switzerland feels again obliged to give no cause of offense to her neighbors. She has recently returned to her traditional and unqualified neutrality. But political action taken by the League on Swiss soil makes her liable to the charge, rightly or wrongly, of being an accomplice to an unneutral and hostile act. Hence she has felt very uneasy when such political discussions have taken place.

This of course is intolerable for the League which must necessarily be completely free to deal "with any matter . . . affecting the peace of the world" and be in a position to "take any action that may be deemed wise and effectual to safeguard the peace of nations."

The mere mention of this problem is sufficient to suggest a solution. Perhaps the nature of the nation-state system will be so changed after this war that the problem will solve itself. But somehow a solution will need to be found.

To sum up: the history of the League has shown that the defects were often serious but not generally irremediable; that there was room for improvements many but not all of which were under way; but the chief reason for failure was lack of support by its members, including the defection by the United States; that the defects were not primarily constitutional and that the League would work if its members agreed to make it work. If they are not so agreed no machinery will work of itself.

And now, what credits stand in the balance? What positive gains may be found in the League's short history?

It can safely be asserted, in spite of the resumption of hostilities in the second phase of the World War, that more progress was made toward the ultimate goal of world order in the last two decades than in any similar period of history. At the same time, the glaring failures were the more regrettable as they were seen to be not only unnecessary, but in some cases so nearly balanced with success. If this were not generally felt to be true, there would hardly be so many plans and proposals for world organization and reconstruction again brought forward and discussed by millions of people. Whether the new settlement will be based on Union, Federation, Confederation, or League; whether it will be universal or regional; geographic or ideological,—the experience of the League of Nations, 1920-40, will doubtless figure largely in any new machinery which may be set up. It should always be remembered that political evolution is rooted in the past, that it is evolutionary rather than revolutionary, and that it is easier to rebuild on existing foundations than to construct something entirely new.

It is not improbable, however, that the range and intensity of the catastrophe immediately ahead may so completely destroy the fragile edifice of cooperation and peace created in 1920 that, figuratively speaking, only a few stones may be left half buried in wreckage and almost hidden by the tall grass of neglect and impoverishment.

But when peace again returns following the war and the armistice, when men have weighed many alternative propositions, it is not unlikely that a reconstructed world organization (perhaps with intermediate regional and continental forms) can make use of some of the following materials already tested by experience:

1. A world-wide health organization comprising, *inter alia,* machinery for reporting and controlling the prevalence and spread of epidemics, researches into various diseases and their treatment, and world-wide studies of nutrition and housing, etcetera.

2. A world-wide economic organization, comprising the most competent individuals from all countries, to deal with the international aspects of trade, commerce, and exchange.

3. A world-wide social organization competent to deal with matters pertaining to child welfare, migration, protection of young people, and refugees.

4. An international narcotics control service, operating effectively to limit the production, manufacture, and distribution of dangerous drugs.

5. The basis for a permanent commission for assistance to backward peoples (colonies) through various forms of international administration, built on the experience of the Permanent Mandates Commission, and working on the two principles of (a) protection and development of native peoples, (b) equality of access to markets and raw materials without exploitation.

6. An international labor organization able to deal with the uniform promotion of labor standards throughout the world, and with a large number of treaties on wages, hours, and conditions of labor already in effect.

7. A functioning and experienced court of international justice capable of rendering judgments and opinions on the basis of both law and equity, with a valuable body of precedents established as a result of several scores of judgments, opinions, and orders already handed down.

8. A network of draft treaties capable of providing for security, for adjustment, and for reduction of armaments, including the constitution of a permanent commission for inspection and control of armaments, ready to be instituted when political conditions permit.

9. An organization for communications designed to facilitate the movement of peoples, goods and ideas, by land, sea, and air in accordance with the developments of modern science.

10. An organization for intellectual cooperation designed to promote reciprocal appreciation of cultural and artistic values of mankind.

11. A political organization with two constituent bodies—an annual assembly, and a quarterly council—having already met ·twenty and one hundred and six times respectively, and capable, if nations agree, of cutting the Gordian knot of sovereignty at a moment's notice by the adoption of the qualified majority vote.

12. A permanent international secretariat, or civil service, capable of performing its tasks efficiently and impartially in the interests of all mankind.

Perhaps the chief contributions made by the League of Nations in its first two decades may be summed up as follows: (1) It has provided for an Annual Assembly which has become a sounding board for the public opinion of the world; (2) there is now an automatic means of bringing statesmen and conferences together and of continuing their tasks until some result is achieved, which may take years; and (3) it has provided a central machinery, expert and equipped, to carry on any common work which states want done.

With these stones a good beginning toward the building of an international cathedral of peace and cooperation could have been, and may yet be, achieved. But cathedrals are rarely built by a single generation. Interruptions and delays invariably occur and often the superstructure remains incomplete for centuries.

But since the essence of world cooperation is essentially a moral or spiritual idea existing in the hearts of men and women everywhere, it is important to recognize that the form should not be mistaken for the substance. The tangible effects of the League of Nations such as building, properties, and official persons may disappear; that would not be an insuperable calamity. What would be an irreparable tragedy would be a loss of faith in the possibility of international cooperation itself. If that should happen, no amount of buildings or constitutions or other tangible instruments could prevent a steady decline toward anarchy. It is the duty of all reasonable men to see that such a calamity shall not happen.

## THE NON-POLITICAL ACHIEVEMENTS OF THE LEAGUE [6]

The anxious drama of the political and economic crises that have convulsed the world during the past twenty years has tended to detract attention from many of the more prosaic yet profound changes that have taken place in the organization of international life. For these changes the League of Nations, more than any other institution, has been responsible. The place which that institution deserves in the history of our time will doubtless be the subject of controversy for decades to come. Some students will feel that it was doomed to failure by the very form of its constitution or by its political environment; others that it might have succeeded if only certain events had turned out differently—if, for instance, the United States had not withdrawn at the start, or if the Allied Governments controlling its destinies had been more positive in conciliating Germany, or if the League Powers (with the United States) had been more firm in putting down aggression when it first occurred in Manchuria or Ethiopia, or finally, if the so-called Have-Not Powers had been content to wait till the operation of the natural forces of history had given them the new resources they desired. But however widely opinion may differ concerning the accomplishments of the League as a whole, there is unanimity of judgment as to the value of its technical and nonpolitical work. Unhappily, that work has been obscured by the more exciting events of postwar history. It is one of the lesser tragedies of this tragic period that few people know and appreciate the great

[6] By Arthur Sweetser, Director without section, League of Nations, since 1934. *Foreign Affairs.* 19:179-92. October 1940.

progress which has been made on the humble level of what might be called the world's daily business. The League's own reverses, particularly in the Disarmament and Economic Conferences and in the Manchurian and Ethiopian disputes, have distracted attention from its solid but less conspicuous successes. This is the more regrettable because, by distorting our understanding of events since 1919, valuable clues as to what the future may hold in store for us have been concealed.

Any political institution is a reflection of the society from which it has sprung. The League is a particularly good example of this rule. Contrary to the picture often drawn of it, the League has not lived a separate life of its own in a rarefied atmosphere detached from the world about it, but has been a very vivid expression of the period into which it was born. Its record is valuable both as an index of the stage which international life has at present attained, and as an augury of the course we may expect it to take in the future. That course cannot be mapped out by following theory alone; it must be based on actual experience, it must grow out of the daily life of nations.

The present moment is peculiarly auspicious for an appraisal of the League's nonpolitical accomplishments. Chapter One of the League's history—a compact twenty-year period from the end of the First World War to the outbreak of the Second—has come to a sharp close. The great and varied work of international cooperation carried on at Geneva for two decades has been suspended. The conferences which had become almost daily events have for the time being ceased; the international staff has been drastically reduced; some of the technical services, beginning with the financial and economic, are being transferred to the United States on the joint invitation of three educational institutions at Princeton—the University, the Institute for Advanced Study and the Rockefeller Institute for Medical Research.

At the same time, thinking people everywhere are taking stock of the assets that remain, for on these will be built the new organization of international cooperation that will inevitably rise when the present nightmare has passed. There can be no

doubt that in the future there will be a need for more international cooperation than in the past, not only because the ravages
of the present conflict will have to be repaired but because
the world is growing constantly smaller.  The advance of science
is relentless; the needs of industry are pushing commerce ever
farther afield in the search for specialized materials; the world's
population is approaching the two and a quarter billion mark.
In a word, the world's highways are becoming dangerously
crowded, and the necessity for some kind of an international
traffic system will thus be more indispensable than ever.  After
this war the greatest single problem confronting mankind will
once again be—how can the world organize life so as to prevent
another and ever more calamitous disaster?

It is hence very important, at this moment of world-wide disruption and discouragement, to understand how great have been
the advances made since 1919 in the field of technical and nonpolitical collaboration between nations.  As Secretary of State
Hull declared on February 2, 1939, "The League . . . has
been responsible for the development of mutual exchange and
discussion of ideas and methods to a greater extent and in more
fields of humanitarian and scientific endeavor than any other
organization in history. . .  The United States Government
is keenly aware of the value of this type of general interchange
and desires to see it extended."  Upon a later occasion, President
Roosevelt, when commenting on the creation of an American
committee concerned with the League's technical activities,
stated that "without in any way becoming involved in the political affairs of Europe, it has been the continuous policy of this
Government for many years to cooperate in the world-wide technical and humanitarian activities of the League.  Certain of
them, indeed, are not only worthy but definitely essential. . .
However governments may divide, human problems are common
the world over, and we shall never realize peace until these
common interests take precedence as the major work of civilization."

The tremendous growth of international cooperation that
marked the period following 1919 was due more than anything
else to the fact that the League provided a center where all in-

ternational activities, particularly those of a technical and non-political nature, could concentrate and draw strength. For the first time in history there existed a central agency where the affairs of the world were constantly surveyed by specially created groups of experts who were provided with a meeting place, a staff and working funds. The significance of this humble and little appreciated fact cannot be exaggerated. Before the establishment of the League, a major diplomatic effort was required to assemble an international conference on any subject, even one of pressing importance; the great majority of questions were of such secondary interest that no attempt was even made to convene a meeting to consider them. With the coming of the League, delegations from all corners of the world met every year in the League's Assembly, under which were plenary committees: Legal, Social and Humanitarian, Financial and Economic, Political, and Disarmament. Any question not sufficiently urgent to call for a special conference could be taken in its stride by the appropriate Assembly committee.

A flexible and efficient mechanism existed for carrying out the work thus authorized. The League Council, a kind of executive committee meeting quarterly, has been on hand to take administrative steps, such as appointing committees and fixing dates of meeting. The Secretariat, an international civil service of some seven hundred officials at its maximum, has been constantly available to collect information, prepare preliminary documentation, and provide for translations, the keeping of records and other secretarial work. Finally, a network of expert committees was built up, ranging over almost the entire field of international affairs. This system, as a system, was as nearly complete as it could reasonably be expected to be; that it did not succeed in its primary purpose of preventing another world war should not obscure its very real achievements in other less important fields.

Among the League's technical agencies the most highly developed is the Economic and Financial Organization, part of the work of which has recently been established in the United States. This organization, set up on the recommendation of the Brussels Financial Conference of 1920, afforded invaluable assistance to such important gatherings as the World Economic Conferences of Geneva (1927) and London (1933). Less well-known yet important activities included the sponsoring of many specialized conferences, in addition to a vast amount of unspectacular but highly useful day-to-day work. The principal agencies of the Organization are the Economic and Financial Committees, composed of experts who are often high-ranking government officials but who for the moment drop their official status in order to exchange views more freely. These two committees are served by the permanent staff of the Secretariat, assisted by specialized committees on subjects as diversified as double taxation, statistics, economic depressions, raw materials, demographic problems, and the gold standard. The result is a kind of specialized economic and financial league within the general League—one with which nonmembers, particularly the United States, have been closely associated. However far the world may have moved in the opposite direction from the liberal policies of free and unrestricted trade recommended by the League's experts, the fact remains that in the end these policies will prove to have been the right ones.

The foundation of the League's work in this almost unlimited field lies in its scientific publications. These, for the first time in history, afford a perspective of the world looking down from above rather than the usual foreshortened view as seen horizontally from the window of a particular nation. The *Monthly Bulletin of Statistics,* the *Statistical Year Book, International Trade Statistics,* and *International Trade in Certain Raw Materials and Foodstuffs* have provided essential statistical information on the world's economic life. Other, more analytical publications such as the *Review of World Trade, World Production and Prices, Monetary Review,* and *Money and Banking,* have been widely used, particularly in the United States and Germany. Other more popular ones such as the *World Economic Survey* have been useful in giving a picture of world economy as a whole; while one specialized study has found its way into use as a college textbook. Though these publications do not claim to be the final word on their subjects, they have demonstrated a new and useful approach to world problems.

The various special committees set up in this field have also made definite, if modest, contributions to the cause of international economic organization. The Fiscal Committee has by years of effort perfected several model conventions on fiscal and double taxation problems which have been used as the basis for over a hundred bilateral treaties. The Committee of Statistical Experts, comprising some of the world's foremost statisticians, has evolved a series of standard forms which have already been widely adopted. The Committees on Raw Materials, Economic Depressions, Demographic Problems and the like have made, or are making, similarly valuable studies.

While most of this work has taken the form of analysis or recommendation, some of it has been given precise or even contractual expression. A number of international treaties have been drawn up dealing with subjects as varied as customs formalities, commercial arbitration, treatment of foreigners, counterfeiting of currency, bills of exchange, regulation of whaling, and veterinary problems. Though these agreements cover but a part of the field of international affairs, they constitute a useful contribution to the international law of economic and financial relations which would hardly have been possible without some such permanent agency as the League.

Mention should also be made of the reconstruction loans totalling something over $400,000,000 issued under League auspices on behalf of such countries as Austria, Hungary, Bulgaria and Greece. These loans undoubtedly saw Europe over a serious crisis and demonstrated a method of international investigation and control far superior to the disastrous and unchecked loans which followed. The experience received from them offers useful suggestions for the large-scale financing which will doubtless follow the present conflict.

Then there is the League's work in communications and transit. This activity made a promising start at the Barcelona Conference in 1920, when a new international law of communications and transit was outlined and an autonomous agency was created, in which participation was later opened to nonmember states on a basis of full equality. Its subsequent development did not, however, fully carry out the early promise, partly because it tended to follow the pathways of international conventions rather than of analytical studies, and partly because several of its most important aspects—such as posts, telegraph, telephone and aviation—were already entrusted to other bodies which were unwilling to pool their activities with the more general agency. Even so, the latter was able to demonstrate its value. Few travelers at sea today realize that the League's Transit Organization has been working for years on the standardization of buoyage and the lighting of coasts; still fewer automobilists in Europe, particularly in Germany, realize that the traffic signs on many roadways were given a standard form at League meetings.

In the field of health, the success of the League has been outstanding. Born during the dangerous emergency when typhus threatened Western Europe after the First World War, its work has been practical to a degree which ought to satisfy even the most cynical critic of international cooperation. It has operated on the principle that disease is no respecter of national frontiers. Two of its foremost officials have met death in its service, an American in Syria and a Dutchman in China.

The League's Health Organization, going far beyond any previous efforts in its field, has woven together a world-wide cooperative system embracing governments and individuals, institutions and foundations, hospitals and laboratories. Its work has been directed by a Health Committee consisting of the foremost authorities, often Ministers of Public Health serving unofficially, assisted by an expert permanent staff in the Secretariat, by a network of committees on special problems, and by an annual review on the part of the plenipotentiary delegates at the Assembly. It has thus been able to move fast and far, with complete independence and impartiality and with full access to existing agencies for the protection and improvement of health. Its first task has been to prevent the spread of diseases. This has necessitated sending commissions to several points of danger, as to Poland in 1920 and in 1937. Far more constant, however, has been the watch which it maintains against the outbreak of disease. These activities are centered in the Epidemiological Intelligence Service, which has an Eastern Bureau at Singapore and which operates a radio service embracing no less than 186 ports, working day and night, unseen and unsung, as a vital part of the world's health protection.

Not content merely to prevent disease, the League has sought to improve health facilities throughout the world. Probably not one person in a million, when treated with any of a score of different serums and pharmaceutical products, realizes that the "international" standard on which they are based and on which depends the patient's health, or even life, is in reality a League of Nations standard worked out with infinite patience by laboratories and experts cooperating all over the world. Still fewer are aware that League committees have studied malaria in London, Hamburg, Paris, Rome and Singapore, have even developed a wholly new drug, totaquina, which is far cheaper and quite as effective as quinine, or that they have organized a leprosy research institute in Brazil, or made comparative tests of syphilis treatment in many countries, or studied sleeping sickness in Africa and pellagra in the rural districts of Rumania. Here, indeed, unperceived by the public at large, has been a world cooperative campaign against man's most ancient and implacable enemy.

Another innovation has been the assistance which the League has afforded to individual governments for improving their own health services. For the first time in history, a nation in need of such assistance has been able to apply for it from an international association, without having to fear political complications. Almost from the start of the League, China has drawn heavily upon the advice and aid of its experts in caring for her colossal public health problem. Greece likewise received considerable assistance when reorganizing her health services in 1928. Various other nations have benefited, though less extensively. The League has also organized collective tours by which over seven hundred health officers from thirty-five different countries have been enabled to study medical methods abroad.

The most timely of all the League's health functions has perhaps been its work in the field of nutrition. Incidentally, this work clearly illustrates the cumulative method of League procedure and the interplay between different zones of interest and authority. The first embryo of this work may be found in an inquiry which the League carried out at the request of the Government of Japan into the food problems of that country. Shortly thereafter, the ravages of the depression led the Health Committee to set up a group of experts to study its specific effects on health. In its turn the International Labour Conference took steps to consider the effect of widespread malnutrition on the health of workers. It remained, however, for the Australian delegation to put the subject on a universal basis by proposing to a somewhat skeptical Assembly in 1935 that the League undertake a study of nutrition in all its aspects—health, social, economic and industrial. As a result, a Mixed Committee on the Problem of Nutrition was set up, the personnel of which included agricultural, economic and health experts. Enlisting the aid of the Advisory Committee on Social Questions, the International Labour Office and the International Institute of Agriculture, it arrived at certain basic principles of nutrition which are embodied in its final report of 1937.

The subject continued to expand, however, and national committees have accordingly been set up in different countries, until there were over a score of them that have proved so effective that their representatives have twice been called into general conference at Geneva. Similarly, a regional approach to specific aspects of the problem has been made through conferences of government representatives. Out of all this study and consultation has evolved a scientific knowledge concerning foods and food values, a maximum and minimum standard of nutrition, a framework of policy for governments and health ministries, and an exposure of the unnecessarily low standards of nutrition prevalent throughout the world. To quote President Roosevelt again: "The world-wide efforts for better nutrition standards have already shown that the way towards solution of health problems may also be the way towards definite improvement of economic conditions."

Housing, commonly regarded as a very individual problem, is another subject in which the League has recently shown an interest. Here again, the subject has been approached from two widely different angles. On one side, a group of health and building experts has, on the basis of the comparative experience of all countries, worked out certain fundamental, scientific requirements for air, heat, light, noise prevention, sanitation and other structural necessities.  On another side, a group of financial experts has elaborated various methods for meeting the problem of financing.  In the field of housing each nation has much to learn from the others, for where one has excelled in design, another has excelled in interior equipment, and still another in financing.  Housing very definitely offers a field of comparative experience in which a free exchange of all available knowledge and techniques is urgently needed in order to aid the millions of ill-housed peoples in all lands.

It is in the sphere of drug control, however, that the League has most nearly approached direct international government. Before the First World War only timid attempts were made to reduce this terrible scourge.  Since the creation of the League, however, these efforts have been accentuated until today they have culminated in the most advanced form of international administration so far accepted by sovereign nations.  As in other fields, an Advisory Committee was created, which in this case was composed of government representatives.  Its domain kept continually widening as the pursuit of the illegitmate drug producer and trafficker went ever farther afield.  Special world conferences were called in 1924-25, 1931 and 1936; and new conventions, some of them the most widely ratified international agreements on record, were adopted.  Control progressed step by step: first, over the international traffic by means of a universally adopted system of import and export certificates; next, over the manufacture of drugs by estimating world needs and bringing about a reduction in production; and then, over national administrations by imposing an embargo against offending nations.  More recently, there has been drafted a Convention for limiting the production of raw materials.  One group of League experts has authority to estimate what quantities of drugs should be manufactured; another surveys the traffic as it actually exists and as it is reported by the separate governments.  In case the Convention is violated, this latter group, sitting as an impartial international tribunal, has the power to embargo further commerce in drugs with the offending nation. Never before have the nations given an international agency such wide authority. The results, however, have been dramatically justified by the 50 per cent reduction in morphine production between 1929 and 1932, the large reduction in heroin and cocaine production and the decrease in the number of drug addicts, *e.g.,* from 100,000 to 50,000 in the United States. This effort has, fortunately, called forth the cooperation of practically all nations, not only of former members like Germany and Italy, but more particularly of the United States, which has been a most militant participant from the beginning.

Such have been the principal technical and nonpolitical activities of the League. Many others less conspicuous or less continuous exist in nearly all phases of international relations, but we need not examine them in detail, for the principles they involve have already been described. The only two we might mention in passing are the League's Child Welfare work and its committees on intellectual cooperation—both typical of the new and useful fields of international action which the League has opened up.

These multifarious activities have come to the League from very different sources. Some, such as opium control, health and the suppression of prostitution, were already in an embryonic stage before the First World War. Others, such as communications and transit, were given special stimulus in the peace treaties. Still others, such as parts of the economic and financial work, originated in plenipotentiary conferences which later entrusted to the League permanent duties that they were not equipped to continue. The great majority, however, represent new activities generated by discussion at the League itself.

As the historical origins of these activities have been different, so necessarily have been their legal bases. Some, though interwoven with the League, are firmly embedded in international convention or treaty, notably the opium work which has behind it the conventions of 1912, 1925, 1931 and 1936. Others are grounded in the League's organization itself, particularly its economic and financial work, which has developed through analysis and report rather than by juridical expression.

Still others, such as the institutes of intellectual cooperation at Paris, cinematography at Rome, and leprosy at Rio de Janeiro, have been established as autonomous agencies associated with the League but having their own governing bodies and, unfortunately, as experience has shown, an ultimate dependence on the governments that give them hospitality.

The various activities have also manifested very different and uneven rates of progress. Some have developed rapidly, others slowly, and often quite contrary to expectations. The speed has depended in part on the nature of the subject and in part on the energy with which it has been pursued. Where a government has taken a strong position, as the British on slavery or the American on opium, progress has tended to be rapid. Where there has been a resolute group of people interested in the question or where a tradition of activity has already been built up, as in the campaign against organized international prostitution, work has likewise gone ahead quickly. In some cases, notably as regards refugees or double taxation, energetic support from individuals has brought great progress. The League method has been simple, informal and receptive; a government or group desiring action could usually secure it unless the opposition was very determined. Very often hostility, if not irreconcilable, has contented itself with mere abstention; an indifferent majority has frequently allowed an energetic minority to have its way.

Any general evaluation of the League's nonpolitical activities inevitably returns us to the point stressed at the beginning of this article: that by its mere existence the League has given an unprecedented stimulus to international cooperation. The very fact that there has been in operation a permanent agency with an annual Assembly, a quarterly Council, manifold committees, a permanent staff and an adequate budget, has made it possible for many international activities to catch the world's attention, receive a hearing, and be given whatever encouragement they deserved.

One of the little understood phenomena of this system has been the development of something which might almost be described as spontaneous combustion in generating new ideas and plans. Bring together the representatives of many nations and many viewpoints in periodic conferences, and the result is almost sure to be the formulation of ideas of the most unexpected sorts. No one would have predicted, for instance, that the most ambitious Press Conference ever convened would develop out of a curious Chilean complex; or that a world-wide campaign for better nutrition would find its origin in Japan and Australia; or that many other activities, in particular those concerning the suppression of the drug traffic and prostitution, would originate among Americans—whose government was not even a member of its League. The League has made it possible for the world to tap its wealth of human experience, wisdom and leadership in a way heretofore impossible. Governments, organizations and individuals which in the past had often had considerable difficulty in discovering a forum in which to present their ideas have found in the League a hospitable medium.

Another important feature of the League method has been its flexibility. It has been able to work without undue haste or pressure, but with periodic revision and checking. It could proceed stage by stage—preliminary study in the Secretariat, more formal discussion in a group of experts, still more formal discussion in the Assembly, and finally full diplomatic action in a special conference. The League has been under none of that compelling urgency so prevalent before the First World War when things were either accomplished suddenly at *ad hoc* conferences or had to wait for years until, as in the case of the old Hague Conferences, public interest demanded the calling of a new meeting.

The League has also been able to carry on its work in a far more scientific and nonpolitical spirit than had been possible in the past. This is well stated in the Report of the Special Committee on the Development of International Cooperation in Economic and Social Affairs (known as the Bruce Committee), which says:

> In the early days of the League, it was perhaps too often assumed that international cooperation necessarily implied international contractual obligations and that the success of such cooperation could be measured by the new obligations entered into. In certain fields, indeed, notably in the control of the drug traffic, and in numerous problems

connected with the régime of international communications and transit—such methods have met with striking success and continue to be appropriate. But it is coming to be realized that many of the really vital problems, by their very nature, do not lend themselves to settlement by formal conferences and treaties—that the primary object of international cooperation should be rather mutual help than reciprocal contract—above all, the exchange of knowledge and of the fruits of experience.

This philosophy has introduced the expert into international life to an unprecedented degree. There, as elsewhere, the first necessity is to know the facts without fear or favor; once they have been ascertained, the action to be taken is often surprisingly clear and is generally accepted. It is when facts are but half known, or are partially obscured by extraneous elements, that conflict is most likely to develop.

Another important and seldom appreciated advantage inherent in a permanent international mechanism like the League is that it permits those working in one field of activity to cross professional lines and obtain assistance from those engaged in cognate fields. The Opium Committee, for instance, has frequently turned to the Health Committee for its judgment on certain drugs; the Nutrition Committee has drawn upon the Health, Economic and Labor Committees; the Child Welfare Committee has turned to the Cinematographic Institute; and so on around the circle. Interesting to note is the fact that the World Disarmament Conference examined the system of international drug control in search of ideas it might use for setting up a similar system of control over world armaments.

The League's twenty years of experience have brought out sources of weakness as well as of strength. First of all, this experience has shown that delegates at Geneva all too frequently vote a resolution only to have their governments fail to carry it out. This has often been interpreted as bad faith, but more likely it is merely a difference of tempo. At Geneva the delegates find themselves in a new atmosphere: as a result of free discussion they gradually come to accept the fairness of other viewpoints; this leads them slowly to modify their own ideas; and thus they eventually come to an agreement representing the greatest common good. The governments at home, however, feel these stimuli but faintly, for their outlook is limited by national interests and in the formulation of their policies they are particularly subject to local group pressures. One can readily understand, then, why there is often a gap between what a diplomat viewing the world as a whole recommends and what a local politician at home is willing to accept. How to narrow this gap is one of the great problems facing the future.

Another difficulty has been the tendency on the part of certain totalitarian governments to make no differentiation between the political and the nonpolitical functions of the League. When Japan left the League, she continued for a while to cooperate in its nonpolitical activities; subsequently, however, she severed her connections with all branches of the League's work. Similarly, when Germany and Italy withdrew, they left the League and all its work. The only exception was that Germany continued to participate in its opium control because this work had originated in a special treaty. It is worth mentioning that the United States, though not a member of the League, has pursued a gradually expanding policy of selective cooperation, until today the American Government is widely represented in the League's technical work.

Another difficulty, this time one of organization rather than of politics, is that several specialized international agencies already in the field before the League's creation have guarded their independence so jealously that they have kept certain important activities from coming under League control. The situation has differed from case to case, but the principle has been substantially the same. The International Postal and Telegraphic Unions, for instance, remain almost without contact with the League; the International Institute of Agriculture has cooperated somewhat uncertainly; the Bank of International Settlements has been kept rather conspicuously apart from the League. The International Health Bureau has, on the contrary, become largely overshadowed by the League's Health Organization. It is true that during the present world upheaval these agencies have been able to maintain a sort of precarious life, whereas the League has seen its work badly crippled. But in normal times, their insistence upon a completely separate individuality often leads to conflicts and duplications of effort injurious alike to the international community as a whole and to the agencies themselves. Another problem to be faced after this war will therefore be to establish a greater degree of unity and cooperation among the various international bodies that render service to the world at large.

The record of the League of Nations in these past twenty years is neither all black nor all white. The League proved inadequate to avert the great catastrophe which many had hoped it might avert. Yet this failure cannot destroy the fact that the League experiment, during its first brief period of life, made appreciable contributions not only to the solution of day-to-day problems but even more to the opening up of new subjects and new methods from which we may derive inspiration and hope for the future. This experience has been deeply valuable, for it marks a phase in the slow transition of mankind from international anarchy to the world community.

## WORLD PEACE: PRACTICAL WAYS
## AND MEANS [7]

*Original Principles of the League and Covenant.* In any discussion of the so-called "Reform of the League," it is well to set forth the leading principles deemed essential to a successful and working system of "collective security," institutionalized through a world organization such as the League. It is also well to indicate how, in practice, these principles have failed of application.

1. The League of Nations was intended to be a world, or universal, peace institution. By gradual extensions, it was designed to embrace all the nations of the world. President Wilson, in answer to criticism of Great Britain's reservations to the principle of the freedom of the seas as one of the conditions of peace, replied that all nations would make common

[7] From article by Charles E. Martin, Professor of International Law and Political Science, University of Washington. *Institute of World Affairs.* Proceedings, 14th Session, December 13 to 18, 1936. p. 190-205. University of Southern California. Los Angeles. 1937.

cause against an aggressor, and that henceforth there would be no neutral rights, since there would be no neutrality.

Russia was not invited into the League at the beginning, and did not join until 1934. Germany was not invited to join, even though she had many of the requisites of membership. Germany joined in 1926, and withdrew in 1935.

The United States, having dictated many of the terms of the Covenant, and even of the Treaty of Peace, declined membership.

Japan, having gained much and lost nothing as a result of the war, retained her membership until 1934.

Italy, while a titular member at this writing [1936], frankly and boldly seeks other means of adjusting her international problems.

With Germany on the Continent, the United States in the Western Hemisphere, and Japan in Asia, all nonmembers, the League's effectiveness for peace in all these regions cannot be other than adversely affected.

2. The League was presumed to be an association of democratic nations. The war had been fought "to make the world safe for democracy." Four great empires had crumbled, and new states, democratic in form, or dedicated to the democratic principle, had succeeded them. The leading states, allied and associated, and enemy, were democracies.

Italy was a parliamentary government. Now it is Fascist. Germany was a republic under a liberal constitution. Now it is a totalitarian state. Japan, with definite parliamentary features at that time, has yielded to the more conservative forces of the military, the bureaucracy, and the great industrial interests. Stateism, nationalism, and authoritarianism have caused democracy and its institutions to recede, with inevitable effects on the peace machinery of the world.

3. The states of the League were to be substantially disarmed through the application of Article 8 of the Covenant. Germany, under involuntary disarmament, was, in a sense, to point the way to what the other states would be expected to follow, under international agreement.

The abstention of the United States from the League settled the point that disarmament negotiations—especially naval—could not proceed within the framework of the League alone. Great Britain declared that she could reduce only as the United States reduced her naval strength. Considerations of "security" took precedence over disarmament measures. The disarmament conferences were deadlocked over certain theoretical and basic problems, and never achieved substantive reductions. Germany, when able to stand alone, followed a policy of "rearmament," in the absence of any substantial reductions elsewhere. The result has been a race in arms, now in full sway.

4. The peaceful settlement of international disputes was provided for in Articles 12-15. Various forms of settlement were provided for, such as conciliation, arbitration, judicial judgment, and decision by the Council. Definite procedure was set up under which member states, parties to disputes, might have recourse to these processes of peace. The Permanent Court of International Justice, through its judgments and advisory opinions, became an indispensable aid in the execution of these provisions of the Covenant.

In this field of activity the League has been fairly successful, and little criticism is attached to its procedure or to its record, where the process has been tried and the decision or the award accepted. It is in other fields where the League has experienced shortcomings.

5. The League provided for the application of sanctions, or collective force against aggression, as set forth in Article 16. The makers of the Covenant realized that the peace problem was a twofold one: (1) to get nations to have recourse to peaceful settlement instead of resorting to war or to hostile measures; and (2) once having submitted to peaceful settlement. to abide by the decision in good faith. It remained to make these two obligations binding on the member states through agreement, and to provide some means for their enforcement. Accordingly, an aggressor was presumed to be a country going to war before submitting its case to peaceful settlement; or having done so, declining to abide by the decision, award, or judgment, as the case might be.

It should be noted that joint action is provided only against the most extreme violation of the Covenant—an act of aggression. Only the enormity of the violation could justify the severity of the mode of redress. Other violations were reserved to other modes of adjustment.

The League members sought, through such supplementary conventions as the Pact of Mutual Guarantees and the Geneva Protocol, to amplify the sanctions provisions of the Covenant, and to define, insofar as possible, what was meant by an act of aggression. An attempt was made to bring together the three doctrines of arbitration, security, and disarmament.

The Sino-Japanese controversy, while involving the interest and the judgment of the League, did not involve the question of sanctions.

The Italian-Abyssinian conflict is the first case of the outright application of sanctions against an aggressor. The application and, later, the lifting of sanctions by the League members, have been the occasion of much attack on Article 16 and the League as a Covenant-enforcing body.

6. The Covenant provided for the registration of treaties, and for the termination of treaties in conflict with the Covenant, or prejudicial to the performance of a country's obligations under the Covenant. Registration of treaties almost became a formality in the whole process of negotiation, following only the exchange of ratifications. The Treaty Series established a body of treaty law never before attempted. And while the Covenant was itself only a treaty, there seemed a determination to negotiate only such treaties as were consistent with it. While these treaties and the Covenant were of equal validity, they were not of the same importance. Moreover, they were presumed to be "open covenants openly arrived at."

A number of supplementary engagements were entered into, supplying certain defects and deficiencies of the League. The Locarno pact, the disarmament convention, and the security pacts were within the general purpose of the League. Certain treaties of alliance, however, were of doubtful validity. Certainly some states sought freedom in treaty-making through withdrawal from the League and from the binding provisions of the Covenant.

7. The *status quo*, in government and territory, was given both recognition and protection through Article 10, under which the territorial integrity and the existing political independence of each member of the League were guaranteed as against "external aggression." Neither in Article 10 nor in other applications of this principle have the justice and ethics of political and territorial settlements been necessarily upheld. It was realized that at some point of political establishment and territorial settlement, mutual respect for such arrangements must begin. It would be impossible to even up all the injustices of the past. Taking the present as a starting point, nations were to be guaranteed that sovereignty, independence, and jurisdiction they are presumed to enjoy under international law.

Respect for the political and territorial *status quo* is found in other peace pacts, such as the Nine-Power Treaty, the Four-Power Pact, the Kellogg-Briand Pact, and the Argentine Anti-War Treaty. The Hoover nonrecognition doctrine, as applied by the United States, and also by the League of Nations, to Japan, is a new form of sanction against a violation of a treaty *status quo*.

While this was, to Mr. Wilson, the "heart of the Covenant," dissatisfaction came from two sources. Few countries desired to guarantee another country's *status quo* to the extent of war. Then, many countries, both defeated and conquering, felt that many settlements had been unjustly or unwisely made, and sought some means of change without violation of Article 10. Finally, it was never known when a country, profiting by the existing *status quo*, might suffer through the establishment of a different equilibrium, political and territorial.

8. Closely related to the *status quo*, was the provision, through Article 19, of means for the peaceful change of the *status quo* after treaties had become inapplicable or the conditions of their continuance dangerous. Unfortunately, Article 19 has received the least attention of the League, and its application is what is today most needed. Little regard has been paid the means of revising treaties and of altering the *status quo* by means of peaceful agreement. Where requests for its application have been made, they have sometimes been ignored.

Had the revision of treaties and of the *status quo* through peaceful means, been tied up with the guarantees of territory and independence in Article 10, as President Wilson suggested and intended, the League and Covenant might have been saved against its present rigidity and inflexibility, apparent and real.

*Fundamental Problems and Issues in League Reorganization*

1. Shall the League continue to seek ultimate universality in the light of the experience of the past? Or shall it decentralize, encouraging the formation of regional Leagues in well-established regions of the world? Should such regional leagues be within the framework of the Geneva institution, or should they be independent of it?

To what extent may bilateral arrangements, such as pacts of nonaggression, and multilateral pacts, such as the Kellogg-Briand Pact, become substitutes for League action?

The fact of nonuniversality, already set forth, proves that now, and for some years to come, the League will not be a universal institution. It is also clear, from what is happening in the Americas and in the Orient, that the League can hardly hope to be an instrument for the effective adjustment of international controversies in those regions. They are too remote from the League machinery and influence. Where the League has spoken as regards these regions, it has not been attended with any appreciable success.

The League, in prescribing for the entire world, has imposed on each member state an obligation to maintain peace in the entire world. It is an obligation as wide as the prescription. However, nations today are not interested in military liability beyond the zone of their special interest or responsibility. Certain tendencies toward regionalism may be noted.

a. The Geneva League, preoccupied with European problems, seems rapidly becoming a European institution. The outstanding problem is the Franco-German frontier, and such security arrangements as will protect one against aggressive attack on the part of the other. To England, in the words of Stanley Baldwin, the Rhine is the frontier, as against interference with France, and with border states, such as Belgium and The Netherlands. The tension between Communist and Fascist states, especially Russia and Germany, is a problem of European concern. The conflict between Great Britain and Italy over the Mediterranean is peculiar to Europe. Perhaps these are the problems to which the Geneva institution should address itself, as within territorial range and within manageable control.

b. The failures of peace arrangements in Europe and the Far East have led to new and independent efforts on this hemisphere toward a new and more effective peace structure. The Inter-American Conference for the Maintenance of Peace, now [December 1936] in session at Buenos Aires, is considering (1) the organization of peace, (2) neutrality arrangements, (3) the limitation of armaments, (4) juridical problems, (5) economic problems, and (6) intellectual cooperation. Under peace organization, it will seek to extend and coordinate existing antiwar treaties; to establish new peace machinery, including an Inter-American Court of Justice; and closer cooperation between the American republics and international institutions such as the League of Nations. A common neutrality policy will be attempted, and it is likely that the Monroe Doctrine will become multilateral in definition and enforcement.

What will be the relation of this collective security to that of the League of Nations? Some states want an American League of Nations, independent of Geneva. Some want a regional League within the framework of the Geneva institution. Others, including the United States, favor cooperation with the League of Nations for purposes of trade and peace, but favor the absolute independence and equality of the Inter-American group of nations. Mr. Hull favors only such League of Nations cooperation as will not complicate or involve the integrity of the American organization of nations. Accordingly, any connection with the League will be nebulous, it is predicted.

c. In the Pacific, we envisage a somewhat different situation from that of Europe and the Far East. There are advocates of League of Nations action, of regional pacts, of bilateral arrangements, and of unilateral affirmation of policy.

Great Britain, committed to the League and to collective security, is opposed both to the pretensions of Japan in this area, and to settlements which ignore the League of Nations and its general principles of peace.

China demands that there shall be an international framework in which all major powers of the Pacific may participate, including Russia, Great Britain, and the United States. It must also involve a peace arrangement between Russia and Japan, for any war between these two would mean also a war with China. Such peace machinery cannot be used, says China, to approve the *status quo* in violation of treaties of peace. China also favors League of Nations peace arrangements in the Pacific area.

Japan, on the other hand, will not be a party to any revision of pacts under the League's auspices. She will not negotiate her special position in the East—it must be admitted. She alone will define this position. She will not agree to any arrangement calling for the application of sanctions. Moreover, any new treaty arrangements for the Pacific and Far East must take into account the *status quo* in North China and Manchukuo.

The United States would insist, perhaps, on all Pacific arrangements being independent of the League of Nations. No sanctions would be agreed to in advance of the contingency. This country would doubtless hold to its present naval position, and to its policy as regards China. And it would go much further here than in Europe to cooperate for peace.

The Pacific area, with countries of an insular and continental character, and with several countries having primary interests, though lying far from the Pacific zone, presents problems altogether different from those presented by continental units.

2. Shall the League retain its sanctions provisions, looking toward the discovery and the punishment of an aggressor, or shall it be reduced purely to a voluntary organization? If sanctions are retained, should there be any difference between the application of economic and military sanctions? Should there be any regional application of military sanctions?

What should be the attitude of neutrals toward sanctions, both economic and military, enforced by a collective body of nations against an aggressor? Should both the League and the aggressor, at war, be regarded by neutrals as on the same basis, and invested with the same rights and obligations?

There are many friends of the League who would like to see it assume a purely voluntary character.  They argue that it should be an organization for the encouragement and the promotion of peace, and for the development of that international solidarity along voluntary lines without which peace is impossible.  They would return the problem of sanctions and action against the aggressor to the foreign offices, where, they argue, it belongs, for the foreign offices, and not Geneva, it is urged, inevitably decide such matters.

Others favor not only the resumption of sanctions by the League, but their extension and improvement, on the theory that a League, to count, must deal with things that matter.

There are others who favor substantial modifications in the nature of the sanctions to be applied, and in the manner of their application.  The suggested modifications are too varied to be listed here.

Great Britain, while favoring sanctions, recognizes definite limits to their effectiveness, and to the possibilities of success growing out of their enforcement.  She regrets the apparent futility of the sanctions against Italy, and insists that this is no argument against collective security, nor against Great Britain's adherence to the principle.  She is particularly concerned over the attitude of the United States toward sanctions.

France and Russia seem committed to the principle of sanctions universally applied.  Both admit the meaning of regionalism, but both seem most concerned with the general peace first, European peace second, and regional arrangements elsewhere, third.  Both are powers in the Pacific area.  Yet both face Germany, and both fear her.  Universal sanctions have long been identified with the case of Germany.  It is not surprising that these countries see in their frontier problems something of a world problem.

Japan, having received the adverse judgment of the League, has no interest in or sympathy for sanctions.  She will enter no peace which provides for them.

Some of the Latin American states favor the limitation of sanctions to definite regions, as do some European states.

Italy, of course, is the greatest critic of sanctions, especially in their more recent form. She might be less opposed to them if a question of continental peace, as between Germany and France, should be at stake.

Germany, having suffered from sanctions of another sort, cannot now, under her revisionist program, be regarded as friendly to coercive measures against an aggressor.

The conviction is growing that military sanctions should be limited to the regions where a country has a particular interest.

On the other hand, it is well understood that economic sanctions, to be effective, must be universal. Accordingly, some measure of universal cooperation in sanctions must continue.

Peace is indivisible. Its preservation must be universal. However, there may be variations in coercive measures taken in its behalf, both in kind and degree.

3. Shall the *status quo* be maintained, or shall some form of peaceful change be introduced? Shall existing international engagements be preserved in their present form, or shall they be revised?

Article 19 of the Covenant provides:

The Assembly may from time to time advise the reconsideration by members of the League of treaties which have become inapplicable and the consideration of international conditions whose continuance might endanger the peace of the world.

Certainly the international law principle of *pacta sunt servanda,* under which a state is bound to carry out in good faith the obligations which it has assumed by a treaty, is implied in the treaty obligations which countries assume under the Covenant. It lies at the foundation of all treaty law, and the fact that some treaty obligations are broken does not establish the invalidity of the principle. It is not only an obligation in good faith, but manifestly a legal one.

The principle of *rebus sic stantibus* is said to be the leading exception to *pacta sunt servanda,* and is frequently said to undermine it. The reconciliation of the two principles is possible to all who do not wish to take advantage of one, at the expense of the other. A country seeking to preserve the *status quo* will urge the first principle above; one seeking to change it will urge the second.

*Rebus sic stantibus* means "that a treaty becomes legally void in case there occurs a change in the state of facts which existed at the time the parties entered into the treaty." What changes shall have this effect? There are three theories:

a. The right to have a treaty rescinded, due to the disappearance of the special circumstances under which and because of which it was concluded, can only arise when there is a difference as to what conditions were implied or contemplated as essential, and not merely possible or existent.

b. The intent of the parties is disregarded in the test which insists that the changes shall be "vital," "fundamental," "basic," or "essential."

c. A third test is whether the fulfillment of the treaty, after the change in the state of facts has occurred, would be so injurious to one of the parties that the right to terminate the treaty exists either under law or necessity.

What will prevent any state from invoking this principle at its convenience, in order to escape its legitimate obligations? The only answer is to commit the dispute to an impartial international tribunal. Article 28 of the Draft Convention of the Law of Treaties of the Harvard International Law Research disposes of this problem as follows:

a. A treaty entered into with reference to the existence of a state of facts the continued existence of which was envisaged by the parties as a determining factor moving them to undertake the obligations stipulated, may be declared by a competent international tribunal or authority to have ceased to be binding, in the sense of calling for further performance, when that state of facts has been essentially changed.

b. Pending agreement by the parties upon and decision by a competent international tribunal or authority, the party which seeks such a declaration may provisionally suspend performance of its obligation under the treaty.

c. A provisional suspension of performance by the party seeking such a declaration will not be justified definitively until a decision to this effect has been rendered by the competent international tribunal or authority.

The *rebus sic stantibus* test under international law does not relate directly to Article 19 of the Covenant, and cannot be interpreted as covering the necessary situations under the League

Covenant, as it applies to executory treaties only, not to executed ones.

Article 19 also applies only to executory treaties and only to those which have ceased to be applicable. Its chief office seems to be "a political procedure for modifying legal rights in the interests of the world community." It was intended to cover territorial adjustments, and to accompany the guarantees of Article 10.

Neither of these devices provides escape from treaties of peace imposed by force, or for the establishment of a preexisting *status quo*. Treaties of peace and of cession, when changed, must be changed by political action rather than by juridical means. The political term applied here is "revisionism." The solutions required must be sought in the political rather than in the legal field.

The need for peaceful change in Europe and the Far East especially may be accepted as a fact, without debate. The so-called *status quo* must yield to certain essential alterations in the present structure of peace. Much change is going on outside the framework of the League. The problem is to make possible legal and legitimate change within the League's Covenant and jurisdiction. Change which is illegal and illegitimate could take place only through the irresponsible and unilateral action of a greatly armed power.

The action of Japan in Manchukuo and in North China; the action of Mussolini in Abyssinia; and the action of Hitler with respect to the Treaty of Versailles and the Locarno Pact are evidences of such change. Some were necessary and may be justified. Some were not necessary, and cannot be approved by any institution dedicated to the preservation of peace, through its provision for a process of peaceful change. Accordingly, not every change which is sought is one which can be granted.

The injustice and the folly of many of the provisions of the treaties of Versailles, Saint-Germain, Neuilly, and the Trianon are being shouted from the housetops. Today the deficiencies of these treaties have the headlines. It is true that these treaties, in remedying certain situations, created other problems. In making changes, we must have in mind the situations remedied, as well as the problems now requiring adjustment. The vanquished nations must have their territorial desires satisfied before there can be any future peace, it is insisted. The peace of the world must await such adjustment. When the treaties are rewritten, or wiped out, then peace and harmony will reign!

It is suggested, however, that the satisfaction of some of the territorial grievances of the defeated countries would mean war, especially on the part of the Little Entente. Peaceful change should not mean a general invitation of the defeated countries to seek a restoration of the political and territorial *status quo ante,* as of 1914. Some of the changes at the Peace Conference must and should be permanent. This is no argument, however, against changes having a foundation in justice and equity, and which an impartial international authority would approve.

The punitive clauses of the treaties have about run their course. Indeed, the peace treaties have been under a constant state of revision since they became effective, and they will be further revised. A chart of the record of revision, item by item, through agreement or unilateral action, would be an impressive one.

Provision for peaceful change is no more important than organization to prevent illegal change. The record of our own country on this score is as consistent as that of any other nation. Through the Nine-Power Treaty, and the Stimson-Non-recognition doctrine, we have supported the established order in the Far East. Through the Four-Power Pact we have sought territorial stabilization in the Pacific. Under the Monroe Doctrine and Pan Americanism, we seek to maintain existing territorial and political establishments against European aggression and also against American attack. More often than not, the preservation of the *status quo* has meant the preservation of peace, and its disturbance has meant war.

Under the general heading of peaceful change, these observations may be considered:

a. There must be some form of peaceful change provided.

b. Such changes should be within the framework of peace institutions, such as the League of Nations.

c. Organization for peace cannot await the completion of all adjustments nations think they are entitled to.

d. International organization should continue in resisting illegal changes, especially those in violation of pacts of peace.

e. Peaceful change is an important, but not the major factor, in the preservation of peace.

4. Shall effective League control be vested in the larger and more powerful states, or shall it be vested in the main body of states, on a basis of equality?

This problem can only be presented here. As with individuals, so is the problem with states. There are the many small and weak states and the few large and powerful ones. Shall control be democratic or oligarchic? The small states declare that the large states, in looking to the interests of the small states, are also following their own interests, in that a satisfactory balance between the large states is preserved. The larger states argue that sanctions, applied for the benefit of the small state, fall on the large states for enforcement. For example, in the Abyssinian controversy, it was urged that all the states might vote sanctions, but France and Great Britain would have to apply them.

There is room for combinations and groups of nations within the ambit of any international organization, especially one pretending to the ideal of universality. Such combinations are expected, and their personnel and character cannot be predicted.

It is not too much to say that states, large and small, will follow their interests in their relations to international institutions. In the long last, national interest must coincide with the maintenance and preservation of peace through collective means.

*The Form of League Reorganization or Reform.* 1. The complete revisionist school. This school of reform would make fundamental changes in the Covenant. It argues that the League should cease to be a war-preventing institution, and should devote itself to peace-promoting. It would demilitarize and desanctionize the League, because of the inability of the state to carry on altruistic warfare, even through an international institution such as the League. The sanctions provisions of the Covenant, it is said, should be eliminated, and the procedure for peaceful change and for amendment of the Covenant should be made comparatively easy.

2. The moderate revisionist school. This school would allow a more liberal use of the process of peaceful change, and would allow certain modifications as regards sanctions. It would not allow the elimination of the sanctions provision, or amendments which would impair the integrity of the Covenant. It would favor the elimination of the Covenant from the Treaty of Versailles. However, it feels that every needed reform can be secured through agreement and through interpretative pacts. To throw the Covenant open to wholesale amendment might mean its devitalization. In this sense, the clauses of the Covenant are deemed to have a protective function to peace essentials similar to the protection afforded by the Constitution of the United States to certain principles of government.

3. The regionalist school. This school would not appreciably lessen the functions of the League, but would decentralize them in the interest of vitality and effectiveness, and thus, it is claimed, reduce them to manageable proportions. The peace principles are not at fault, it is urged, but the area of operation is too large.

*Changing peace methods and procedure and the collective system.* In view of the foregoing problems, what can be done to make the principles and machinery of the collective system adequate to the peace problems of the day? Something must be done, taking into account the questions of regionalism, sanctions, and peaceful change, without sacrificing the institutions and processes of peace which have been established.

As one possible solution, and only one, for the purpose of discussion, there is submitted the plan of General Sir Kenneth Wigram, British delegate to the Yosemite Conference of the Institute of Pacific Relations, held in August, 1936. It created much attention, and is as follows:

It has been generally agreed that there is still ample machinery for peace, though it has failed to function.

What are the causes of failure?

Of the League, surely because of the absence of membership of some of the greater and more important powers which tends to make it selective rather than collective.

Of the Pact of Paris, surely because of the absence of power to deal with an offender.

Of treaties, surely the disinclination to respect the sanctity of treaties. In addition there has been a general refusal on the part of nations to submit disputes to arbitration.

Now, the League as constituted at present attempts to prescribe for the whole world, thereby imposing on each assenting state member an unlimited liability which may turn out to be a military liability or economic liability or both. The conception, based as it is on altruism, is good. Is it practical? What can Ecuador know or care about affairs in Manchukuo? Why should the United States of America be implicated in the domestic squabbles of Europe? How can Japan take a hand in the settlement of a dispute in the Dardanelles?

In this matter of security, I suggest that the world is over-rationalized, and that consequently the machine has become unwieldy. Particular regions have their own particular problems, and particular states have particular interests in these problems.

My first suggestion, therefore, is that we would decentralize our existing organization and concentrate more on the idea of regional organizations—call them regional Leagues if you like—composed of those powers only which are immediately interested in the region concerned.

My second suggestion is that in order to furnish the Pact of Paris with the requisite sanctions it should be linked in some way with the regional leagues.

Finally, in order that the regional leagues may obtain the support of the whole world, should they see fit to name an aggressor and to impose sanctions, they should be affiliated in some way with the main league at Geneva.

The idea underlying this proposal is: first, to provide the Pact of Paris with some weapon with which it can bring pressure to bear upon an offender; second, to limit the military liability of members to the regions in which they have particular interests; third, to insure that in the event of aggression in any part of the world the full force of economic pressure of the whole world would operate against the offender as Public Enemy Number One by the stoppage of exports to the offender's country, by every member of each regional league thereby limiting the liability of members, other than those forming the regional league, to economic sanctions only.

All organization of these lines could, I suggest, provide effective machinery for collective security.

It allows, however, of no place for neutrals, and I contend that there is no basis for world peace so long as there can be neutrality when a crime is committed.

## INTERNATIONAL UTOPIAS [8]

There is, more than ever before, eagerness to establish something new which will prevent this ruin of our race. And the opportunity will come after victory. What shall we do with it? What sort of new world is desired? Several sorts, in fact. Many books and magazine articles have already broached different schemes, although the subject of postwar organization has not yet received much attention in daily newspapers. There is some danger that people will get so bewildered by all the overlapping and conflicting proposals that they will throw up their hands in despair and stop thinking about the whole matter. That would be a great misfortune, for an enlightened public opinion on the right use of the victory for which we strive will do much to save us from throwing that victory away.

On the other hand, some persons incline to seize on a single scheme and fervently hail it as a cure-all with no thought of adverse criticisms and alternative possibilities. Fanatical devotion to one plan at all costs wearies listeners and alienates supporters of other plans. Competing zealots may raise such a clamor that they will silence each other and disgust everybody else. So no features of any international scheme will win general acceptance, and we shall be back to some form of the balance of power.

Consequently, it is wise for Americans to consider more than one scheme, yet not too many schemes. There are four main types of international utopias that have considerable influence. Each of them stands out pretty distinctly despite many divergences among its supporters about details. Consequently, it will simplify the problems of postwar organizations to distinguish these four schemes from one another, and illustrate each of the four by means of a brief description of a significant book.

At the outset, I want to make it plain that all four plans are like the famous recipe for hare soup, which began: "First catch your hare." Every international utopia presupposes the downfall of Hitler and the other Axis rulers.

[8] By Zechariah Chafee, Jr., Professor of Law, Harvard University. *American Academy of Arts and Science. Proceedings.* 75:, no. 1:39-53. October 1942.

The first plan is to improve and strengthen the League of Nations. In twenty years it showed several kinds of defects. Its most outstanding failure was the breakdown of economic sanctions against Italy during the invasion of Ethiopia in 1935. Hence there has risen a strong movement in favor of stronger sanctions and more effective methods for bringing sanctions into operation. It is to be made really a League to Enforce Peace. An able and very thorough presentation of methods for this purpose is made by an Englishman, Lord Davies, in a book of seven hundred pages entitled *The Problem of the Twentieth Century*. . . .

After a full and informative analysis of older proposals for international unification, like those of the Abbé Saint-Pierre and Kant, he takes up more recent expressions of the idea of an international police force. I was surprised to learn that in 1910 both Houses of Congress passed a resolution asking President Taft to appoint a commission of five to consider among other aspects of disarmament, "the expediency of . . . constituting the combined navies of the world an international police force for the preservation of universal peace. Taft took some steps but no cooperation then seemed feasible. Although Wilson at Paris dropped force out of the League, this was inconsistent with his utterances of January 22, 1917, in his speech on Peace Without Victory. . . .

Lord Davies would carry out this proposal of Wilson and expand the idea in the congressional resolution so as to include an army and an air force as well as a navy.

Under his plan there would be three types of police: (1) the ordinary police we have now to maintain local order; (2) a national body of police in each country to maintain national order and supplement the local police; (3) an international police force to maintain international order. Their two principal functions would be to repel aggression and to enforce the decisions of the World Court and arbitration tribunals. Unlike the Holy Alliance, the League is not to intervene in the domestic affairs of either members or nonmembers. *A fortiori* another state is to be kept from so interfering.

One of Davies's most interesting points is that the progress of invention has now made possible a differentiation of weapons, so that the international police can be armed much more powerfully than will be allowed for any national body. Some sort of differentiation has long been common inside a country. The local police carry clubs or at most revolvers, while the national guard and the army carry rifles. According to the plan of Lord Davies, each national army would be limited to weapons existing before 1914, whereas the monopoly of the newer and more powerful weapons would be possessed by the international police. These would include submarines, airplanes, poison gas, tanks, the new heavy artillery and bombs. All these weapons would be forbidden to the national armies. Such a differentiation was proposed by France at a disarmament conference in 1932. The Washington conference of 1921 also furnishes a precedent, for differentiation was there used in a negative fashion to forbid certain powerful weapons and reduce others while some weapons were left unrestricted. If the proposal of Lord Davies could be effectively carried out, it would have two great merits. In the first place, it might very well make the international force more powerful than any combination of member states with their limited equipment. A combination of outside states would be met by an even stronger force as I shall show later. On the other hand, his plan would not impair the ability of each state to maintain law and order in its own territory. The burden of the international force would be met by contributions from member states in personnel, arms, and money. States which failed to contribute would be unable to participate in the management of the League, whereas in the past no such penalty was imposed and Peru even obtained a seat on the council after it had been years behind on its annual assessment. A delinquent state would also be denied the use of the international force for the protection of its own frontiers. Another new device would be in international general staff which would render the international police effective and mobile. Thus sanctions would be organized before the crime was committed, whereas the actual League has been greatly handicapped because the economic sanctions which it could use had to be worked out after the violation of law. For instance it was several months after Italy invaded Ethiopia before the League could decide what to do. The international force would embrace all the instruments of coercion. If it consisted of a navy alone, as Congress proposed in 1910, it could not have prevented the German army from overrunning Europe in 1914. Hence an army and air force must be included. Perhaps the development of aviation will eventually make an international air force sufficient.

How shall the international police force be organized? Davies describes three alternative schemes:

1. It will consist entirely of quotas furnished by the member states, each of which will control its own quota and pay its cost in time of peace. However, a general staff at international headquarters will organize these scattered quotas, and on mobilization it will take them over under international command. This was the French scheme at the Versailles Peace Conference. One advantage is that it would cause a minimum amount of interference with existing national establishments and yet bring about considerable disarmament in each country. However, there are several disadvantages. There is no adequate guarantee that a nation would meet its obligations when the crisis arose, and thus the League might lack the support it had counted on. This uncertainty would discourage apprehensive nations from diminishing their national forces. Also, it would fail to eliminate competition between the war offices and admiralties of different countries. A national staff would resent the intrusion of the international staff. When each nation retained financial control during peace it would be tempted to spend more in making more, to prepare peace industries for transformation into munition factories, and to invent new weapons for its own use. Secession is made easy, just as the southern state militias in 1861 became the Confederate Army. Finally, this scheme disregards the hopeful new opportunity for differentiation of weapons.

2. At the other extreme is a complete self-contained international force, with the abolition of all national forces except as they are necessary to maintain internal order. This scheme would have the advantages of eliminating all competition between countries, obtaining comprehensive disarmament at once,

producing increased mobility of the international force and simplifying the problem of organization. On the other hand, the disadvantages are numerous. The League would have to possess a bigger force than it would ever be likely to use. This force would be much more expensive to maintain than national quotas. Even if some of it could be kept within international territory, considerable portions would have to be garrisoned inside states, which would cause disputes. The problem of maintaining internal order would become much more difficult. Each country would be stripped to its local police who would have no national army to fall back on. Finally, since there would be no liaison between national and international staffs, the people of each state would be wholly cut off from the international force and might cease to regard it as a genuine part of their own defense system.

3. Therefore, Lord Davies favors a compromise scheme. He would have a composite force: both national quotas and a specialized contingent which should be enlisted, equipped, and controlled by the League. This plan was proposed by General Gerard, a far-seeing Frenchman, in 1923. Here Lord Davies's ideas of differentiation of weapons would have full scope. The separate national quotas would be armed with older weapons, and the international contingent with newer weapons. He finds many advantages in this scheme. First, the central contingent would have unmistakable superiority over the armies of member states, which would be decisive in an emergency. It could also hold off outsiders long enough to give time to assemble the national quotas, and the combined force would then be overwhelming. Second, competition in the invention and manufacture of new weapons would be abolished. Third, substantial disarmament would be produced unless a nonmember state starts competing. Fourth, it would give permanence to the League, for a member would be unlikely to withdraw once it had surrendered its most potent weapons. Fifth, the sovereignty of states is preserved for they would control their quotas, and the central contigent is dependent on their contributions. Sixth, the scheme is practicable. The technical arrangements of each country go on, of the older sort. The international police is

small with specialists as aviators, tankmen, etc.  Its small size simplifies the problem of international barracks and bases.  It also renders the central force very mobile.  Seventh, the continuance of a liaison between the national staffs and the international staff makes every nation directly interested in the efficiency of the central contingent and in fruitful cooperation with the League military authorities.  Eighth, self-defense is recognized in a relative form.  The frontiers will be guarded by their own national quota, then by the rapid arrival of the central contingent, and finally by the later mustering of the quotas of other members of the League.  Thus the third scheme meets the objections to the first two.

The international force will owe allegiance to the League like the present Secretariat and will presumably cease to be citizens of their former states.  The headquarters and bases will be independent territory of the League, like the District of Columbia and the federal forts in our country.  During a twenty-five year experimental period, which Lord Davies shrewdly advises, these territories might be merely taken on lease.  The bases should be chosen for their strategical position, access to the sea, and suitability for fleets of airplanes.  They should not be too close to any great powers.  He proposes Palestine as the District of Columbia, because it satisfies these requirements and has strong associations for citizens of so many countries.  Other strategical points to be occupied include Suez, Panama, Singapore, Djibouti, Corsica, the Hawaiian Islands, Constantinople, the Aaland Islands, and Yap.  It might also occupy neutralized zones like the Rhine Valley, the Dardanelles and Bosphorus, and the Great Lakes.  Small states might lease part of their territories as part of their contribution, receiving full protection in return.  For example, Albania, Monaco, Latvia, Honduras, Newfoundland, and Haiti.  The League would have its own aircraft factories; and it would ration orders for other munitions among many states, storing them at international bases.

Although this sounds very elaborate and some details would certainly be rejected by the United States, it seems possible that the international police would become less costly as the world became increasingly habituated to peace. Lord Davies wisely observes that a good centralized police force tends to eliminate all force, including itself.

In order that the international police force may be satisfactorily organized and operated Lord Davies would remove a second usual objection to the Covenant, namely, the requirement of unanimity for most acts of the Council. He would have an executive body capable of managing the police and of enforcing sanctions and the decisions of international tribunals. The prompt action of the executive must be assured by the residence of representatives of the member states at the capital. The actual executive must not be too large or unwieldy. Countries should be excluded which do not maintain international order or fulfill their obligations, including the payment of contributions. The apportionment of contributions would be based on wealth and other factors as well as population. This does give big states an advantage, but they already possess this now for the purpose of piling up armaments. They will be equal in the judicial sphere, the privilege of representation on the assembly and freedom to criticize. Small states as a class will be represented on the executive body. Instead of the rule of unanimity he would substitute a two-thirds vote, thinking a majority too much liable to make mistakes.

Several objections to the plan of an international police are discussed by Lord Davies himself and also in a shorter book on *Theory and Practice of International Police,* by Professor Hans Wehberg, a German scholar long teaching in Geneva (1934). Here are some of them:

The force may suffer from disloyalty within, because policemen will be more devoted to their countries of origin than to the League. In reply writers point to the success of the French Foreign Legion, the Swiss Army, the composite army of the Allies in the World War, and the frequency with which men change their allegiance on migration.

Secondly, it is urged that a single nation or group of nations could overcome the police either by a sudden attack or by secretly acquiring a considerable supply of the strong weapons. Lord Davies deals pretty well with the danger of sudden attacks, in view of the mobility and strategic locations of the international contingent. The quota of the attacked nation would be able to hold up the invasion for a while, so long as the invaders possess the same sort of weapons. However, this reply is greatly weakened if the invaders have secretly acquired airplanes and tanks. Lord Davies does not sufficiently show how the monopoly of these strong weapons in the central contingent is to be maintained, or how a member country is to be prevented from inventing and using new devices. This seems a particularly serious danger.

Third, one power might try to get control of the central contingent. Fourth, this might go in for politics on its own and behave like Wallenstein's army in the Thirty-Years War or the Roman army in bad periods of the Empire, ready to go anywhere under a leader who promised high pay and abundant loot. The reply of Lord Davies to these two objections is that treachery and conspiracy would be difficult in a force with three divisions for land, sea, and air, each having a separate head for a limited period of time, and all paid by the executive. He doubts if one state or one leader could influence all the heads and all the divisions. Although I am not entirely satisfied by this reply, Lord Davies goes on to give a better reason: "Every scheme has its risks. Every federation has been faced with the possibility of the disruption of its central force. Every government is liable to be deprived suddenly of its sanctions. These possibilities are inherent in any political system, national or international, but it does not follow that they will be realized. The effective safeguards are to be found in the public opinion of the countries participating in the confederation, and in the common sense of the international police."

Over and above this, the international police must not be viewed in isolation. The success of this device depends much on the general strength of the League as a guardian not merely of formal international law but even more of the idea of justice in a broad sense. The peoples must want to cooperate in the League, not in order to keep down a certain group of states, but in order to serve the well-being of the world. In other words, security and disarmament and just international relations are three interdependent factors. Lack of any of the three interferes with the two others. It is proper to isolate each of these factors for purposes of study and detailed discussion, but in the end they must be considered together and all treated satisfactorily.

Therefore, it is important to cure not only the two defects in the Covenant already mentioned—weakness of sanctions and the unanimity rule, but also to remove other defects which have produced a strong sense of injustice. Three of these may be mentioned. First, the handling of minorities is poor, and produces a feeling of insecurity in the majority and of injustice on the other side of the boundary line. One suggestion is periodical visits by a League inspector, who would ascertain the facts, deflate peevish complaints, cut through the excuses of the majority, and often be able to effect compromises before quarrels become serious. Also a Minority Commission at the capital would receive periodic reports from governments with minorities and be able to question their officials. Next, although the mandate system is an advance on previous practice, several writers advocate that all non-self-governing territories should be administered directly by the League, which should undertake to fit them for independence and conserve their raw materials for the benefit of the natives as well as that of consumers generally and not to profit investors or governments. Finally, there must be an effective machinery for the peaceful change of treaties and boundaries which have been rendered unsuitable by new conditions. The powers of the League under Article 19 have been narrowly interpreted and never used. Some writers would transfer the power to make just changes from the Council to the World Court, but any lawyer will realize the danger of trying to combine the judicial settlement of disputes which are suitable for the application of general rules of law with the uncontrolled exercise of a vague sense of fairness. It would be much as if our Supreme Court added to its present functions the power to determine how big an income tax the rich should pay in order to provide funds for the WPA.

Even if defects in the Covenant are remedied by the establishment of an international police and other devices like those described, the League is not likely to succeed unless there be also a new spirit. Of this I shall have something to say later.

Instead of a League, it has been widely proposed that nations should form themselves into a Union. The difference between these two types of international organizations is very important. In a League the nation is the unit. Each national government selects its representatives for the central legislature and executive groups. The central government is financed by contributions from the treasuries of the member nations. In case of any violation of international agreements, coercion is exerted on the government of the nation which is committing the violation. A Union, on the other hand, makes every human being within it the unit. The citizens of the member-nations elect their representatives to the central legislature and perhaps also vote for a chief executive official. The central body imposes taxes directly on citizens. The force of the central body is exerted against the individuals who are responsible for international wrongs. The central government takes charge of matters of common importance like defense against aggression, while the national governments confine themselves to the affairs of their own respective territories. The difference between a League and a Union is, in a general way, like the difference between the Confederation of our thirteen states which fought the Revolution and the national government which was set up by our Constitution in 1789.

The leading advocate of a Union is Clarence K. Streit. His *Union Now,* a book of three hundred pages, has gone through many editions, and societies with local offices in numerous cities to support his plan are active both in this country and in England. The book first appeared in October, 1938, shortly after the Munich crisis.

Under the Streit plan, the Union government would deal with five matters of common importance—citizenship, the maintenance and use of defense forces, customs with international free trade, money, and the postal and communications system. Other powers would be reserved to the national governments, and the Union would guarantee to each nation protection against enemies, foreign and domestic, and the maintenance of democratic self-government and those rights of man that exist in all the democracies.

In Streit's illustrative constitution the Union will have a Congress of two houses, elected by popular vote. The lower house will be roughly apportioned among the member-states according to population, while each state will have two senators except that four would come from France, Great Britain, and the United States. An Executive Board of five men will be chosen, three by popular vote, one by each house of Congress. The judicial power is vested in a High Court.

Streit argues at length that such a Union is superior to conceivable alternatives. The old balance of power can no longer keep peace, and neither can limited alliances. "We get peace by putting so much weight surely on the side of law that the strongest possible lawbreaker cannot possibly off-set it and is bound to be overwhelmed." He stresses the weakness of any League of Nations. It cannot act in time, because as he thinks, a League cannot escape the unanimity rule. To get the agreement required for action not only all the delegates must be persuaded, but also the governments behind them, and in democracies this means that the legislatures must be persuaded too. By contrast, a Union can act swiftly through a majority vote of those on the spot. Consider the speed with which the New Deal measures were adopted in the United States. Furthermore, a League cannot enforce law because it must operate against a state. No big state can be coerced. You cannot indict a whole nation. Even if the League succeeds, the condemned people is resentful. What makes matters worse, the nation which is the lawbreaker in one incident still sits as judge over a different lawbreaker. Thus Italy while undergoing sanctions still took part in League hearings on Germany's violations of the Locarno Treaty. There is no sheriff in a community where every man is equally sheriff. Streit raises similar objections to a permanent League police force.

Objections about the difficulties of inaugurating the Union are met by the persuasive analogy of our own situation in 1787.

The makers of our Union went straight ahead, unafraid of the future.

Yet they lived in a time when New York was protecting its fuel interests by a tariff on Connecticut wood and its farmers by duties on New Jersey butter, when Massachusetts closed while Connecticut opened its ports to British shipping, when Boston was boycotting Rhode Island grain and Philadelphia was refusing to accept New Jersey money, when the money of Connecticut, Delaware and Virginia was sound, that of all other states was variously depreciated and that of Rhode Island and Georgia was so worthless that their governments sought to coerce the citizens into accepting it. In those days New York was massing troops on its Vermont frontier while the army of Pennsylvania was committing the atrocities of the "Wyoming massacre" against settlers from Connecticut.

Variations of this plan for a Union have been set forth by other writers. Thus Grenville Clark, a leading New York lawyer and a Fellow of Harvard, published at the end of 1939 *A Memorandum With Regard to a New Effort to Organize Peace and Containing a Proposal for a Federation of Free Peoples.* His scheme differs from Streit's in limiting the powers of the Union at the start to defense only. Also he would add to Streit's fifteen members Argentina, Colombia, and Chile. The most influential English book appears to be W. B. Curry's *The Case for Federal Union,* which adheres closely to Streit's plan. This pamphlet of over two hundred pages was published in the autumn of 1939 after the outbreak of war.

Many of these proposals for international political organization remind me of some plans for an international language. An American urges that life would be much simpler if everybody spoke English, while Mussolini predicts a Europe where Latin will once more be universally used. The originator ends where he starts, in his own country. In the same way the draft constitutions of Streit and Clark, both Americans, bear a close resemblance to the Constitution of the United States. On the other hand, an Englishman, John S. Hoyland, has produced an interesting little book of one hundred pages, *The World in Union,* which though falling within Streit's general scheme makes considerable use of English experience with administrative bodies of experts. For instance, he proposes a world economic council, composed of representatives of employers, employees, and citizens generally, which would be in charge of reconstruction of areas devastated by war, and readjustments due to the introduction of free trade from which some regions now having a high tariff would suffer for a time. This council would also bring oriental countries up to the same standard of living as western countries in order to prevent the latter from being flooded with cheap labor, and would seek to eliminate poverty all over the Union.

Hoyland has given us a better book than Streit's which I find very heavy going. Some of the divergences are due to Hoyland's strong religious feeling, which is especially prominent in the last chapters. Unlike Streit, he wants no sanctions. "The peoples must want to come into the Union." Also Hoyland would include the Axis powers and Russia despite the undemocratic nature of their institutions. To the objection that Union is then risky he replies that it is risky anyway and even more so if sanctions are inserted and several great powers are excluded from membership. "You have to trust the future. Take one step at a time. Do the right thing now; and believe that as you do the results will be sound and attractive enough to quell the spirit of violence and separation before it comes to strength." On the other hand, he says "There is no future for national sovereignty." It will shatter civilization.

The diminution of democracies since Streit published *Union Now* after Munich has led him to write a second book *Union Now With Britain* (1941), proposing that the United States should at once federate with the British Empire.

Some kind of association of the English-speaking countries seems more probable than world union or the other three schemes I am discussing. China and Russia, for which Mr. Streit did not allow, are likely to be partners too. However desirable such cooperation of the victors, it is not an international utopia. An association to enforce the terms of peace upon the vanquished and nurse the occupied countries back to order and prosperity may prove necessary and do its work very well, but it is only a temporary receivership although it may last for years. No four governments, however enlightened, are wise enough to run the rest of the world altruistically for decades. Sooner or later the conquered and occupied peoples will demand the return of self-government and a share in the process of world administration.  If this demand be denied indefinitely, trouble is bound to arise.  Our Congress will get weary of paying a quarter of the cost of policing the world.  The excluded nations will try to band together against the Big Four inside, and the so-called Union will be little more than one alliance against another.  Finally, not all the internationally minded statesmen live in the United States, the British Empire, China, and Russia.  Whatever the shortcomings of the League, it revealed such statesmen in France, Germany, Scandinavia, Latin America, and elsewhere.  The task of international organization will be very difficult, and it would be fatal to reject the help of the best men wherever they live.

Therefore, an association of victors should be regarded as only a transition to something wider, and the problem still remains—what shall this something else do?  Even if the four principal allied nations now form a union like Mr. Streit's, this cannot be forced down the throats of other countries when they do revive.  When general participation becomes practicable, it will not succeed unless the scheme is reasonably satisfactory to the new members as well as the old.  Everything must then be reconsidered.  The result may be an expansion of the arrangement among the victors, whether union or something looser; it may be a strengthened League of Nations; it may be one of the two schemes still to be described.

The difficulties of world federation have led some writers to substitute a more modest scheme for federation in Europe alone.  An interesting book of this type is *The United States of Europe,* by Alfred Bingham, who is an American and edits the magazine *Common Sense.*  His book was published in 1940 before the fall of France.

Bingham favors a union resembling Streit's, but with smaller powers over a smaller area.  He believes it best to use what we have whenever possible, rather than attempt to build a completely new and more logically perfect structure.  He would omit the United States because we are less prepared to surrender our national sovereignty than are European countries; the Soviet Union, because it covers two continents and has different institutions; and the Far East, because it has its own problems. "Federations have grown up where there were some fairly obvious common interests and the possibility of a common loyalty." Europe meets these tests. The idea of European unity, though subconscious, has always existed in the European heritage. There is the common background of Greek thought, Roman Law, Christianity, the use of Latin, even the same habits and clothes. Unity was approximated by the French Revolution and Napoleon. The idea has lately been popularized by Count Coudenhove-Kalergi, Rathenau, and Briand, who was partly moved by the desire to confront American prosperity with a strong Europe. Plans for a customs union have been brought forward. European workmen have been joined together by a single song, the Internationale. Bingham stresses the long establishment of numerous international bodies for mail, telegraphs, health, the navigation of the Danube, copyright, electric power, agriculture, banking, and the regulation of maritime affairs like lighthouses and buoys. These bodies have been called bricks without mortar. They need something vital to draw them together. Also Europe has had a considerable experience in the theory and practice of federalism in Switzerland, Germany, and the British Commonwealth, besides Russia which he would exclude.

Bingham's union is looser than Streit's. He would not speak of secession one way or the other. He would not require the internal government of member states to be uniformly democratic. India shows the possibility of diverse institutions within a federation. Instead, he would meet persecution by allowing the victims to emigrate freely and take their property with them. Then he would wait for the dictatorships to alter, believing that the federal structure of Europe as a whole will encourage local democracies. Unlike most postwar plans, this book does not emphasize disarmament. Bingham believes that armaments are a superficial symptom of deeper disorders. Peace within the United States of America, he says, is not due either to the national army or to abolition of state militias. He would like to forget the term "international police force." Coercion of a state or its inhabitants is war. The only genuine protection against civil war inside the federation is good government. Although he would meet external aggression with an international army which should have the monopoly of offensive weapons, somewhat in accordance with the plan of Lord Davies, Bingham believes that the real answer to competitive armaments is the maintenance of high standards of government which will rapidly demonstrate the advantages of European union. War will be abolished when government has replaced anarchy in areas now left to the arbitrament of force.

As to boundaries, Bingham says that ideally Europe, at least west of the Vistula, should be a single economic area with complete freedom of movement for men and materials, having merely those administrative subdivisions that prove convenient. It is not practicable to go that far now. However, one practicable and valid principle for political boundaries is to make them mean as little as possible. This is better than attempting to redraw political boundaries. "New boundaries raise as many problems as they settle. The less tinkering with boundaries the better." One way to make boundaries mean less is to have different boundaries for different purposes as in our country, where the federal reserve districts are not co-extensive with a state or with other kinds of federal regions. In the same way European political boundaries need not coincide with cultural boundaries for the language used in schools, etc., or with economic boundaries set up for labor regulations, river traffic, or the efficient industrial administration of a coal and iron area. The desire for cultural autonomy, which has been so troublesome in the past, can be better satisfied in a federation than with independent nations on a military basis. For example, Alsace might then develop in its own way without being suppressed by either France or Germany.

The central government would maintain the army (for defense and not as a police force) and a navy. It would carry on foreign relations though national diplomacy would continue. It would have power to tax individuals, protect minorities, and hold a plebiscite in any region on the question whether it should become partly or wholly autonomous.

Sub-federations would be possible, for instance in Scandinavia or the Balkans. This would be like the New England Conference of Governors. Indeed, European federation may, Bingham thinks, be preceded by several attempts at partial federation, already illustrated by the close association of England and France during the first months of the war.

Colonies outside Europe seriously complicate any plans for European federation. It is too simple to throw them all into a single melting pot. You could not include the Dominions, India, or Algeria. However, colonies are less important than the "have not" countries think. Instead of pooling or redistributing non-self-governing colonies, Bingham would give the Union considerable power over colonial administration. The greatest need is that the resources of a colony should benefit its inhabitants. He compares a colony to the zinc and lead region in the Ozarks, which enriches outside investors and leaves the natives poor and unhealthy. International agencies should be set up to regulate investments and the conservation of scarce resources; and this should be done for the benefit of the inhabitants, consumers all over the world, workers, investors, governments, and future generations. The mandate principle is sound when really applied, but he thinks the European Union would carry out this principle better than the League.

The United States of Europe would exist within the League of Nations. There might also be other international organizations like the Pan American Union, the British Commonwealth, the Soviet Union, an association of Far Eastern nations, and perhaps one of the desert peoples of North Africa and the Near East. These regional unions in Europe and elsewhere may prove only a brief interlude before world federation.

In conclusion, Bingham warns us that perfection is not just around the corner any more than prosperity. Our own Constitution succeeded only through compromises, political deals, and the accidents of personality.

A somewhat different plan for European Federation is proposed by Arnold Brecht, a professor at the New School for Social Research, in a stimulating article in the *Harvard Law Review* for February, 1942. Mr. Brecht, being a German, escapes from the usual analogy of our Constitution. Instead, he derives several interesting suggestions from the German Confederation of 1815-1866, which as he observes, worked better than the League of Nations. "It soon resulted in sweeping eliminations of tariff barriers and it succeeded in preserving peace for about fifty years. Its end was not anarchy, but a more perfect union, plus an alliance." This article suggests the reflection that we need a cooperative endeavor to frame a plan for international organization. In a group of experienced men from different nations, each would be able to contribute fruitful ideas from his own governmental system. The resulting combination would be more likely to win acceptance from many countries than would a plan shaped largely by the political institutions of the United States or any other single nation.

The last book to be considered at length is very hostile to the views of the other three books. It is *Federal Illusion?* by D. M. Pritt, a prominent English barrister and a Labor Member of Parliament. This was published in 1940, apparently before the fall of France. It advocates a Socialist Union like that in Russia.

The chief position taken here is that war cannot be ended by proposals which leave our main economic structure untouched. The causes of war are economic, as socialists said long ago, and only socialism will insure peace. War is due to the effort to get into closed markets and obtain new fields for investment and new sources for raw materials. However, war is impossible between socialist states. They cannot quarrel over exports. There are no private interests, and the socialist system of producing what the people need and enabling them to buy it eliminates the whole element of scarcity of markets. Your country is your own market. You produce all you can consume, and consume all you produce. Nobody fights over water when there is no drought. International trade in a commodity then becomes just a question of convenience; it does not make the rich profit or the poor starve. There is no quarrel over the exploitation of colonial races, when there are no colonies, no exploitations, no private capital.

Because war is inherent in the nature of modern industrial states and the men who hold power in these, all previous schemes for peace have failed. Arbitration, formerly regarded as a panacea, does not affect the deeply-rooted conflicts of interest between rival states. The League of Nations failed because it was always designed to be an instrument for securing the protection of the imperialist and economic system of the major powers. If these interests prevented the League from fulfilling its limited functions, they would *a fortiori* prevent any wider federal union from operating under the present economic system. So Pritt's argument runs.

The requisites of a successful federation are then analyzed with considerable shrewdness. Not every group of states will be willing or able to federate effectively or even ineffectively. Dicey laid down two conditions for federation: (1) A body of countries like the Swiss cantons, the American colonies or the Canadian provinces so closely connected by locality, history, race, or the like, as to be capable of bearing an impress of common nationality in the eyes of their inhabitants. (2) The existence of a very peculiar state of sentiment among the inhabitants of the member countries—a desire for union and not for unity. There is no basis for federalism if there is no desire to unite. For example, the scheme in Cromwell's time for uniting England and the Netherlands was one of those dreams which may haunt the imagination of politicians but can never be transformed into facts. On the other hand, a desire for unity will lead to a single nation rather than federalism. Dicey adds that the distribution of the different powers of government between the central body and the member states, which federalism necessitates, requires courts to possess authority to act as interpreters of the Constitution. Federalism substitutes litigation for legislation. Hence it can flourish only among communities imbued with the legal spirit and a reverence for law. Furthermore, each federation has grown up under historical conditions peculiar to itself and its own reasons for existence. The United States grew out of common aims in a revolutionary war and a rising capitalist economy which demanded for its proper functioning a national market.

There was no probability that competitors would amicably federate with it. Even the extension of American sway over our present area was not idyllic, for the Indians were exterminated, new territories were acquired by war with Mexico, and a great Civil War occurred.

The federal union advocated by Streit and others fails in Pritt's opinion to satisfy the requirements laid down by Dicey. The great powers have no real desire to surrender any part of their sovereignty in the political, financial or industrial field. They want to hold on to every fragment of power they possess. Even if disputes were settled by the executive or the legislature, it would be hard to get acceptance. There is even less chance that the decisions of courts would be accepted, and such acceptance is essential in federalism.

There is no force to the argument that tariffs and other barriers to commerce can be abolished by the establishment of a federal state. They are really weapons of the economic warfare between the ruling groups in a modern industrial state. The powerful interests which depend on these restrictions for their prosperity, for example, in the United States, will not consent at the behest of the federal state to lay their industry bare to foreign competition. Differences in labor costs alone show the impossibility of this. Pritt reminds us of the difficulties caused by the color bars at Versailles, although it is not quite clear just why he blames this on the rich.

The plan for the federal legislature rests, Pritt thinks, on two false assumptions: (1) That elections can be taken at their face value without investigating the conditions under which they are carried on. It is notorious that many ostensibly democratic elections are fictitious and dishonest. Wealth controls. The results would be even more warped in dictatorships and undeveloped countries. The ruling interests of different nations would merely carry their fatal rivalries into the new legislature. (2) It is assumed that all states in the federation are equal. This completely ignores the distinction between great powers, small powers, and client states under the influence of the great powers.

Then comes a sharp thrust. Streit's proposed Union is not really a world union, but limited to fifteen states. It is the preliminary syndicate and not the operating company. Many states are still left outside to fight. It excludes China, the East Indies, and Russia, which make up half the human race. Indeed, if we disregard small states and client states, the so-called world union comprises only Great Britain, the United States, and France. It is just like the proposed abortive alliance of 1918 and merely revives the Versailles grouping in place of the Four-Power Pact at Munich. The omission of Russia is extraordinary because it is the biggest example of a federated union, the most modern and the most thoroughgoing. Yet its constitution is wholly ignored as a model. It is more democratic than France where women cannot vote, or South Africa where the majority of adults cannot vote, or the United States where Negroes have been practically disqualified. It treats the Jews better than do other countries. Russia is a democracy where people manage affairs in industry as well as in strict politics. So Pritt reprints the Soviet Constitution in his book as an illustrative substitute for Streit's revamped American constitution.

Russia proves that a federation of socialist republics is easy, whereas a federation of capitalist countries would at most amount to a Holy Alliance of a few powers and their satellite states. Some republics came into the Russian federation on their own initiative, but the capitalist states wihin the former Russian area showed no dispostion to enter and would not have been welcomed. A socialist country is unified while a capitalist country is split into hostile sections. Colonial problems are not met by Streit's union, for it omits India and puts other dependencies under control. So likewise, the United States of Europe is bound to turn into a joint plan for the plunder of the colonies. But in a socialist federation colonies become people with equal rights.

If the Union be made broad enough to include Russia and other omitted countries, states which are so different cannot achieve Dicey's requisite of a feeling in favor of uniting, either for sentiment or for industrial and commercial interests. It would be impossible to federate effectively without eliminating conflicts between wealthy groups, and only socialism permits this. Consider the difficulties of an attempt to allocate markets for cotton goods between manufacturers in Great Britain and Japan. The old conflicts of interest will remain in the member nations which are not socialistic, such as restricting production to keep up prices, oil and wheat, desire for expansion, unemployment, wealth, and poverty. Union is a smoke screen for the reactionary war aims of British and French ruling classes.

It is true that a real federation greatly reduces the danger of war. This is not because the states are federated, but because the very connections between them which led them to federate also reduce quarrels and frictions to small proportions. Federation and friendship are not cause and effect, but effects of the same causes. The attempted federation of groups of states with no real inclination toward union contains no genuine peace-making qualities. It will solve none of the real problems.

However, socialism removes the real causes of war. Countries which have abolished capitalism then have a strong common interest and a freedom from conflicts which facilitate union, as in Russia. The U.S.S.R., Pritt concludes, must be our model.

This completes my survey of four postwar schemes. One more book is worth mentioning, although it proposes no scheme. This is a pamphlet issued by the Carnegie Endowment for International Peace, entitled "Preliminary Report and Monographs of the Commission to Study the Organization of Peace." It appears as *International Conciliation* No. 369, for April 1941. This is written by many different experts. Each gives a brief but meaty account of some difficult problem of international organization. I have found this the most helpful of all the books I have consulted.

A few remarks of my own may be ventured about these four schemes. I find it easiest to start with Mr. Pritt and work backwards.

The plan for a Union open only to socialist states seems to me the least promising of all the schemes. To begin with, the U.S.S.R. is the only nation now able to pass the admissions-test, so that great internal changes must take place in Great Britain, Canada, the United States, China, France, and several other countries before the new world federation can be formed. Even a European federation must be put off until the same drastic process has taken place on a smaller scale. All this offers a gloomy prospect for peace during our lives or our children's lives. The establishment of socialism in Russia was accompanied by a long civil war and followed by a good deal more bloodshed for political and economic reasons. If, as Mr. Pritt contends, there are no conflicting interests inside a socialist state, this harmony may not be due to the inherent capacity of such a régime to produce a persuasive unification of human desires, but merely to the elimination of everybody who ventures to disagree with the people in power. Similar civil wars and purges may very well occur in the United States and the countries of western Europe before they are fit to form an international socialist Union. As I am one of those who would doubtless be liquidated, it takes more self-sacrifice than I possess to view with equanimity this cheerful sequel to World War II. Even if dissentients are allowed to emigrate or slip away, they will have to live somewhere, and they will tend to increase opposition to the federation wherever they go. When the longed-for second armistice has at last arrived, will there be no practicable road to world peace except through a long series of violent revolutions, mass exiles, and massacres?

Of course, it is possible that the present war will produce such extensive expropriation of private property that every state will be virtually socialistic when it ends. Then the nations may be able to slide into a socialist union without any preliminary turmoil. Even so, it is rash to assume that socialism will automatically end war. Mr. Pritt argues that the inhabitants of a socialist state will not be aggressive because their government will produce all they need. This seems inconsistent with the occurrence of several great famines in Russia. Political and economic equality will not produce world-wide geographic equality. Even without rich men, there will be rich lands. The inhabitants of a fertile region may decline to stint themselves drastically in order to feed a famine-stricken state, and so the underfed people may surge outward into the golden wheatfields and green pastures of neighboring states. . . .

Even if your government gives you all you want now, this does not prevent you from wanting still more and perhaps persuading your government to find it beyond the frontiers. The disappearance of capitalism will remove some of the present causes of war, but others will still remain. In the present combat between Germany and Russia, both sides call themselves socialists, and certainly there is very little opportunity for private profits in either country. Future wars may result from conflicts of interest between different races or regions, between rice-eaters and meat-eaters, between clever people and plodders.

In order to adjust such conflicts peaceably, we shall need a more complex scheme than the constitution of the U.S.S.R. In spite of Mr. Pritt's praise, this does not offer a close parallel to a federation of Europe or the world. One of its member states, Russia, contains three quarters of the area of the U.S.S.R. and two thirds of the population. Under such conditions, one partner is likely to be predominant and the rest satellites. Even if such a system has worked satisfactorily within the Soviet Union, this tells us very little about the probable success of a greatly expanded socialist federation with several approximately equal large members. So if we proposed to set up an organization including, say, Great Britain, the Dominions, the United States, Germany, the U.S.S.R., China, and Japan, then even though they have all become socialistic states, still we shall have to draw on schemes like those of Lord Davies, Streit, and Bingham, in order to determine the best form of organization.

Our next question is, should the world unite in some way or other, or only Europe? It is significant that Mr. Pritt's telling objections to a proposal of federalism for the world are much weakened when applied to Europe. Here is a body of countries which have belonged for centuries to an intellectual and spiritual confederation, which form an economic unit, whose boundaries have lately become less important.   There is sufficient likeness and pressure in this crisis to foster a desire for union, sufficient divergence in language and traditions to make them stop short of complete unity.   A respect for law is strong in western Europe at least, and even the Balkans are probably not more lawless than our frontier states a century ago.

On the other hand, a union of Europe alone presents serious perplexities.   Great Britain seems an essential member, but what are you going to do with the British Empire?   If you bring in Russia, half of Asia comes in too, but her omission leaves her a potential disputer with definite interests in the Baltic and the Balkans.   Non-European dependencies ought to be run by a world organization, not just European, if they are to be administered for their natives and their raw materials handled for the benefit of consumers everywhere.

In short, a European union seems feasible, and it will be desirable if it be subsidiary to some sort of world organization.

Finally, League or Union?   Here I feel still more cautious, but I shall throw out a few ideas for what they are worth.   I began my reading with a strong feeling that the League had hopelessly failed, and that Grenville Clark's plan of Union, which I already knew, was a better way out.   The more I have read, the more I have found myself swinging toward something based on the League.   With all its timidities (which Congress can often imitate) and its defects, the record of unspectacular achievement is much more impressive than I realized.   The so-called technical services, in particular—health, labor, etc.—must not be abandoned.   Perhaps they could be merely transferred to Mr. Streit's Union, but there is more to it than that.

In the first place, it is not fair to balance against a League with bad failures a Union with no failures.   The Union never existed.   We do not know what it would do.   My guess is that Mr. Streit's Congress might have hesitated about sanctions against Italy in 1935 as much as the Council did, and applied them no better if it lacked an international police.   I also surmise that the elected representatives from Italy or Germany in a Congress would have been *alter egos* of Mussolini and Hitler as much as their appointed delegates to Council or Assembly.

A dictator can control elections easily, at least if there is no effective federal supervision, and would that have been likely?

Next, the League is a going concern, or at worst was such until Munich. You have something to start from. You know its weak points so as to remedy them. Its strong points have been operating for two decades. At least, we should be rather slow to junk it for something entirely new.

The parallel with our own Confederation and Union is tempting, but is it sound? American conditions were far more favorable to Union than are world conditions. Large areas lie outside a common tradition, and others have not developed a respect for law as we know it. A looser form of association may be appropriate, at least for some decades.

The failures of the League are not necessarily due to its structure. Causes hampered it which may not be repeated. There was its entanglement with a dictated peace—this time we may negotiate, especially if the dictators are previously replaced by democratic governments. The strains in the early years were terrific. Would the United States have survived if the Dred Scott case, secession, the recent depression, and several state dictators like Huey Long had all come within two decades after 1789? The League had to go through all that. Our Union had sixty years to become rooted before the first great strain of 1850. Finally, the League may not have worked because its members did not want very much to make it work. Rappard in his "Quest of Peace" (March 1, 1940) writes:

> The nations which had been at war with each other . . . had never concluded a real peace in that they had never succeeded in regaining each other's confidence. . . . Those who . . . had won the World War and settled the terms of peace were unwilling to prolong those efforts and to exert their influence to insure the maintenance of those terms. . . . The present plight of Europe is due less to the excessive ambitions of the men of 1919 than to the excessive debility of their successors.

It seems possible then that we shall be wise to begin with what we have, the League of Nations. It will be wise to use its experience of twenty years with legislative sessions, executive sessions, a judicial tribunal, and numerous administrative bodies of high quality. Knowing what were the mistakes of the

League, we have some ideas what to avoid. This may require drastic changes in the Covenant, and very likely some of these changes may approximate ideas suggested by Streit's Union and other schemes. For example, the League finances would be on a sounder basis if the contributions from member states were supplemented by some kind of League tax. This might conceivably be levied on all international movements of goods, money, and persons.

Getting away from details to a broad outlook on the problem of postwar international organization, the previous discussion suggests two points for the future.

In the first place, it is very important to avoid strains during the early years of the new international body. Whatever our impulses, there will be no time for vengeance. The world after the armistice will resemble a town which has to rebuild itself after a flood. The incompetents must be removed, but any other sort of punishment will be a luxury which we cannot afford. There will be too much else to do. The lesson of our own Reconstruction Period and Europe since November 11, 1918, is that when a war is over, it ought to be over. Briand's words *"Pour nous, c'est fini,"* ought to be spoken on the day of the armistice and not eight years afterwards. . . .

Another way to avoid strains is the immediate freeing of economic life after the armistice, so as to produce on both sides a feeling of great relief that the war is ended. This time there must be no food blockade.

Also, there must be no raids, like those on Vilna and Fiume. No matter what the costs, those in charge of the peace must make everybody realize that fighting has got to stop. Perhaps frictions could be reduced by establishing a temporary *status quo,* say for twenty-five years, with a definite method for later adjustments.

Strains can be reduced by the restoration of normal life through rapid reconstruction on a great scale. International understanding might be increased if this were carried out co-operatively. For example, suppose some German workmen came over to help in England and *vice versa.* Each visiting group would soon realize that people very much like themselves had suffered in a common disaster. Who will pay for this vast work of reconstruction? The answer is simple, though perhaps unpalatable. Who pays for the war? For the most part, we do. I suspect that we must also bear a heavy share of the expense of reconstruction in order to avoid an infinitely greater outlay in preparation against a Third World War.

Secondly, no scheme is enough. The spirit is even more essential. Years ago André Siegfried remarked to me that the League of Nations lacked "Geist." It had no personality. To the ordinary man it was just a distant piece of machinery in Geneva. One strong reason for the success of the United States in the early years was that the nation was immediately brought before the eyes of every citizen through flags over postoffices, federal judges and officials in every state, naval vessels in harbors, and the government stamp on coins. In some such way, the new international body must become a reality for the common man everywhere. It would be very helpful if the League could fly its flag widely and take over a considerable number of everyday things like postage stamps and coinage. The League symbol should be put on all the great public works built during reconstruction. Its officials and benefits should be made generally visible. Recreation is an excellent way to make the League a drawing force. It might take over all youth hostels, which formed one of our most hopeful international organizations before the war. It might arrange international excursions at public expense, taking a leaf from the book of the Nazis and using these excursions for mutual understanding instead of nationalistic pride.

The spirit is all important. The new international organization requires a desire to make it work as well as a desire to start it. In this respect practically all the books I have read are at fault. They possess little emotional appeal. They lack the quality which shone so clearly in the speeches of Woodrow Wilson. We must make people everywhere want to join a world organization.

Some such organization must come into existence for the alternative of perpetual defense and repeated total warfare is hideous. Still we must not minimize the difficulties. When the local contractor in the little Maine village where we go for the summer engages workmen from the next village, there is an outcry against the employment of "foreigners." This illustrates the frictions which must be overcome between inhabitants of different countries and different parts of the world. There is no simple solution. We must be patient and remember that cathedrals are rarely built by a single generation. We must know much—we must hope much.

## IS A NEW LEAGUE WANTED? [9]

There are a large number of alternatives, but for purposes of discussion they can be reduced to three: (1) a new form of world league, (2) world or regional federations, (3) an independent U.S. policy.

The first proposal would call for the restoration and strengthening of the League of Nations. The League was essentially an American idea. And despite its dismal failure in averting the outbreak of World War II, statesmen still pay it tribute. Curiously enough, the most generous tributes come from America. On February 2, 1939, Secretary of State Hull declared that "the League [of Nations] . . . has been responsible for the development of mutual exchange and discussion of ideas and methods to a greater extent and in more fields of humanitarian and scientific endeavor than any other organization in history." Recently an even more generous tribute came from ex-President Herbert Hoover and ex-Ambassador Hugh Gibson, who wrote in their *Problems of Lasting Peace* that the League "constituted the greatest experiment and the greatest effort that mankind has ever made to assure the peace of the world."

The League Covenant emphasized collective security—the reinforcement of the *status quo*. League members promised to refer disputes to pacific settlement and not to resort to war except in certain extraordinary cases. They also promised in the famous Article 16 to impose "sanctions" against any aggressor state.

[9] By Raymond Leslie Buell, Round Table Editor of *Fortune*. From "Draftsmen of the New World, a Report on the Principal Plans for Postwar Political Reconstruction." *Fortune.* 27:128-9, 152-4. February 1943.

The Covenant held out the hope for peaceful change; but no such change could be imposed upon any member without its consent. The League developed many nonpolitical agencies to transact world business. But, in fact, it was little more than a loose, if supposedly universal, alliance of sovereign states. From the constitutional standpoint, the League could make no important decision without unanimous vote.

More serious than the constitutional defects was the unwillingness of public opinion in any important country to take the League obligations seriously. The refusal of the United States to join the League set an example that inevitably influenced every other government, even though accepting membership. Public opinion in neither Britain nor France—let alone the United States—was willing to go to war to stop aggression in a supposedly distant land; nor was any nation willing to curb its economic nationalism or revise controversial boundaries for the sake of world reconciliation. Consequently the League system broke down when challenged by the aggressors. As a result the entire world again finds itself at war.

On paper, the League of Nations still remains in existence. Forty-five members continue to pay their annual dues. A phantom secretariat of around eighty members remains at Geneva. The High Commissioner for Refugees has his office in London. A League mission also carries out certain functions in Princeton. The staff of the International Labor Organization, a semi-League organization, is now in Montreal.

As Mr. Sean Lester, Acting Secretary General, wrote in his latest annual report, "All these organizations of the League of Nations are thus in being, ready at the appropriate moment to take their respective parts in the reconstruction of the world, or to serve as the foundations on which the new order can be built."

While there are some people who want to see the old League automatically revived at the end of this war, perhaps the majority of the League idea proponents want either to see changes made in the existing Covenant, or to create a similar type of world organization under a different name, possibly developing out of the loose alliance now called the United Nations.

Profesor Hans Kelsen, the noted jurist, proposed before the outbreak of war not only the separation of the League Covenant from the old peace treaties but the redrafting of certain articles. Mr. C. J. Hambro, Norwegian President of the League Assembly, in his recent book, *How to Win the Peace,* admits that the equality rule in the old Covenant should be changed, and increased voting power given to the larger states in at least one League body to correspond with their greater financial contributions and responsibilities. Numerous suggestions have been made to waive the unanimity rule, particularly so that no state can judge its own cause. Others propose that the League anti-war machinery be tightened up. An automatic system of sanctions, they urge, should be worked out against aggressors in the future, rather than be left to national discretion as in the past. Some plans would give the new world authority a monopoly of bombing planes, while gradually reducing national armaments within the requirements of collective security.

Still others propose that the new association control various technical and humanitarian organizations of an international character, such as the Universal Postal Union, the International Institute of Agriculture, and the International Labor Organization.

While such developments could take place within the framework of an amended League Covenant, many believe the old League was too intimately associated with the disasters of Europe to make it psychologically acceptable in the future. They would therefore change the name of the world association and move its capital away from Geneva.

Field Marshal Jan Smuts, addressing the British Parliament on October 21, 1942, declared that the United Nations is a "new conception, much in advance of the old concept of a league of nations. We do not want to be a league, but something more definite and organic, even if, to begin with, more limited and less ambitious than the League."

Under Secretary of State Sumner Welles, in an address last December, spoke of the need for a United Nations association. Even more striking have been recent addresses of Harold E. Stassen, Republican Governor of Minnesota, the latest of which

(December 14) called for a continuing organization of the United Nations of the world, which would establish temporary governments in each of the Axis nations, a commission controlling the greater international airways of the future, an administrative body controlling the gateways to the seven seas, a United Nations commission to increase literacy throughout the world, and a United Nations legion to police the world.

Whether it be the old League of Nations, a new United Nations association—or possibly both—this concept rests on the belief that the like-minded nation states of the world should voluntarily join in a *confederation* gradually evolving common institutions, with an independent power of action within a delegated sphere. As Lord Simon, British Lord Chancellor, has said: "The conception is not that we should aim at forcing upon as many people as possible the dictates of some international organ, but rather that we should aim at getting agreement between as many sovereign communities as may be, each of them, we trust, enjoying rights of self-government, so that as the result of consent, not as the result of externally applied force, this international authority is able to speak in the name of all well-disposed people."

The idea that after the war the seventy-odd sovereign states can ever reach agreement on preserving the *status quo* or peacefully changing it strikes another school as highly unrealistic. These critics insist that in this complicated world no universal solutions are possible; and that even though, in the flush of victory, the great powers promise to repress future wars in any part of the globe, they will soon forget their obligations. History has proved that the more wide-sweeping the guarantee, the less likely it is to be observed. Despite the technological revolution through which the world is now passing, its component parts have little in common according to this school. Confronted by differing levels of culture and by incompatible political and social systems that have already resulted in an international civil war, the world, it maintains, cannot hope to find any universal solutions now.

Commenting on the old League, the English writer Lionel Curtis, in *Civitas Dei,* wrote several years ago that "all the states which signed the Covenant have broken their pledge in the letter as well as the spirit. These pledges are dead. No miracle can restore them to life. . . . The League has failed in its primary duty of revising treaties. . . . I see no hope that the League can revise its own Covenant."

Dr. Egon Ranshofen-Wertheimer, a former member of the League secretariat, has expressed a similar view in his *Victory Is Not Enough*: "We must squarely face the fact the next step cannot be a world peace agency. . . . There must be no guarantee of territorial integrity, as there will be no international army to enforce it; no sanction clause, as there will be no common power to conduct sanctions; no compulsory jurisdiction by a world court, as there will be no policeman to execute its decisions."

Such pessimism was recently echoed in an editorial in the London *Times*: "We shall not again attempt to found the peace of the world upon such a basis as the League of Nations, noble indeed in the vision and purpose of its creators, but untried in action, discontinuous with the history of the immediate past, and vaguely defined at the very points where precision was most essential."

## METHODS OF PRESERVING PEACE: THE LEAGUE [10]

The plans for perserving peace, and which have been suggested, fall into eight major categories:

1. Restoration of the League of Nations under the Covenant as it stands.

2. Restoration of the League with a revised Covenant giving it absolute military power to enforce peace.

3. Restoration of the League of Nations with a revised Covenant constituting it as an effective Council of Nations to preserve peace solely by pacific settlements and for building international cooperation.

[10] By Herbert Hoover, former President of the United States, and Hugh Gibson, Ambassador to Belgium, 1927-1933. From their *Problems of Lasting Peace*. p. 253-63. Doubleday, Doran and Company. New York. 1942.

4. Proposals for a separate military organization by the leading allied nations to preserve order.

5. Proposals that each great region of the earth should separately organize its own preservation of order while co-operating in pacific settlement through some form of the League, Council of Nations, or other world organization for pacific settlements.

6. Extreme isolation.

7. Federation of nations.

8. Pax Americana

. . .

Without here expressing opinions of our own, we give the arguments, pro and con, and state such experience as the world has had with such methods.

1. *Restoration of the League of Nations under the Covenant as it stands.* The League of Nations represents the greatest and most comprehensive experiment in all history in deliberate organization of nations to bring lasting peace. Indeed, we can grasp the value of this experiment only if we realize that the world has to learn its lessons in preservation of peace by trial and error.

The League failed to preserve peace. Yet it was by no means wholly a failure. We have sought to analyze fully its workings in Chapter VIII, to which we refer the reader for the background of these immediate observations.

There were many causes for this failure. Among them were the failure of the Treaty of Versailles to allay the six dynamic forces which make for war; the disastrous political climate arising out of the competition of power diplomacy, balance of power; military alliances which constantly ignored the League; the failure to support representative government in the enemy countries; and, finally, the economic miseries of Europe.

Despite these handicaps from outside, the League did succeed in developing a considerable measure of accomplishment in one field and an unparalleled measure of success in another. It did settle many controversies by pacific means; it did advance the technique of such settlements. Its outstanding success was in the development of cooperation between nations in the fields of public health, in advancement of welfare, in intellectual exchanges, and in economic improvement.

We have referred to the outside influences which militated against the success of the League. There were, however, weaknesses in the League itself. We have analyzed these weaknesses elsewhere, but we may condense them here.

1. The Covenant of the League was at the same time too elaborate, too precise, and not precise enough in its provisions. The text became a yoke under which nations chafed or became fearful concerning their sovereignty. The attempt to commit nations to certain procedures and at the same time to give them each a veto power action led to destructive effects. In consequence, there were incessant disputes over interpretation, jurisdiction, and authority.

2. The original theory of the League was that all controversies between nations should be submitted to pacific settlement and that if any nation refused and began military action, it was to be dealt with as an aggressor. Thereupon, collective economic or military force should be applied by the other members. This definition of an aggressor proved to have great difficulties. But more important, the compromises in the Covenant by which nations did not bind themselves to this procedure and with the provision of a full veto power to each member the original theory never had a chance.

3 The League was thus founded upon two different concepts, one organizing the preservation of peace by economic or military force; and the other, for the prevention of war by settlement of controversy through pacific methods. The two concepts clashed. In any event, attempt to summon economic and military force against important aggressors proved beyond the practical capacity of an international body, and with these failures the strength and prestige of the League in the field of pacific settlement were fatally injured.

4. The League did not recognize, or was prevented from undertaking, one of the first functions of preserving peace: that is, the need for comprehensive consideration of the political

forces in different areas which were developing strains and the formulation of longview policies and action for their correction. Regional development of such policies in Europe and Asia comparable to the work of the Pan American conferences in the Western Hemisphere was a constant and urgent necessity.

5. The League failed to provide for or secure any reality in the revision of onerous treaties or those made from the heat of war which could not endure. Thus, it became the defender of the *status quo* and left to war the dissolution of such strains.

It seems improbable that the membership of the League could be voluntarily restored without considerable amendment to the Covenant. Even if nations were forced to join, they could obstruct and withdraw unless the whole Covenant were revised.

Two categories of amendments are proposed. The one would take the League fully into the field of military force, the other would take it wholly into the field of pacific settlements.

II. *Restoration of the League with a revision of the Covenant giving it absolute military power to enforce peace.* One proposal for revision of the Covenant is to preserve most of its present structure but with revision so as to give the League complete power by making arbitration or judicial determination compulsory in all disputes; making refusal the sole criterion of aggression; making the economic and military sanctions follow automatically upon military action of such an aggressor; doing away with the veto power of each nation; making League decisions by majority or two-thirds vote; and giving the League an international army, navy, and air force to enforce its decisions.

It is asserted that this would "put 'iron teeth' in the League" and would make peace impregnable. This method would assume that "aggression" can be defined in these terms, but the experience which we have discussed indicates that it is not this simple.

And such an armed force would necessarily have to be larger than any combination of other armies, navies, or air forces, all of which implies that the disarmament of all nations must be very thorough, or, alternatively, that the League force be a very large one.

These ideas were discussed at length and rejected at Versailles. They, of course, mean a wholesale surrender of national sovereignty. The refusal of nations to join or abide by the much milder provisions of the present League would seem to indicate that it would not have many voluntary members. It would, in fact, be a blind acceptance of super sovereignty which nations in practice would probably refuse to accept, or, if they were compelled to accept, they would not abide for long.

A further criticism is that a majority of nations would not necessarily represent a majority of population. And that a combination of small nations, even if a two-thirds vote were required, might use the machinery for aggression on the larger ones. A further objection is that such an army, navy, or air force would have to be commanded by human beings of some nationality, and they would not be likely to attack their own people; and conversely, they might on nationalist or other grounds be influenced to attack others. When such proposals were raised at Paris in 1918, they were rejected, partly because no considerable adherence could be expected, and partly because it was recognized that a group of nations or the commander in chief of such an army could become dictators of the world.

III. *Restoration of the League of Nations with a revised Covenant constituting it as an effective Council of Nations to preserve peace solely by pacific settlements and for building international cooperation.* Another proposal is made for amendment of the Covenant which takes account of the weaknesses of the present League idea and its structure and seeks to build up and strengthen it in the directions where it has proved to have been most successful. The proposal amounts, in fact to a transformation of the League into a continuously sitting Council of Nations—each nation to be permanently represented by the highest-caliber men of more than ambassadorial rank, with the purpose of the League confined to developing broad regional policies for peace; to bringing about settlement of controversies under existing treaties through negotiation, arbitration, and judicial settlement; and to promote revision of onerous treaties. The use of force would be divorced from its proceedings. The League is to be, it is suggested, a continuous round table of nations through direct representatives of chiefs of states and ministers for foreign affairs.

This would also be a radical departure from the practice of the League, which was seldom to convene the nations until after a crisis had arisen.

Broadly, it is proposed to preserve the name and that the Covenant be revised:

1. To eliminate all clauses dealing with military and economic sanctions.

2. To eliminate all clauses presuming to commit nations to specific procedure in the settlement of disputes.

3. To substitute for these clauses the simple declaration that it shall be the duty of the League to promote pacific settlements.

4. To substitute for the Council and Assembly as at present constituted a body composed of ambassadors from all nations, resident at all times at the seat of the League, with no binding votes except upon procedural questions.

5. To elect annually a President from its membership with an annually elected Executive Committee on procedure and organization.

6. The Executive Committee to appoint subcommittees from its membership upon a regional basis to formulate regional policies of peace. For Europe, for instance, it would be, in effect, a Concert of Europe constantly operating. Its president, upon such regional committee's failure to secure settlements, to have power to appoint a more general committee from members not parties to the dispute.

7. All committees simply to negotiate, conciliate, urge adoption of pacific methods, report on facts and recommend to the whole body, with no penalties or obligations.

In fact, the proposal seeks to get away from rigid organization to a constantly functioning clearinghouse and round table of international questions, where each nation is effectively and at all times present in the person of a leading personality acting in close collaboration with his own foreign office.

Fundamentally, this is a modernization of diplomacy. It would tend to hold the heads of states and their foreign ministers more directly in the picture of responsibility instead of in a stand-off attitude negotiating with a separate body, as the League was regarded. It is proposed that the League should preserve and encourage all the treaties of arbitration, all the machinery of the World Court and the Hague Tribunal—it being one of the purposes of the League to secure that controversies be referred to and solved by such agencies or special committees as the occasion might require.

The plan proposes that the admirable organization of the existing secretariat be reestablished with all of its excellent machinery of international cooperation under the direction of this reorganized League.

No machinery of enforcement is suggested. It would rest solely upon good faith, world opinion, and the value of immediate discussion directly between nations rather than through the intervention of an outside body.

Carrying no commitments or delegations of sovereignty, it is contended not a single voice in any country could object to full membership.

It is held that such council, out of experience and successful precedent, could be expected to build up the fabric of international law and steadily guide the movement of nations toward abolition of war.

One objection to this plan is that some organization of force methods to preserve peace will be necessary for some years to come, but the contentions of its advocates are that experience has demonstrated that the two functions of force and pacific settlement are incompatible and mutually destructive when exercised by the same organizations, and that ultimate hope must be in the growth of pacific methods. The proposers hold that force measures to preserve international order should be separately erected elsewhere, somewhat as described next.

IV. *Proposals for a separate military organization by the Allied Nations to preserve order.* The history of 140 years amply indicates that among the multitude of nations in Europe and Asia there must be some kind of military restraints if there is to be peace. The long catalog of a hundred military alliances and interventions of the balance of power intended to prevent war is in itself ample proof of this.

After the Napoleonic wars the Quadruple Alliance performed this function during the readjustment period. After the First World War the military power of Britain, France, and Italy served after a fashion until their joint relationships began to disintegrate and the League failed with "collective security." The job was bigger in 1919 than in 1815 partly because of the multiplication of independent states.

The organization of economic, military, or other force action to preserve peace is, however, the most difficult problem that civilization has to confront. The world is today not only divided by its nationalisms, but it is also divided by militant ideological groups whose emotions and devotions to their ideas are not going to evaporate with peace.

One lesson the world should have learned by this time. That is that economic sanctions mean war when they are applied to a strong nation and therefore can be abandoned as a method of force more likely to make for war than peace.

The foundation of any police measures must first be laid in general disarmament. Technically, for reasons given elsewhere, this is simpler than hitherto. The possibility after general disarmament of stopping aggressive action by a comparatively small air force as distinguished from large armies and navies offer more arguable approach to the problem than hitherto.

Most students agree that it is a reasonable deduction from all history that after the present war, with its even larger number of states which "self-determination" will create, and the increasing hates from total war, there must again be some strong military supervision if Europe and Asia are to keep the peace, at least until the malignant forces in those areas have had time to abate and the constructive forces to dominate.

The proposal of those advocating the transformation of the League into a Council is that the Allied Powers must, after the peace, take on the burden of policing the world for some period after the war, but should act only after the League, reorganized as above, had exerted its full energies to keep the peace.

In any event, if the realistic experience of former world wars is any criterion, even with definite organization, the victorious powers will, with military means, jointly dominate the world for so long as their interests do not clash. They will need to do so at least during a period for political and economic recuperation.

## BUILDING ON LEAGUE FOUNDATIONS [11]

All the criticism of the League of Nations has not come from the outside. In 1936 the Assembly set up a Special Committee to Study the Application of the Principles of the Covenant, which devoted itself to the underlying problem of why the League had not accomplished its central purpose of preserving peace. Among the major questions which the Committee found had a bearing on this problem were peaceful change, enforcement of obligations, universality of membership, and regionalism. Undoubtedly the statesmen who make the new peace system—whether it be the League revamped or something with a new name—will debate these questions further.

There are other questions connected with this problem that have not yet had as much public attention as they deserve. Among them are two of special importance:—first, whether new methods of representation can be devised; and second, whether the governments should and can be brought to abandon their sovereignty in certain fields. The proposed Union of Democracies is one answer to these questions. Enthusiasts for the International Labor Organization believe that its scheme of functional representation points the way for the future. Some of the study committees referred to in the introductory paragraphs of this pamphlet are trying to devise ways in which these principles could be worked into the League structure. It is to be hoped that the subject will be discussed thoroughly in public before the time comes for governments to make decisions about the new system.

[11] By Esther Caukin Brunaer, Associate in International Education of the American Association of University Women. From pamphlet *Building the New World Order*. p. 28-37. American Association of University Women. Washington, D.C. December 1939.

The sum and substance of the debates in the League's Special Committee was:—How can the forces for war be restrained and the forces for peace be given freer play?  One thing that it was thought could be done to raise the prestige of the League of Nations and therefore its influence for peace, was to separate the Covenant from the Treaty of Versailles.  The importance of such a move was chiefly psychological.  The Treaty of Versailles had not caused the defeat of Germany, but only registered it.  Much had already been done to wipe out the bitterest aspects of the defeat, especially during the Stresemann-Briand period.  However, it had not been done rapidly nor generously enough to overcome the resentment which helped the Nazis into power in Germany.  By 1938 the lesson was fairly well learned.  In September of that year the Assembly recommended changes in the Covenant that would make the League of Nations technically and legally independent of the peace treaties.  Within two months forty-two states members had approved the amendments, but the changes have not come into force because all the members have not agreed to them.

By the time this war is ended the connection of the League with the Treaty of Versailles will probably be an academic and fairly meaningless question.  It is necessary to note it in discussing proposals for a better peace system, however, because the principles involved in the question will still be important.  One problem will be whether to make plans for a new or renovated international body in the course of the peace conference, or to hold a special meeting for the purpose.  Presumably, a conference for the express purpose of establishing the postwar peace system would include the defeated nations on a basis of equality.  To make them a part of the new order from the beginning and make them equally responsible for it might help to prevent them from trying to wreck it later.

To demand that the new international government should be completely divorced from the peace settlement would be highly unrealistic.  If it is to deal with political questions at all, they will be actual and not theoretical questions and the most vital ones will have some connection with the peace settlement.  What people really mean when they insist that a going international organization should be separated from the treaties that mark the end of a war, is that it should not be simply an instrument to perpetuate the terms of the treaties, and that its decisions should not continue to be determined by the same array of forces that ended the war. This is a part of the larger problem of peaceful change, which has also been discussed widely in recent years, both within and outside the League.

The problem of peaceful change can be solved only partially by institutional devices. Political habits, traditional attitudes, the will to power, internal economic and social maladjustments, vested interests,—all these enter into the endless pattern of shifting boundaries and populations. They determine demands and refusals, and they also help determine whether war is to be used as a last resort to back up either the demands or the refusals. Today it is the national states that exert the greatest control over these forces. An international body that is weaker than the individual states that compose it can deal only slowly and indirectly with them. Persuasion and education here, compulsion there, compromise at another point will gradually change habits and attitudes, relieve internal strains, curb vested interests, and direct the will to power constructively. In every nation there are forces ready to ally themselves with any agency that will work in these directions. In some countries these forces are suppressed for the time being; in others they are free to work. As long as national governments hold the reins of power, the pressure for improvements needs to be exerted on them in the first instance. The ability of international government to create and preserve stability with freedom will grow as the peoples of the world become more and more convinced that peace and justice are indivisible,—that they have to be worked for and attained together.

The League of Nations has by no means ignored the problem of peaceful change, although it has not registered any conspicious successes in that field. The Covenant of the League of Nations gives authority to the Assembly, in Article 19, to "advise the reconsideration by Members of the League of treaties which have become inapplicable and the consideration of international conditions whose continuance might endanger the peace of the world." Article 19 was never specifically invoked, even by the members that complained most bitterly about the injustices of the Treaty of Versailles, so that there is no way of knowing how well the provision might have worked. A number of changes were made in the Versailles settlement by peaceful means, such as the revision of the reparations system and the withdrawal ahead of time of the armies of occupation in the Rhineland. This was not much of an advance over the pre-war situation, however, because every general peace treaty has been modified in some respects in the course of time, by diplomatic methods as well as by the use of force.

Perhaps a periodic survey of the state of the world, noting sore spots and suggestions for healing them, might be required in the basic law of the new international system. It is true that such a forum might keep alive some grievances that had better be buried and forgotten, but that are kept alive anyhow. Any group of people with a little time, money, and a mimeograph machine can keep on agitating any subject in the hope that if the world becomes sufficiently unsettled they may get a sympathetic hearing. There are plenty of serious grievances, however. In the beginning they often present themselves in a mild form and mild measures would settle them. Really dangerous subjects do not get taken care of by being ignored, although human beings have a natural tendency to think that if they will not acknowledge the presence of something disagreeable it will cease to exist. Reviewing the state of the world from time to time as a matter of routine and not in the excitement of a crisis would help to keep various types of grievances in their proper perspective. It would also underline the responsibility of all nations for dealing with serious problems before they reach a state of emergency.

More fundamental than devices for review and discussion would be to make certain kinds of grievances less important. For example, boundary lines need not irritate people all the time if they are not made a symbol of perpetual fear, hatred, and suspicion. The fate of minorities need not cause conflict among nations. This is demonstrated by the fact that Hitler, who could stir up crises over the Sudeten Germans and Danzig could also abandon the Germans in the Southern Tyrol to his ally, Mussolini, and could enter into a scheme to take the Germans out of the Baltic countries so that they would not cause friction with Russia. With freedom of trade and equal access to markets and raw materials, colonies would become less important economically. As they become less important economically, colonial possessions would cease to impart the prestige that is today so hard for imperial nations to give up and so much sought after by would-be imperial nations. The whole complex problem of nationalism needs to be worked through before we can solve the problem of peaceful change in the international scene. As long as nationalism is raised to the emotional pitch of religion, grievances that might be soothed by a little common sense and good will are exaggerated into crusades. If nationalism could be shifted over to cultural realms and taken out of politics and industry, it would be a creative and not a harmful force. Here, again, the solution is less a matter of setting up new international institutions than of changing attitudes and habits.

It is easier to talk about making change seem less important both to those who want it and those who oppose it, than it is to create such a happy condition. We are in a vicious circle, because change would come to seem less important only in an atmosphere of confidence and a spirit of cooperation. It is difficult to develop such an atmosphere when nations are constantly being threatened with destruction either because they stand in the way of a desired change or because they insist on change as essential to their own welfare. In other words, as long as the threat of war hangs over the scene the nations cannot get very far in an effort to develop the habit of seeking change by discussion and negotiation. That brings us to the twin problem of how an international body can enforce peace.

In our analysis of the existing peace system we have seen that one of the greatest weaknesses is the fact that the actual power remains in the hands of the individual members and that they must also decide each time whether and how to use this power. The decision of each government is influenced by many factors. The depth of respect for an obligation is one. The judgment of responsible officials as to the importance of a given threat to peace in comparison with other interests of the nation is another. Assurance that other nations will fulfill their obligations also influences such a decision. Since the collapse of the Disarmament Conference there has not been any discussion in official circles about providing the League of Nations as such with power to enforce the decisions of the Council or Assembly. At that time, it will be recalled, the French Government proposed that the nations give up what could roughly be called the offensive armaments and put them at the disposal of the League. In the Committee to Study the Application of the Principles of the Covenant, set up by the Assembly in 1936, the Soviet government proposed a scheme to hasten consideration of threats to peace. The Soviet proposal included making a vote of three fourths of the Council members, excluding the disputants, decisive, and forcing a decision to be taken within six days after the outbreak of war. These particular proposals may or may not be renewed in the conference that plans the new peace system, but the underlying problems of an independent police force and decisions by something less than unanimous vote are certain to be discussed.

The makers of the new international government will probably still have before them the question that was considered by the Committee to Study the Application of the Principles of the Covenant. That question is, how can all nations be brought within the system and subjected to its influence? The answer has an important bearing on the problem of enforcing peace. It has been recognized that, for various different reasons, it was the peace obligations of League membership that prevented at least one nation from joining and caused some to withdraw. It is also recognized that nations could not be compelled to enter or stay in the system against their will except by force, and that even if they acceded momentarily under pressure, their presence would contribute nothing unless they came to see advantages for themselves in membership. Such nations need to be educated, and on the modern educational theory of "learning by doing" it can be argued that a sort of associate or transitional membership might be provided. The obligation of nations in this stage would extend only to loyal cooperation in nonpolitical fields. In serious emergencies they might be called in to consult with the full members of the central body, and be permitted but not required to join in enforcing their decisions. The difficulty with such a scheme is that most nations would prefer associate membership, unless the obligations of full members could carry certain advantages of protection and security against aggression.

The question of universal *versus* limited obligations has been discussed in the League of Nations since the failure of the Geneva Protocol in 1925. The Locarno Pact was the first important step in what was expected to be a network of regional security agreements. These agreements, which included specific procedures for settling various kinds of disputes, were intended to establish confidence, so that the nations would cut down their arms and thus, in turn more confidence would be created. A regional security system was developed outside the League of Nations by a series of nonaggression pacts between the Soviet Union and its neighbors. These nonaggression pacts have gone to pieces in the present conflict. The Locarno Pact vanished when Hitler remilitarized the Rhineland. Mussolini, smarting under sanctions, refused to discharge the obligations of Italy as a guarantor, and the British government would not permit France to take military action. The idea that Germany might be subjected to the procedures carefully worked out for peaceful settlement got nowhere at all, and the whole issue was soon swallwed up in the crisis of the Spanish Civil War. The fate of the Locarno Pact demonstrated the difficulty of establishing regional security when the members of such a system are at the same time likely to be involved in situations that go far beyond the area covered in the agreement.

Another attempted answer to the problem of unlimited or limited obligations is the idea of a network of little leagues of nations. The theory is that the major problems of Europe are peculiarly European, of Asia are peculiarly Asiatic, and of the Americas, are peculiarly American. On this assumption it is felt that the nations on those continents should deal with their own problems. Under present conditions very little can be done along these lines in Asia, although the situation in that part of the world may become stable by the time the European war is over. There have already been some efforts to create a federation of European states. A "United States of Europe" was an ideal promoted by Briand and in 1930 the League of Nations set up a Commission of Enquiry on European Union. The Commission was able to do little toward building up a sense of European solidarity. This was partly because of the antiquity of certain rivalries and suspicions and partly because the larger European nations had heavy interests and commitments outside of Europe. The Commission recommended that the European countries should cooperate in certain measures to relieve the economic crisis that was then becoming acute, but even this project got no further.

While a policy of European solidarity seems to be ruled out for the time being, it may be possible to organize some parts of Europe. The "Oslo Powers," that is, the small neutrals of western and northern Europe, have acted together at times, and they may take the lead in measures to stop the Russian advance in the Baltic. A closer union of the countries of the Danube Valley and the Balkans has been forming since the war broke out. If these two groups could create a system of freer trade among their own members and cooperate closely on both political and nonpolitical projects they would set an example which might eventually be followed by other European countries. However, the far-flung interests of the larger countries of Europe lead to the observation that if partial federations are to be set up as units of a world-wide League they will have to be on other than continental lines.

The subject of continental solidarity as a foundation for world peace brings up the question of the western hemisphere and the Good Neighbor Policy. The next section will take up more fully the relationship of Pan Americanism to the whole problem of organizing the world for peace. Since we are discussing here the ways in which the League of Nations might be changed or extended we should call attention to a few basic facts. One is that the Covenant of the League already recognizes the Monroe Doctrine as a "regional agreement,"— which it did not become in fact until 1936. Also, the Chaco War was finally settled as a regional problem, not by the intervention of the whole League. On the other hand, both the Latin American countries and the United States have many interests and commitments outside the western hemisphere. The United States is heavily involved in the Far East. Many countries of South and Central America are bound by strong economic ties to European countries, and Latin America looks to Spain, France and Italy, rather than to the United States for cultural inspiration. All of these facts do not exclude the possibility of working for a higher development of Pan Americanism as both a direct and indirect contribution to the organization of the world for peace, but they do urge caution in promoting the idea of a federation of continental leagues as the framework of the new peace system.

## AMERICA'S FAITH—A CALL FOR REVIVAL [12]

The terrible implication which such resolutions [as the Burton-Hatch-Hill resolution and the Fulbright resolution] unintentionally but unavoidably carry is that after the last World War our government broke faith with our soldiers and our allies and violated the conditions upon which our enemies sought peace. That is not only the implication, it is the resolution's *raison d'être.* Except for that bit of history the resolution would not have been thought of. Such a commitment was never thought necessary before.

If the bald statement of our default is shocking to one's chauvinistic sensibilities, a brief review of events will nevertheless convince one that it is true. The initial and main

[12] By Robert N. Wilkin, United States District Court Judge, Northern District of Ohio. *New York Times Magazine.* p. 10, 30. July 18, 1943.

attack on the treaty of peace which President Wilson submitted
to the Senate in 1919 was directed by the opponents of the
treaty against Article 10 of the Covenant.  Now Article 10
was in substance the same as the last of the "Fourteen Points"
which President Wilson in his address to Congress on Jan.
8, 1918, had announced as essential to peace.  It provided
that members of the League would respect and preserve
the territorial integrity and political independence of all members as against external aggression.

When Germany in October 1918, transmitted through
the Swiss Government a request for an armistice, it accepted
"as a basis for peace negotiations" the program set forth
by President Wilson in his speech of January 8.  The Fourteen
Points, with but a few additions or amendments, had proved
acceptable to our allies.  They were for the most part a statement of allied war aims prior to America's entry into the
conflict.  The fourteenth point was new, and some of the
older statesmen were skeptical, but a general willingness
to try the experiment prevailed.  In this country the Fourteen Points had been received enthusiastically.

Nevertheless, when the peace treaty was finally submitted
the Senate declined to approve it.  More accurately stated, a
minority defeated it.  There were 57 votes for and 39 against
it.  It lacked by seven votes the constitutional requirement
of two thirds of those present.  Now the Senators who opposed
the treaty advanced the argument that there was no default
or breach of faith in their conduct, that they acted within
their constitutional rights, and that the other parties to the
treaty knew of the requirement of our Constitution regarding
Senatorial approval.  But that argument is mere legalistic
rationalization.  Such specious reasoning cannot justify the
moral wrong of our government's failure to complete what
it had definitely led others to expect that it would perform.

Such an argument would not be accepted in a court of
equity in an analogous case.  A corporation which had ac-
quiesced while its president negotiated a contract on terms
announced to its directors, would not be permitted to escape
its obligation on the ground that the contract lacked formal

approval by the board of directors as required by the constitution of the company, if in the meantime others had acted
on the contract and the contract was in substantial compliance
with the previously announced terms.

But consideration of such an argument brings the discussion down to a level beneath its proper import. The
wrong consisted not so much in the breaking of an implied
promise to our allies as in the breaking of the sacred obligation owed to our soldiers. One who lived through the
First World War can never forget the high emprise which took
our soldiers forth. They were assured it was a war to end
war. And then, after the soldiers had won the war, the
Senate quibbled and haggled and passed reservations and
finally declined even to attempt any fulfillment of the soldiers'
noble purpose. It even declined to support the Permanent
Court of International Justice, although the proposal to join
was no part of the peace treaty and membership in the League
of Nations was not prerequisite to membership in the Court.

The failure to accept the covenant for a League of Nations was not only a breach of faith, it was a denial of faith.
It was a denial of that ever-growing and often-affirmed faith
of America in international cooperation for the maintenance
of world order. As early as 1910 that faith had waxed so
strong that a resolution for a commission to consider utilization of international agencies for limitation of armaments
and of the combined navies of the world for preservation of
peace, was adopted by the Congress without a dissenting
vote in Senate or House. In spite of the slighting references
to the Fourteen Points and the League of Nations Covenant
as "Wilsonian idealism," the truth is that those principles
were thoroughly developed and generally accepted American
policy prior to their lucid pronouncement by Wilson or their
incorporation into the treaty of peace. Although the general
idea back of the League had been growing for fifty years, it
may be said that the plan ultimately adopted in the peace
treaty was originated in the League to Enforce Peace, which
had been founded in Philadelphia in June 1915, with William
H. Taft as President. . . .

Another proof of America's faith is found in the history of the Presidential campaign of 1920. Both major parties promised to support the League of Nations. The Democratic candidate made a forthright and able defense of the covenant, and with heroic courage and prophetic insight foretold the calamity which now we endure. The Republican candidate, never definite as to international affairs, was not so forthright regarding the League, but certainly he did not dare to denounce it. Some of the outstanding members of the Republican party organized the Committee of Thirty-one to support the Republican candidate and the covenant for the League, listing among its members such political and intellectual leaders as Hughes, Hoover, Wickersham, Wilbur, Lowell, Butler, J. G. Schurman, H. W. Taft and William Allen White. But in spite of all endorsements, recommendations and assurances, the proposals for our participation in the League and the World Court were defeated by the Senatorial minority. This sudden reversal of policy and denial of faith was accurately characterized by Ex-President Eliot of Harvard as "America's great apostasy."

The chief responsibility for our nation's default must rest with the Senatorial minority. They set in motion and pressed to conclusion the obstructionist tactics that resulted in the defeat of our war aims and the frustration of our peace hopes. In their excess of determination they took the name of "Battalion of Death," and the terrible portent of that appellation becomes apparent in the ever-growing list of fatalities of the present war. . . .

But while the chief burden rests on the minority Senators, the people as a whole must bear a great responsibility. In a democracy the people cannot evade the duty and destiny which is implicit in their influence. If there had not been a general spiritual decline and moral apathy the Senatorial minority would not have dared to do what it did. The people did not study the covenant; they turned away from its consideration. Domestic problems and irritations from war restrictions absorbed their attention. The soldiers were bent for homes and jobs. They were war-weary and disintegrated.

The post-armistice era gave unrestrained vent to cynicism, self-indulgence, and crass materialism. Under the banner of "Back to Normalcy" the nation entered "the most corrupt and extravagant period of our history."

The extent of our spiritual decline is made manifest in one incident. When President Wilson realized the strength and determination of the "irreconcilables" in the Senate, he set out on a tour of the country to rally public sentiment in favor of the League. But he was followed by Senators Borah, Johnson, and others, who did their utmost to nullify his efforts. In the course of his address in St. Louis, the President said:

> I feel like asking the Secretary of War to get the boys, who went across the water to fight, together on some field where I could go and see them, and I would stand up before them and say: "Boys, I told you before you went across the seas that this was a war against wars, and I did my best to fulfill the promise, but I am obliged to come to you in mortification and shame and say I have not been able to fulfill the promise. You are betrayed. You fought for something that you did not get." And the glory of the armies and navies of the United States is gone like a dream in the night, and there ensues upon it, in the suitable darkness of the night, the nightmare of dread which lay upon the nations before this war came; and there will come sometime, in the vengeful providence of God, another struggle in which not a few hundred thousand fine men from America will have to die but as many millions as are necessary to accomplish the final freedom of the peoples of the world.

That statement has been quoted recently as an instance of prophetic utterance—and for that it is remarkable. But the greater significance of the words lies in the moral tragedy which they reveal. When it came to pass that the President of the United States could stand in the center of this nation, confess mortification and shame over his inability to fulfill his promise to its soldier sons, and say to them, "You are betrayed," and there was no response, then the spiritual life of the people was indeed at low ebb.

The President returned to Washington a broken man. The Commander in Chief of the Army and Navy fell in action. He gave his life to the cause. The great intellect that had so magnificently voiced the aspirations of humanity for peace and brought unity to the efforts of all the Allies, could not maintain the unity of his own people; that courageous and patient soul who had gained acceptance of our faith from all the rest of the world had to witness the loss of that faith at home.


## WILL WE SUPPORT A WORLD ORDER? [13]

The League, most people may now admit, was well enough so far as it went. It did not go very far, because we had not thought very far. We had not thought about peace, not only because we were very busy thinking about war, but because we did not suppose that thinking about peace was necessary. We did not see the enemy, obscured in peace. We did not appreciate the dangers inherent in maldistribution of raw materials and markets, in the use of quotas and tariffs. We did not assay the disunity of the Allies: we ignored the fact that Japan was fascist, that Italy was anything but democratic, that France and Britain disagreed basically as to the manner in which Europe should be run, that Russia was in confusion and fighting off her old allies, that America knew little of international affairs and wanted to know less. We ignored the fact that democratic world government must rest, not only upon "the consent of the governed," but upon a desire of the governed to be governed. We forgot that the world had not been regenerated; Germany might have been regenerated, but she was held down; China and Russia were being regenerated, but regeneration takes time. France and Great Britain had been lusty and grasping imperialists; They remained mature and jealous imperialists. America was too naive to understand what was happening and provincial enough to feel like the country bumpkin done for a cleaning by the city slicker. The little countries which were at once practical and idealistic were too small and too few.

[13] From article "Literature for Defense," by Charlton G. Laird, Professor of English, University of Idaho, Southern Branch. *American Association of University Professors. Bulletin.* 28:319-23. June 1942.

Of the big nations, Italy wanted Fiume, Japan wanted a free hand in Asia, Russia wanted a world revolution, France wanted a Syrian mandate, Great Britain wanted her world trade, and we wanted our war debts. The few who were willing to sacrifice for world peace did not appreciate that hard jobs cannot be legislated, that success grows from work, mistakes, intelligence, and education; that a League of Nations cannot be set up. We did not understand that world government, and its resultant world peace, has to be earned and learned; it cannot be established.

True, we might have done better at establishing. We should have recognized that a world government must be world-wide and must be a government. We might, however, have succeeded. In spite of the gerrymandering in conference, in spite of the ethnic horror that was solemnly pronounced a map of Europe, in spite of great gaps in the "world" government, the makeshift League of Nations might have grown big enough for its job. At the time, all was confusion. Looking back we can see several possibilities. Had the Treaty of Versailles been revised earlier, and democratic elements in Germany given more support, the basic trouble might have been curable. Had the signatories been a little more willing to implement their puppet super-state, the League might have survived its critical years. Above all, had the United States joined and supported the federation it had seemed to sponsor, the League might have had the resources it needed.

In 1919 there was one nation strong enough in money, in goods, in manpower, and in vitality to do almost anything it wished, to get almost anything it wanted. There was one nation sufficiently isolated and sufficiently dominant in its own geographical area to be immune from attack—as attack went in this days. There was one nation wealthy enough to be able to afford to gamble, to lose a few millions of anything for the sake of world peace for all time. These nations were all one, and we were that nation. To glimpse what we might have done, we have only to remember the tremendous power of Herbert Hoover in 1919, although he was but meagerly equipped and his power erratically used. The rest of the world was sick, and we had the medicine; it was starving, and we had the food. We could have bought as much decent international behavior as we wanted. But we did not much want it. We wanted to go home and collect our war debts. Who would not now give up the war debts we never collected, for the war in which, apparently, we are to be paid with good interest?

Thus, although the Allied armies and navies seemed to win the First Phase of the World War, Allied statesmen started to lose it and Allied populations—particularly the American population—finished the job. We were probably too ignorant to write a world peace, and were certainly too provincial to make one work if it had been written. That we were provincial is understandable, but it was not necessary. We were provincial because we wanted to be. New England intellectualism had given way, first to the frontier, then to immigration and industrialization; the average American read something trivial, if he read anything at all. If he went abroad, he went to say he had been there, and to have the fun of coming back. Typical was the pronouncement of a mid-western judge who returned from across the Atlantic: "All the castles of Europe are not so beautiful as one Iowa cornfield," and the significant detail is that scores of small-town editors reprinted the words with a triumphant headline, "The Judge Was Right!" The average American had not read a hundred pages of Tolstoy, Goethe, Balzac, nor of any other continental master, and he felt no lack. The "cultured" American was not much better. As a democratic people we were in no condition to take leadership in a world order, nor to accept a peace that would make world order possible.

Now we are in the Second Phase of the World War, and whether there is to be a third, or a fourth, or a tenth phase probably depends much upon the understanding of the American public. Since Warsaw, we had known that if culture as we know it was to be preserved, we must preserve it. Since Sedan, we have known that no one can preserve the kind of world we thought we were living in, and that if we want a part in making a different world, we shall have to fight for the privilege.   Since Pearl Harbor, we have known that we shall fight; we may or may not avail ourselves of the opportunity to make a better world.   Thus, the question raised by Pearl Harbar is not, "Was the Navy asleep?"   It is, "Will the average American continue to sleep?"   That is, shall we have an enlightened public that will demand and support a world order? . . .

## EXCERPTS

I hope we shall not lightly cast aside all the immense work which was accomplished by the creation of the League of Nations.   Certainly we must take as our foundation the lofty conception of freedom, law, and morality which was the spirit of the League.   We must try—I am speaking, of course, only for ourselves—we must try to make the council of Europe, or whatever it may be called, into a really effective league with all the strongest forces concerned woven into its texture with a high court to adjust disputes and with forces, armed forces, national or international, or both, held ready to enforce these decisions and prevent renewed aggression and the preparation of future wars.—*British Prime Minister, Winston Churchill.   Address, March* 21, 1943.   *Congressional Record.   Mr.* 23, '43.   *p.A*1474.

The League's failure has caused this Second World War; or, if one cares to say the same thing in another way, the conditions which caused the League's failure also produced this war.   But the idea behind the League is exactly as good, exactly as necessary to the peace of the earth, as it was in 1919, when President Wilson proclaimed it.   In organization it had defects.   In action, despite its rejection by American Senators as a "super-government," it was inherently weak.   In purpose, in clear acceptance of mankind's joint task, it was superb.

The League is dead—and it lives.   Though fifty nations failed to make it operative by discussion, twenty-six are now engaged in making it operative by all their armored strength and all their spiritual devotion. Woodrow Wilson's body, like John Brown's, lies moldering in the grave, but his soul is marching on.—*Editorial. New York Times. Ja.* 10, '42. *p.14.*

What of the conclusions of the Institute [on World Organization] and its results? . . . It was recognized by all that the only permanent solution would be a world union in which all law abiding states would have a fair share.

As to the form of this organization for justice, peace, security, and welfare, the Institute talked in terms of a universal League or Association of nations combined with more closely knit regional organizations, which might include a European federation or federations. There was surprisingly little reference to a world federation, which was regarded as unrealistic, at least beyond some special fields. Not all nations are prepared to surrender their sovereignty to that extent. But the adoption of federal solutions for the regional organization of Europe was a different matter. This was generally thought possible and even likely. How far the peoples of Europe would be willing to go in that direction, when they were once more free to express themselves and to determine their own destiny, could not now be determined. One could not foresee whether such solutions would apply to the whole of Europe or only to groups of neighboring states within Europe. The area involved might not be the same for all matters which would be considered as of federal concern. Neither was it possible to foresee which matters would be considered. Thus, many hypotheses would require study and consideration from the point of view of the interests of the European peoples and also from the broader point of view of those of the world community.

On the whole the Institute discussed functions rather than forms but there was a tendency to talk in terms of a modified League rather than a new organization, whatever it might be called. Yet it came as rather a fresh idea to most of the members when they were reminded by speakers that the

League of Nations has a legal existence involving legal commitments which cannot be ignored, and that after the war the Assembly is bound to meet, if only to be dissolved.—*Laura Puffer Morgan and Jan Hostie. World Affairs. D. '41. p.215.*

The lessons learned from the League of Nations experiment have been immensely valuable. It has charted rocks and reefs to be avoided by mariners of the sea of international politics of the future.

The fate which befell the League was forecast from the start by the history of similar loose associations, and particularly by the complete inability of the confederacy of the thirteen American colonies to cope with the problems which sustained government constantly meets. The League Covenant copied too closely and too crudely our own Articles of Confederation of 1776 to provide a permanent constitutional document.

Many there were who earnestly hoped that history would repeat itself and that, before the present cataclysm engulfed us, a veritable written constitution for the Society of Nations could be promulgated, fitted to the peculiar problems which government of the Society of Nations presents. That did not seem possible, but we must not lose heart and we must try again.

The Peace Conference at Paris was not entirely barren of proposals which would have yielded a firmer federation. The French and the Dutch delegations were leaders in perceiving the possibilities presented. Both the British and the American delegates stood firm, however, against the creation of any representative legislative bodies, and against any international police force. The original American draft of the Covenant even omitted any provision for a judicial system.

The plan for financing the League which was finally adopted, i. e. a basis of voluntary graduated national contributions, provided no revenue whatever which the League could collect in its own right. By 1934 thirty-five nations, among those then remaining in the League, were in default. Several had defaulted as early as 1923. The League's total annual income in 1933 and 1934 from all sources whatever, including special contributions from our own government, from the Rockefeller Foundation and from the contributing member governments, was about $6,000,000 to $7,000,000. It had available to apply toward world government less money in a year than our single national government will soon be spending for munitions every hour of the day!

The system of voluntary national contributions, plus the unrestricted right of withdrawal from the League, were complete obstacles to the erection and permanent maintenance within the League of Nations of effective governmental institutions.—*Amos J. Peaslee, Lawyer and Author. "Some Financial Problems of World Government." My.* 15, '42. *p.9-10.*

In its essence the problem is no more than the extension to large communities of those habits of order and obedience which, in any group of civilized beings, regulate the relations between man and man. That same balance between rights and duties which in the long story of mankind has progressively regulated the relations between members of a family, members of a tribe, and members of a nation ought, it would seem, to be capable of almost unlimited expansion so as to embrace the nations of the world. It would appear at first that there can be little difference in kind between those processes which have rendered Great Britain or the United States comparatively ordered communities and those processes which could create an ordered community of nations.

The analogy between national fusion and international fusion might, indeed, be pressed farther. It is possible to trace in the several experiments which have been made in world government the same variations with which we are familiar in the evolution of national states. We have had the autocratic or tyrannical experiment, as under the *Pax Romana* or the European dominance of Napoleon. We have had the oligarchic experiment, as in the Castlereagh system of diplomacy by conference and in the ensuing Concert of Europe. We have even had mystic or theocratic variations, as in the Greek amphictyonics or in the Holy Alliance. And we have had in the League of Nations what might be called the democratic experiment, under which the nations of the world were to cooperate on a basis of theoretical equality. None of these experiments has proved permanently successful, and one is tempted in moments of pessimism to believe that the mind and soul of men are too narrow to admit expansion beyond a certain limit or to pursue enlightened self-interest beyond a certain horizon of awareness. Are we to admit, therefore, that man is only capable of subduing anarchy within prescribed limits, and that whereas he can achieve national order over wide areas of the earth's surface he is unable to achieve order as between nation states? I refuse to accept so negative an assumption. But I remain aware that for three thousand years man has tried and failed to achieve any form of international governance comparable in certainty to the rule of state law. I approach the problem therefore, not in any mood of despondency, but in a mood of scientific doubt. And I view with alarm the optimism of those who believe that past failures have been due to evident and remediable errors and that all will be feasible now that so many of us have seen the light.—*Harold Nicolson, Parliamentary Secretary to the British Ministry of Information. Nation. D. 28, '40. p.651-2.*

The desire and need for a more comprehensive League, including the United States, should be satisfied by the continuance of a world-wide League, to which the European body as a whole (in federal matters) or its individual members may form a party. The League of Nations, to be strengthened in its turn by structural reforms, would then be relieved of the unsavory business of pacifying Europe and darning or patching up hopelessly torn and outworn clothes. It could concentrate on problems of the globe.

The two headquarters should not even be located in the same city. While the League would continue in Geneva, the European federation may set up headquarters, say, in nearby Strasbourg, or some other city at an approximately similar distance from London, Berlin, Paris, Rome, and other capitals.

If it be Strasbourg, this city may thus be compensated for the involuntary role it has been forced to play through a thousand years of West European history as the apple of Eris. The headquarters of the European federation might well be organized as a federal city on the example of Washington, D.C.

Every detail of what has been said here has been considered and reconsidered many a time from the point of view of one who has known the practice of European politics and European domestic life under various regimes, has gathered considerable practical experience with the working of federal machines, has studied the great contributions of America to federal and democratic institutions, and is not prepared to abandon hope for a better world. If one might call these proposals optimistic, he should not forget that they purport to set standards—standards for the democratic alternative—not to predict the course of events. If one would call them pessimistic, because of their modest character, he should not forget that the perfect union of the United States was attained through the detour of an evidently imperfect confederation, as was the German union of 1871. Although in both cases a belated civil war was waged to produce the ultimate decision in favor of a more perfect unity, in both the initial stage of confederation with all its imperfections was necessary to bring about the later stages of union.

The idea of a European federation, long favored by democrats, is basically sound. Scholars and politicians should vie in giving it realistic shape, equally remote from utopian dreams and inactive pessimism.—*Arnold Brecht, Graduate Faculty, New School for Social Research. Harvard Law Review. F. '42. p. 593-4.*

# RECONSTITUTING THE LEAGUE

## OUR  FUTURE  INTERNATIONAL  SOCIETY [1]

The peace conference will, like the last conference, be faced with two types of problems: those of the immediate liquidation of the war and those of future organization.' The former we cannot foresee in detail at the moment, particularly as regards frontiers, damages, disarmament, and the like.  There are, however, two questions that developed in the last conference and that will have special importance in the next.

The first is the self-determination of peoples. . . .  The second question is the control of certain backward or special areas. . . .

Beyond all of this, however, remains the greatest and most vital problem of all: the creation of some kind of permanent organized method of international collaboration for the promotion of cooperation among nations, and the prevention of war.  This was the very last problem taken up, almost in fleeting moments of spare time, at the last peace conference out of deference to a President of the United States.  Surely it ought this time to be given the first position of honor and put ahead of the other more material and less permanent problems.  There is no question in the world so important as this, no national or local problem that equals it; it conditions everything we do and underlies our whole life.  World disorganization has twice within one generation led to war; has taken us into one conflict and to the edge of the second; has twice brought national conscription; has led to one world economic crisis and already forecast another; has piled billions of dollars of taxation upon us all and diverted a great share of our national wealth from the good things of life to engines of destruction.

[1] From article by Arthur H. Sweetser, Director in the Secretariat of the League of Nations.  Institute of World Affairs.  *War and Society; Proceedings of the Eighteenth Session,* December 8 to 13, 1940.  p. 271-84.  University of Southern California.  Los Angeles.  1941.

This brings us to the League of Nations.  Deeply I wish there was time to answer some of the truly preposterous charges that have been either willfully or carelessly directed against it; seldom indeed has a great movement for human betterment been more outrageously misrepresented.  This is not, however, the time for that; let us simply try to draw objectively and dispassionately some of the lessons, both good and bad, that grew out of what might be called Chapter I of the League, the organizing period between two world wars, and that will serve as guidance for Chapter II of the League, which is as sure to be written as that dawn follows night.

It would not seem to me an exaggeration to say that the League of Nations was the most ambitious effort in human organization ever attempted.  Whatever one's judgment as to American membership or as to the League's own work, it would seem difficult to deny that the effort to unite all nations, in all continents, into a single permanent agency of peace and co-operation was without any comparable precedent in human history.  The League did not prevent a second world war; nevertheless, it laid out broad lines and suggestions for the future relations of peoples that will be invaluable.

First and foremost, the experience of the League in these twenty years has demonstrated that it is definitely possible and practicable to establish an agency of international cooperation complete in all the principal details of international life.  It has demonstrated that there does definitely exist such a thing as an organic international community and that the nations can function together simply and effectively in many definite fields through a machinery proceeding in an orderly and almost automatic fashion.  There were developed, indeed, whole paraphernalia of association and cooperation: an annual Assembly of all member states, which brought together automatically every September for twenty years over a thousand delegates and experts from three-score nations; a quarterly Council of the more important states, which met one hundred and six times in that period; a permanent international civil service of some seven hundred officials; a Permanent Court of International Justice with judges serving no other interests; an International

Labor office with a complete machinery for discussing and advancing social, labor, and economic problems; several institutes on matters of culture, cinema, and cancer; and a host of committees on practically every subject that has reached the international stage. The machinery was there, complete, moderately financed and staffed, and ready to do what the nations wanted it to do.

The great lesson that developed from it was that this mechanism is like any other; its speed and strength depended, and will always depend, on what the nations were willing to put into it. One of the great errors of present-day thought is to assume that all that is necessary is to create a mechanism and leave it to function alone on a level of its own entirely disconnected with anything else.

Another most interesting and unexpected result was that the amount of work to be done, far from remaining stationary, kept ever increasing. At the outset, League authorities were self-conscious and uncertain, did not know what to do, but thumbed through the various peace treaties in search of activities. As international interests widened, men's minds opened onto new horizons, and subjects that had never been recognized as having an international angle were found to be decidedly international. Bring together diplomats, politicians, experts, journalists from all corners of the world, and there is bound to develop something that very closely resembles an intellectual spontaneous combustion. A whole chapter could be written on new lines of work unexpectedly suggested from the most divergent quarters: a world press conference, by a Chilean delegate; a world nutrition study, by a Japanese; codification of law, by a Swedish foreign minister. Such a system represents the extension of democracy to the international field; it allows any nation, however small, and very often even organizations or individuals to put an idea before a world gathering simply and informally, for any study that may be justified.

Through such a central system, moreover, the various elements in international life can give and receive of each other's strength. A problem can be split into its various component parts—political, economic, social—and studied each in its competent section. A health committee, for instance, alarmed about the spread of drugs, can call on the services of an antidrug committee, or inversely the antidrug committee, if uncertain of the danger of a new drug, can have the advice of a medical committee. The problem of housing can be studied for its financial aspects in the financial committee and for its health aspects in the health committee. A disarmaments conference, perplexed with the problem of how to control and supervise armaments, can appeal to the experience acquired in a worldwide control of drugs. Never before the League has this been possible; there can be no doubt that it will be greatly extended.

The existence of a permanent central system of international cooperation serves, as it were, to depoliticalize problems. No longer is it necessary to have all problems, no matter how nonpolitical and technical, handled hastily by overburdened politicians or statesmen. On the contrary, it is now possible to call in the world's foremost experts, whether the problem be double taxation, biological standards, or control of armaments. Once a problem is thus given over to its qualified experts, it follows a normal course of development free from exaggerated political considerations. One of the great contributions of the last twenty years has been the uncovering and opening up of untold intellectual and scientific riches which heretofore have not had opportunity to be put at the service of the world community. The fervor with which many of the world's foremost authorities have responded, without remuneration or reward beyond that of service, has been inspiring.

Another unexpected development has been the immense byproduct of such a regular, permanent system. It is a fair guess that as much work was done at Geneva outside the formal agenda as within it. Statesmen who either did not or could not meet on their own soil constantly rubbed elbows at Geneva without causing the usual diplomatic turmoil. Similarly, experts in all kinds of fields, who had never had opportunity to meet their colleagues from different countries, came into intimate association with them at the League. The degree of stimulus thus given to the world's business, entirely beyond the formal agenda, is almost inestimable.

But, striking as these developments have been in comparison with any precedent, they are only the beginning of what will surely develop as international interests come ever closer in the future. There would not seem the shadow of a doubt that, as the interests of nations extend and intertwine as they surely will, there will be a still wider development of the conference and central service system initiated through the League. It would seem inevitable that, instead of a dozen or so international officials who did such yeoman service in the world's health field during the League's first chapter, it will be essential to have many times that number. Similarly, instead of a score of officials attempting to follow world economic and financial progress, there will need to be a far larger staff. The difficulty has been that there was not too much, but rather too little, League. The world's common interests have gone far beyond the point where they can be handled by a few hundred officials operating on an almost negligible budget.

One of the striking examples of the provincialism of our time is the way in which nations spending almost limitless sums on armaments for war have haggled over the few pennies they have spent for peace.

The possibilities of international organization are infinitely greater than commonly realized. The experience of the last twenty years has thrown open the portals of the future and shown what the world might be. It indicates that we are far richer in international relationships than we have thought, that we have far greater assets, and that we do not need to stand inactive and frozen. It also ·proves, despite the outbreak of war, that it is possible to bring about a more closely unified world, with common services, common interests, and even common possessions.

At the same time there will be large questions as to the method of international cooperation. While it is impossible to be dogmatic as to the eventual decisions until the outcome of the war is more definable, nevertheless, there would seem to be certain permanent questions which must eventually be faced. These questions follow these broad lines: Shall world life be organized (a) on the international or on the federal basis, (b) on the universal or on the regional basis, (c) on the centralized or on the autonomous basis, (d) on the coercive or on the cooperative basis, (e) or on a combination of several of these elements?

Let us take the problem of the international as against the federal principle first.  The League was organized on the former basis; recently, however, have come projects on the latter basis, some for a federation of the European states on a geographical basis and others for a federal union of the democracies on an ideological basis.  The international basis is obviously the more simple and conventional.  It has many precedents in international life, particularly in the League, and it is certainly easier of adoption among nations that differ greatly in viewpoint, that are far apart geographically, and that jealously guard their own individuality.  The federal idea, while demanding far greater sacrifice and becoming increasingly difficult in ratio to the distance and the differences between the component parts, is obviously a tighter and more binding agreement.  How far either will be utilized in mankind's next step in political evolution will depend on the outcome of the war, the amount of chastening the nations will have received, and the consequent degree of sacrifice they are willing to make.  A fair guess would seem to be, however, that neither principle will be followed exclusively but that both may be followed simultaneously.  Certain states close to each other either geographically or ideologically may come together in closer federation than now exists, while all states are likely to come together in a looser, universal association such as the League.  The two principles are not contradictory but complementary.  The wise course would seem to be to explore both against the day when parts of either can become operative, rather than to enter, as some have, into a conflict of principle that is premature at the moment and of assistance only to mutual enemies.

Next is the problem of universality versus regionalism.  Here the answer of experience is even clearer: not one but both are essential.  Many problems involving specific regions can be most effectively handled in a regional meeting of those immediately concerned.  Other questions of world-wide interest can be handled only if all nations come together. The most probable system for our present stage of development would seem to be to have close regional associations of states with a universal association spanning the whole. The various elements could play back and forth as occasion required, with cooperation rather than hostility between the regional and the universal groupings, on the basis that both are seeking the same objective of international cooperation and peace. No inflexible line can be drawn between universal and regional problems; the two types weave and interweave; elasticity in their treatment is extremely desirable. For example, the League of Nations and the Pan American Union, after rather stuffily ignoring each other for years, despite their identity of purpose, have at last thrown a small bridge between themselves that in time will be highly traveled.

The third question, whether international organization should be highly centralized or divided into autonomous agencies, has taken increasing importance as different branches of work have had a chance to organize and gain strength. Before the war the Universal Postal Union and the International Telegraph Union were organized as distinct entities; as a result of the war the League of Nations, the International Labor Office, and the Permanent Court of International Justice, while associated administratively, were made autonomous in their work and functions. Since then, as other activities have taken form, they have tended to establish a personality of their own. Within the last year the technical and nonpolitical activities of the League have been grouped together through the new so-called Central Committee and further removed from political interference. Similarly, the League's opium work has been recognized as having a somewhat distinct status. The probability is in favor of a considerable extension of this type of autonomous organization, with its foundation grounded in distinct agreements but with its administrative arrangements centered around the common agency. The suggestion has even been made that the League, which heretofore has been a fairly unified central agency, should divide into a series of autonomous organizations, each with its own basic law, annual conference, and specific duties, but all staffed and financed from the central organization.

Fourth is the fundamental question whether international cooperation should be organized on the coercive or on the purely voluntary principle; whether, in other words, there should be any form of sanctions against a nation violating its agreements. This is obviously the greatest question of all, as to which recent history has been very differently interpreted. What is clear beyond doubt is that sanctions go to the very heart of state policy. They will not be imposed simply because they are in a treaty, as witness many recent cases where in all logic they should have been imposed. On the other hand, they may be imposed even without being embodied in a treaty, as they have in many cases of national policy, even to a considerable degree in our own recent neutrality or embargo decisions. The system of sanctions elaborated in the League Covenant was undoubtedly the most ambitious effort ever made by sovereign states to pool their resources for the prevention of aggression and war. It can hardly be claimed, however, that the system has had anywhere near a fair trial. It was handicapped at the very outset by the absence from the League of the United States, the most powerful single economic unit in the world. This inevitably led from the outset in 1920 to a considerable caution on the part of the other states and a steady whittling down of their commitments.

The only case where sanctions were formally imposed, the Ethiopian affair, was far more effective and less a failure than thought, for not only were sanctions accepted and put into operations by some fifty states, with partial parallel action by the United States, but they might quite well have proved decisive if the war had lasted, not the seven months it did last, but the two years it was expected to last. At the worst the experiment was inconclusive; the principle was put into operation, but the execution was incomplete. What seems probable in eventual international organization is some kind of combination or regional agreement, with strict obligation of sanctions to preserve peace, accepted by states within an immediate neighborhood, together with a wider and more universal agreement not to trade with a state violating its international agreements. As force is an underlying element in all human life from the family straight up to the state, it is difficult to say how it can be left completely out of the most complicated relationship of them all, that between different races and nations. The very minimum would seem to be an agreement of nonintercourse with an outlawed state, to prevent the wealth and resources of a peaceful, treaty-abiding state from being used, as is now too often the case, to destroy another peaceful, treaty-abiding state.

But all this is mechanism. It will have but little importance indeed if it is not actuated by a spirit and philosophy different from any that has operated in international life up until now. After the last war the world created a mechanism that, if properly supported, could have averted the present catastrophe. It did not, however, so support it, and the world finds itself today in another holocaust.

The first, the most fundamental, and the most difficult of all steps to secure world peace is a complete revolution of thought and philosophy. Men and women the world over must see and accept the world as it is today to appreciate that we have left the days of unlimited, uncontrolled, unco-ordinated, and competitive national sovereignties and entered into the first phase of world life. This does not at all mean the abolition of nationalism or nationality, the creation of a super-state, or the leveling of individual cultures and differences. On the contrary, it foresees the development and extension of all these values in a regime of security for all.

Without this shift of viewpoint, nothing certain can be done for world peace. We have got to take into our con-sciousness that we have entered an era different from any we have ever known. Industry has became world wide, with its quest for raw materials going to the far corners of the globe. Population pressure is increasing nearly everywhere, with the frontier gone for the world as it is for the United States. Ideologies now span the globe, with a well-directed wireless station often more important than a naval base. The nations are going even farther and farther afield: Germany sprawling over most of Europe, Russia bulging out from the Baltic to the Black Sea, Italy reaching nervously into Africa and the Balkans, Japan creeping through East Asia, even our own country spreading its defenses out into the Atlantic and the Pacific. The nation's highways are becoming desperately crowded; the world has passed from the nomad to the community state.

Yet, the acceptance of this change represents the greatest psychological adaptation mankind has ever attempted. To come together in families, clans, towns, cities, or states is child's play in comparison with coming together in organized international association. Differences of outlook, of custom, of language run to the roots of our being. Deep in the subconscious lies all that dynamite which unscrupulous politicians exploit against "the foreigner." It is that emotion which produced the rallying cry of "the foreign devil" in China, the platform of racial arrogance in Germany, and part of the substratum of our own isolationism.

A fundamental change there must be in the moral conception of nationhood. Till now nations have been a law unto themselves. "My country right or wrong" has often been the unrestricted adage, with no recognition of responsibility that the country be right and no thought of the injustice to others if it be wrong. That is gunman philosophy, well exemplified in the international depredations of today. A nation's immediate duty following that of its own self-defense should be not to injure other nations, but to recognize that there is a higher community law. Japan could have had a peaceful settlement in Manchuria if she had accepted the constructive proposals of the League of Nation's Commission instead of trying to impose her will by force. Italy could have had a settlement of the Ethiopian dispute if she had not gone through by military power. Germany had righted one by one her various complaints and could eventually have found satisfaction for her demands without war. And for ourselves in the United States, could we not have made a settlement with Spain short of war, effected an arrangement to build the Panama Canal without a subsequent conscience-grant, met a valid immigration difficulty by an arrangement not entailing a political affront, found an adaptation to the League of Nations without abandoning it entirely, worked out a way of entering the only permanent international court of law in the world without the sordid misrepresentation which occurred?

If we really want peace, the sovereignty of nations must be limited, as the sovereignty of individuals is limited, at the point where it does injury to others. This limitation must go further than commonly thought. It must be not only negative in the sense of not attacking other nations, which corresponds to the limitation in individual society not to commit murder, but also positive in the sense of limiting other actions, which, while justified within national sovereignty, might nevertheless react unjustly toward others. We in this country, for instance, have the right to impose what tariff or immigration restrictions we wish; yet by all laws of community responsibility we have the highest moral obligation not to adopt either a tariff or an immigration policy that will suddenly and without warning disrupt the world's regular channels without opportunity of adjustment.

Man's economic and material interdependence has far outstripped his progress in political organization. The world as an interdependent economic unit exists in a barbarism of militarized states. It has not drawn the consequences of its own startling growth; its modern mechanism seeks to function in a system surviving from archaic days.

This means that isolationism must go for good and all. No longer is it possible for any people, no matter how great, to hide its head in the sand and pretend that the rest of the world does not exist. It is all very nice and comfortable thus to try to hide from the evils of the world; it gives a feeling of complacency to consider oneself superior to them, but it simply does not work. China tried it with her contempt of foreigners and her Chinese wall; Japan tried it until the guns of a subsequently isolationist nation forced open her ports; Britain tried it until her rude awakening at Munich; the little nations in Europe tried it until today they lie crushed in the dust; we in the United States tried it until now we are paying

to the tune of our first peacetime conscription in history and
eleven billions of dollars of armaments annually.  Not only
is isolationism crassly selfish, dangerously contemptuous, and
morally indefensible, but it is even actually impossible.  It is
because the nations have sedulously sought it in these various
ways that the world is in chaos today.

Peace is the most precious thing in the world.  It cannot
be had for nothing.  It demands and must receive some kind
of sacrifice.  There is no use in talking, talking, and talking
peace and yet taking no positive action to secure it.  The record
of the last twenty years is tragic; peoples and statesmen forever
uttering these rich, sonorous words, yet never substantiating
them.  Peace is not an unconscious Nirvana or a static
somnambulance; it is in itself a conflict, a constant effort to
harmonize different views and to lead people to accept changes
peacefully.  It is fine to pray for peace, as we are often asked
to do, but it would be far more effective to act for peace.

Let us in the United States adopt a very humble attitude
in this regard.  Too often we have had a holier-than-thou attitude, as if we were guiltless and the other nations incorrigible.
But it was we who made the first and irreparable breach in the
organization of peace after the last war with our refusal not
only to enter the League of Nations but to propose any amendment or alternative that would have allowed our participation.
No one who did not live in Europe at that time, who did not
feel and sense the reactions, the discouragements, even the
despair of exhausted peoples abroad can appreciate what a
desperate blow this was to the world's hopes.  And the small,
narrow-minded period of normalcy that followed, the withdrawal into a kind of contemptuous superiority, the failure
even to recognize the League which we had created, the general
nonnegotiability of the United States, the unwillingness to assume any responsibility, the sudden desperate barrier of the
Hawley-Smoot Tariff, the bewildering reversal during the World
Economic Conference, all served further to disintegrate what
little of international unity had come out of the last war and
to depress the world's moral standards still further.  Several
generous initiatives we did indeed take, on our own very neat

terms, but in the broad concept of world life we not only took our hands off the rudder and let the ship drift but we even contributed by successive pushes to driving it to the brink of the falls where we see it today. This is said, not in bitterness or in mere empty criticism, but, on the contrary, with the conviction that America shortly will face a second and greater opportunity for constructive leadership and that, having seen the disaster which came so quickly and so inevitably out of the last disintegration, she will make it her deepest and profoundest resolve that "it shall not happen again."

Let me conclude with one pointed statement: War, the greatest scourge of mankind, is not an act of God. It is a scourge that man inflicts upon himself. War is man made. It can be man cured. It is the hardest, the steepest, the most difficult path in mankind's long progress up from the swamps. It will require his best and most devoted service. There is hope for the world today if, instead of sitting around and waiting for peace, we go forth courageously, constructively, and agressively to fight for peace, and for the philosophies that underlie it and the agencies that sustain it.

## THE CHALLENGE OF INTERNATIONAL LAWLESSNESS [2]

The League of Nations, for all of its defects and in spite of all that it has left undone, has had a wholesome influence on the international thought and habit of our time. The Covenant required publicity and registration of treaties, and it authorized recommendations to reconsider treaties which became inapplicable. A more enlightened concept of trusteeship underlies the system of mandates for backward people created by the Covenant. It required mediation, arbitration, or conciliation of certain classes of controversies, and it provided for the establishment of a Permanent Court of International Justice for the adjudication of justiciable controversies. Moreover, the League

[2] By Robert H. Jackson, Associate Justice of the Supreme Court of the United States. Address before the American Bar Association, Indianapolis, October 2, 1941. *American Bar Association Journal.* 27:690-3. November 1941.

Covenant, in limiting the right of war, created new obligations of good conduct.  It departed sharply from the older doctrine that, in respect of their right to make war, sovereign states were above both the discipline and the judgments of any law, and that their acts of war were to be accepted as legal and just. Instead, for its members it created a category of forbidden and illegal wars—wars of aggression.  It made resort to war in violation of the Covenant an act of war against all other members of the League.  It provided economic sanctions to be invoked against the aggressor.  Even if it was not able to end unlawful wars, it ended the concept that all wars must be accepted by the world as lawful.

The League, which we rejected, was followed by the Pact of Paris.  By it the signatory nations renounced war as an instrument of national policy and agreed that the settlement of all disputes or conflicts of whatever nature or of whatever origin should be sought only by pacific means.  While the United States became a party to this treaty, Secretary Kellogg said that it was out of the question to impose any obligation respecting sanctions on the United States.  The Senate proceedings make clear that its ratification was due only to the assurance that it provided no specific sanction or commitment to enforce it.

This treaty, however, was not wholly sterile despite the absence of an express legal *duty* of enforcement.  It had legal consequences more substantial than its political ones.  It created substantive law of national conduct for its signatories and there resulted a *right* to enforce it by the general sanctions of international law.  The fact that Germany went to war in breach of its treaty discharged our own country from what might otherwise have been regarded as a legal obligation of impartial treatment toward the belligerents.

Regardless, however, of these juridical consequences, the disillusioning fact is that neither the League nor the Pact of Paris proved adequate to prevent war.  Whether they did not actually induce a false sense of security which contributed to the undoing of those who relied on their promise is an open question.  That a signatory state may lawfully support a war to punish an illegal war may mean merely bigger and better wars. It is a rough international equivalent of the ancient "hue and cry" procedure, which involved the whole community in the troubles of an individual. What we seek is to prevent, not to intensify and spread, wars. And that tranquility can rest only upon an order that will make justice obtainable for peoples as it is now for men.

Our institutions of international cooperation are neither time-tried nor strong, but it is hard to believe that the world would forego some organ of continuous consideration of international problems or scrap what seems to be a workable, if not perfect, pattern of international adjudicative machinery.

It is not difficult with the aid of hindsight to point out structural defects in the League or to complain of the timid use made of such powers as it had. But we can no more dismiss as a failure all international organization because the League did not prevent renewal of war between nations than we can dismiss our federal government as a failure because it did not prevent a war between its constituent states.

Intelligent opinion should not visit upon struggling international instrumentalities that condemnation which rightly may be visited upon the selfishly nationalistic policies of several nations. We must place blame only where there was power. Too many people forget that the League was merely a collective annex of foreign offices. The dependence of the League on the policy of home governments was never better stated than years ago by Sir Arthur Salter:

> The League is an instrument through which the real desire of the world for international cooperation can find expression and be put into effect. . . . But it is not, and cannot be, a short cut to supreme control. It cannot enable the best part of the world to impose its will upon a hostile, an indifferent, or an apathetic majority. It is an instrument and not an original source of power. It is a medium, but a medium only, through which the desire of the world can find expression.
>
> Moreover, the League under the Covenant is based upon existing national authorities. The members both of the Council and of the Assembly are nominated by governments. It therefore expresses the will of the world indirectly, not directly by a parallel form of popular representation. Those who care most for the ideals on which the League was founded can indeed use the League itself in many ways

to mobilize and concentrate their forces. But the route to *action* lies first through the national electorates and the various national media through which the policy of national governments can be affected.

The League's position as foreign office subsidiary was probably inevitable, but it was unfortunate for the peace of the world. A diplomat suffers less risk to his personal career if he can hush a delicate issue than if he brings it to the surface and tries to meet it with long-term remedies. The foreign office genius for suppressing issues rather than solving them was the common denominator of all nationalistic representation and became the chief, if not in fact the only, policy of the League.

Sumner Welles, in a really notable address, has aptly said:

> The League of Nations, as he [Wilson] conceived it, failed in part because of the blind selfishness of men here in the United States, as well as in other parts of the world; it failed because of its utilization by certain powers primarily to advance their own political and commercial ambitions; but it failed chiefly because of the fact that it was forced to operate, by those who dominated its councils, as a means of maintaining the *status quo*. It was never enabled to operate as its chief spokesman had intended, as an elastic and impartial instrument in bringing about peaceful and equitable adjustments between nations as time and circumstances proved necessary.
>
> Some adequate instrumentality must unquestionably be found to achieve such adjustments when the nations of the earth again undertake the task of restoring law and order to a disastrously shaken world.

We now see that such an instrumentality, if it is to compose the world's discord, must have flexibility. Neither maps nor economic advantages nor political systems can be frozen in a treaty. Peace is more than the fossilized remains of an international conclave. It cannot be static in a moving world. Peace must function as a going concern, as a way of life with a dynamic of its own. Unfortunately, however, the internal structure of the League loaded the dice in favor of the perpetuation of the *status quo* which was also the policy of the dominant powers and the governing classes within them. Any peace that is indissolubly wedded to a *status quo*—any *status quo*—is doomed from the beginning. The world will not forego movement and progress and readjustments as the price of peace. Where there is no escape from the weight of the *status quo* except war, we

will have war.  Perhaps if that is the only escape, we should
sometimes have war.

The Assembly of the League could advise "reconsideration
by members of the League of treaties which have become inapplicable and the consideration of international conditions
whose continuance might endanger the peace of the world."
That promise to the ear was, however, broken to the hope by
the provision that action be only by unanimous consent.  Any
one dissenting member government could thus perpetuate the
*status quo,* though all the world knew it was at the price of
eventual war.  This was a fatal situation when the *status quo*
in Europe was an experimental and in some respects an artificial
one established by victors in an hour of heat and hate.

The world will not, I trust, be naïve enough again to believe
it has so reordered its affairs as to prevent conflicts that might
provoke wars.  The supremacy of domestic law is not based
on an absence of individual conflicts.  It is predicated on a
settlement of them by means that do not violate the peace of
the community.  The law anticipates a certain amount of wrong
conduct, for which it provides damages or punishments.  It does
not end injustices, but it requires the victims to seek redress
through the force of the law, rather than through their own
strength.

In this we have to abide the imperfections of legal institutions.  I am not convinced, even by my own transfiguration
into a Justice of the Supreme Court, that courts have overcome
the hazard of wrong decision and of occasional injustice.  The
triumph of the law is not in always ending conflicts *rightly,* but
in ending them *peaceably.*  And we may be certain that we do
less injustice by the worst processes of the law than would be
done by the best use of violence.  We cannot await a perfect
international tribunal or legislature before proscribing resort to
violence even in case of legitimate grievance.  We did not
await the perfect court before stopping men from settling their
differences with brass knuckles.

But even if we achieve a formula for order under law among
all or among a considerable number of like-minded nations, we
may as well recognize that its instrumentalities of justice and of

adjustment will give us little security unless we give them a more real support than in the past. There is no dependence on a peace that is everybody's prayer but nobody's business. Peace declarations are no more self-enforcing than are declarations of war. Peace without burdens will no more come to a world that will not assume its risks than domestic peace would come to a community that would not assume the burdens and risks of a force of peace officers and courts for judging offenders and a form of political organization that commits the physical force of the community to support the peace officer, if necessary.

The American people seem to have believed, and some scholars have asserted, that international law can operate by the voluntary acceptance on the part of well disposed powers. But Mr. Justice Holmes pointed out that we cannot test our law by the conduct of the good men who probably behave from moral or social considerations. The test of the efficiency of the law, he said, is the bad man who cares only for material consequences to himself. Said Holmes:

> A man who cares nothing for an ethical rule which is believed and practiced by his neighbors is likely nevertheless to care a good deal to avoid being made to pay money, and will want to keep out of jail if he can.

The world is in war today chiefly because its civilizaton had not been so organized as to impress the "bad man" with the advisability of keeping the peace.

The German people might not have supported a war of Nazi aggression, had there been explicit understanding that it would bring against them the array of force they now face. Everything indicates that Hitler's early steps were cautious and tentative and calculated to test out the spirit and solidarity of the rest of the world. Shirer asserts, and we find little reason to doubt, that Hitler was successful in creating the conscript army in violation of the military provisions of the Treaty of Versailles, only because of default of opposition from the former Allies. He also says that when Hitler sent troops to occupy the demilitarized zone of the Rhineland, in violation of the Locarno Treaty, the troops had strict orders to retreat if the French army opposed them in any way. They were not prepared or equipped to fight a regular army. Peace appears to have been lost, not for the want of a great supporting force, but for the want of only a little supporting force.

It is in the light of such facts that America will face a tough and fateful decision as to her attitude toward the peace. It is a grave thing to risk the commitments that are indispensable to a system of international justice and collective security. It is an equally grave thing to perpetuate by our inaction an anarchic international condition in which every state may go to war with impunity whenever its interests are thought to be served.

But it is a perilous thing to neglect our own defenses as if we were in a world of real security and at the same time to reject the obligations which might make real security possible. At the end of this war we must either throw the full weight of American influence to the support of an international order based on law, or we must outstrip the world in naval and air, and perhaps in military, force. No reservation to a treaty can let us have our cake and eat it too.

The tragedy and the irony of our present position is that we who would make no commitment to support world peace are making contributions a thousandfold greater to support a world war. We who would not agree to even economic sanctions to discourage infraction of the peace are now imposing those very sanctions against half the world in an effort to turn the fortunes of war.

The Roosevelt-Churchill "Atlantic Charter" promises aid to all "practical measures which will lighten for peace-loving peoples the crushing burden of armaments." Certainly, the present competition, if continued, threatens the financial and social stability of free governments. Vast standing military establishments and the interests that thrive on them and the state of mind they engender are no more compatible with liberty in America than they have been in Europe. Five years of the sort of thing the world now witnesses and twenty centuries of civilization will not be worth a tinker's damn.

The Roosevelt-Churchill statement affirms that all nations "must come to the abandonment of the use of force" and it envisions the "establishment of a wider and permanent system of general security." Such happy days wait upon great improvement in our international law and in our organs of international legislation and adjudication. Only by well considered steps toward closer international cooperation and more certain justice can the sacrifices which we are resolved to make be justified. The conquest of lawlessness and violence among the nations is a challenge to modern legal and political organizing genius.

Men of our tradition will take up the challenge gladly. We have never been able to accept as an ultimate principle the doctrine that, in vital matters of war and peace, each sovereign power must be free of all restraint except the will and conscience of its transitory rulers. Long ago English lawyers rejected lawlessness as a prerogative of the Crown and bound their king by rules of law so that he might not invade the poorest home without a warrant. In the same high tradition our forefathers set up a sovereign nation whose legislative and executive and judicial branches are deprived of legal power to do many things that might encroach upon our freedoms. Our Anglo-American philosophy of political organization denies the concept of arbitrary and unlimited power in any governing body. Hence, we see nothing revolutionary or visionary in the concept of a reign of law, to which sovereign nations will defer, designed to protect the peace of the society of nations. We, as lawyers, hold fast to the ideal of an international order existing under law and equipped with instrumentalities able and willing to maintain its supremacy, and we renew our dedication to the task of pushing back the frontiers of anarchy and of maintaining justice under the law among men and nations.

## A NEW INTERMEDIATE LEAGUE [3]

Immediately after victory, it will not be possible to organize this better world for which we are hoping. A transitional period will be necessary, characterized by the following facts: complete

[3] From "Discussion of Professor Whitehead's Paper," by Professor Hans Kelsen, University of California. *American Academy of Arts and Science. Proceedings.* 75, no. 1:11-13. October 1942.

disarmament of all states now under national socialistic or fascistic régimes or military dictatorship; political and military control of these territories exercised by a body of representatives of the United Nations, above all in order to win the population of these countries for democracy and international cooperation, and to educate their youth for these ideals. No illusion is more dangerous than to assume that these Germans and Italians, these Spaniards, French and Rumanians, these Japanese, (more than two hundred million people) are democrats and pacifists, and that only their dictatorial masters prevent them from having the same political organization as this country or Great Britain.

How long will this transitorial period last, and which is to be the political form of the Union which finally may be established? The first question cannot be answered now. Everything depends upon circumstances which cannot be foreseen today. As far the the second question is concerned, two different plans are suggested: one is to reestablish the League of Nations, the other to create a completely new international organization. The difference between these two plans is, however, not so great as it might appear at first sight. For, should the League of Nations be revived, it could never be the old, it must be an entirely reformed League of Nations. And if a new international organization is to be established, the lessons which can be drawn from the breakdown of the old League will be indispensable for building up the new community.

The decisive question as to the constitution of the new League refers to the degree of centralization which shall and can be realized in the law-creating and law-applying function of the new community. It is the question whether the international community shall or can have the character of a federal state or only of a confederation of states. There is no doubt that the aims of the intended organization would be achieved in the best and most effective way if this community would be organized as a federal state; that means the establishment of a world parliament and a world administration which is, of course, incompatible with the sovereignty of the member states of the union. On the basis of our experiences with attempts to create international organizations, the idea of a world federal state must be considered—this is my personal opinion—a utopian scheme. Even if such a federal world state should be desirable, it is, seen from a realistic point of view, quite unlikely that within a reasonable time great powers like the United States of America or the British Empire will unite with dwarf states like Denmark, Norway or Switzerland, that republics and hereditary monarchies will from one day to the next give up their sovereignty, will found a federal state, will submit their own governments to a world government in which all the members participate. It is more than likely that this aim, if one accepts it as such, can be reached only in various stages. From the political point of view, the only serious question is, *what is the next step on this road to be taken with a view to success?* Obviously, it can at first only be an international union of states, a confederation of states, not a federal state that one should set up. It can be only a confederation of states, and not a federal state, if the new community of states shall be created by an international treaty concluded by free and democratic governments and not by unilateral coercion exercised by a victorious power. Such a federation of states is not incompatible with the existence, within its framework, of closer and more centralized unions of single member states. Such a closer union may be established especially by the United States of America, Great Britain and some others of the United Nations, and must be established if these states accept the responsibility of a political control of the vanquished countries.

As far as the constitution of the wider League is concerned, the breakdown of the League of Nations has furnished us a valuable experience. One of the most important, if not decisive, causes of its failure was a fatal fault of its construction, the fact that the authors of the Covenant placed at the center of this international organization not the Permanent Court of International Justice, but a kind of international administration, the Council of the League of Nations. The Covenant placed the Council, not the Permanent Court, at the center of its international organization, because it conferred upon the League not only the task of maintaining peace within the community, by settling disputes and by restricting the armament of the member states, but also the duty of protecting them against external aggression. This protection of member states against external aggression is possible only if the government of the League disposes of an armed force, if the League has its own army, navy and air force. Such a centralization of the executive power means the establishment of a federal state. Because it was impossible to organize the League of Nations as a federal state, the League failed completely in its duty to protect the member states against external aggression. The experiences of the League of Nations show that it is necessary to make a clear distinction between the maintenance of internal peace within the League, and protection of the members against external aggression, and that it is hardly possible to fulfill the second task by the specific means at the disposal of a universal international organization embracing many different states. As long as it is impossible to constitute this union of states as a federal state, it seems to be more correct to limit the task to the maintenance of internal peace, and to leave protection against external aggression to political alliances between the member states. To maintain peace within the international community, its constitution should try to establish the strongest possible guarantee within the compass of international law: the obligation of the member states to submit all their disputes without exception to the *compulsory jurisdiction of an international court* and to execute in full good faith any decision of the court. That means that the members of the League agree to *abandon the use of force* in their mutual relations (Point 8 of the Atlantic Charter), except against a member which in disregard of its obligations refuses to execute a decision of the court or resorts to war or reprisals against another member, without being authorized by a decision of the court.

If the treaty constituting the international community does not establish a central executive power, an army, navy, and air force of the League independent from the armed forces of the member states—a central armed force at the disposal of a central government—the decisions of the international court can be executed against a member state only by the other members of the community, if necessary by the use of their armed forces under the direction of an administrative organ, such as the Council of the League of Nations. The Covenant of the League may determine the size and the organization of the armed force which each member state has to keep in readiness to execute the collective sanction according to the orders of the Council. The Council may be authorized by the Covenant to appoint an organ whose function should be to control the military obligations of the member states and, if a military sanction is to be executed, to appoint a commander-in-chief of the League. But the Council of the new League should be an auxiliary organ of the Court. The fact that its task will chiefly be to execute the decisions of a court, will facilitate considerably the composition and particularly the procedure of this administrative organ, especially as its decisions must be adopted according to the majority-vote principle.

A new League of Nations whose central organ was to be an international court with compulsory jurisdiction would constitute an extraordinary progress in the field of international organization. It would be the technical realization of an idea which the Kellogg Pact first tried to put into operation: the elimination of war as an instrument of self-help. The Kellogg Pact could not succeed because it pursued its end with technically insufficient means. The League here proposed would be an intermediate stage between the old League of Nations and a future world federal state with a world government; an intermediate stage which is inevitable in the natural evolution of international law. The next step, not the last one. After we have succeeded in establishing an international community uniting the most important states of the world under a covenant instituting compulsory jurisdiction, and after this political system has worked successfully for some time, we can try to make a further step, we can hope to succeed in organizing a centralized executive power, a world police, and later perhaps a world administration under a world parliament.

As far as the economic purposes of the new League are concerned, its constitution must contain certain provisions which guarantee to the members of the League the right "of access, on equal terms, to the trade and to the raw materials of the world which are needed for their economic prosperity" (Point 4 of the Atlantic Charter), and secure for all members "improved labor standards, economic adjustments and social security" (Point 5 of the Atlantic Charter).

But I would like to lay stress upon the fact that, contrary to a widespread opinion, it is not the economic element which determines the political one, it is the political element which determines the economic one. If the history of the last decades has taught us anything, it is the primacy of politics over economics.

It is a political task to win the war; it is a very difficult task, but even more difficult will it be to organize the peace.

## THE ESSENTIALS OF INTERNATIONAL STABILITY [4]

The existing procedures for the settlement of international disputes are not adequate to eliminate war. What is needed, then, is the establishment of a dynamic world order which will facilitate peaceful changes in the *status quo* as they become necessary, and will minimize belligerent contests for power and material benefits. The question now arises, are there any aspects of the world situation from which we may draw hope? Are such ambitions possible of realization?

The answer, to begin, is that there are certain characteristics of the modern world which definitely strengthen efforts directed toward the creation of international order. In spite of the frequency of war, peace is accepted by thinking men as the normal condition. We have, in actuality, an international interdependent community. The world is no longer composed of disparate and barbaric aggregations of people. As Joseph Avenol, Secretary-General of the League of Nations, put it a few years ago, "The community of nations exists already; it is merely a question of defining and regulating it."

Within this community, if we have not a single common language we can get along satisfactorily anywhere in the world

[4] From article by Dell G. Hitchner, Instructor in Political Science, Coe College. *Social Science.* 18:72-7. April 1943.

with only two or three. We have rapid and efficient means of international transportation and conmunication. The dissemination of goods or information is no longer limited by lack of physical facilities. Our economic productivity is such that we have recently worried more about surpluses than about deficiencies. The science of governmental administration has made possible the role of larger communities and a wider domestic order than has ever before been possible. We have, in the development of democracy, the means of effective self-government based on a peaceful reconciliation of conflicting interests. In our Christian heritage, we have the basis of a common ethical system. All these are tangible accomplishments —developments essential to the creation of any international order—and they are already won.

Still more specifically, and contributing an important solution to our problem, we have twenty years' experience with the League of Nations. Difficult as is the position of the League in the world at war today, it can still claim some noteworthy accomplishments. True, its scope of operation is greatly limited by recent withdrawals of some members caused by the war, and many of its activities are temporarily at a standstill. Yet 48 nations—about five sixths of those in the world—are at present still parties to the Covenant. Member states still provide the League's financial support, and last year, even some of the invaded states made token payments toward its expenses. But whatever the temporary eclipse of the League, the facts of our experience with it remain. Whether the League is revived, or whether a similar organization takes its place, we cannot afford to overlook the valuable precedents which it has established.

The idea of organizing a number of states in the interests of peace in not a new one, and excluding the age of the ancient empires, proposals looking to that end are found in successive centuries as early as the fourteenth. These dreams of world order found their realization only with the creation of the League of Nations at the peace conference in 1919. Founded "to promote international cooperation and to achieve international peace and security," this agency sought to associate the states of the world on an equal footing by means of an Assembly, which gave each state a voice in its control; a smaller Council, which concentrated responsibility and leadership; and a Secretariat, to serve as a permanent administrative body in carrying on the functions of the League.   Without attempting to delve further into the machinery of the League, let us examine its outstanding contributions to the cooperative solution of world problems.

The first of these is that it embodied the idea of a universal organization as the proper machinery for dealing with international problems.   The League was not organized to be a tool in the hands of a few ambitious states.   Participation was open to any state which could meet the responsibilities of membership and accepted the obligations of the Covenant.   The universality of its organization is indicated by the fact that only the United States and two small Arabian states were never at any time members among all those of the world.

Next, the League could reach decisions of an international character without requiring every state to accept each single decision.   Unanimous acceptance of a principle by all the members of a body is always difficult to obtain, and this is particularly the case in international matters.   And while it is true that most of the League's decisions did require unanimous acceptance, this unanimity was interpreted as requiring only the favorable vote of those representatives actually attending any particular meeting.   States might abstain from voting, and thus would not hinder action which they might not fully approve; and still further, there were some questions which could be settled by a two-thirds majority.   The importance of this precedent is often overlooked, yet without something approximating majority rule, nothing but colorless compromises can ever be expected from any association of states.

Another of the League's contributions was the establishment of the premise that the problems of international society must be viewed as a whole.   The League had a world-wide sphere of action and could deal with any matter "affecting the peace of the world."   The fault of too many previous efforts in this direction was that they were narrowly limited to their outlook and sought to deal with only a single aspect of the difficulties of the world community. The League sought to develop order by attacking social, economic, political, and other maladjustments as aspects of a whole problem—which, indeed, they are.

Fourthly, the League was able to create and maintain an efficient administrative force on the international level. International administration on any large scale, was, before this, somewhat of an experiment. The League Secretariat functioned with the employment of over 600 persons, representing some 50 nationalities. Thus, the delicate problem of obtaining what amounted to an international civil service, whose members owe a primary allegiance to an international personality, was demonstrated to be solvable. Indeed, the efficient work of the Secretariat was considered to be an important League success.

Finally, the League proved that there could be an international institution capable of evoking national enthusiasm on a fairly large scale. It is not suggested that support for the League ever exceeded feelings of national patriotism in any country. Yet in England, in an unofficial peace ballot in 1935, 10,000,000 votes were cast in favor of supporting the League and the use of sanctions. Even in the United States, where League sentiment has been least in evidence, a Gallup poll not so long ago indicated that some 8,000,000 Americans favored support of a reconstructed League. That body could not hope to develop a supernational patriotism; yet few institutions in world history have made a greater appeal to man's imagination.

The sum of the arguments here presented is simply that the League has definite accomplishments in its favor. The League has undoubtedly been more thoroughly grounded on political realities than most proposals looking toward peace; it has been able to function successfully in fields never before entered; it proves that the problem of organizing the necessary machinery of international government is not insuperable. We need not start over when peace is won; we can go ahead from these advance posts.

Our need now is to consolidate our experience and follow it in projecting the essential elements of a new stability in world society. What follows, to be sure, is not a plan in detail. It is rather, within reasonable dimensions, a suggestion of the underlying reasoning necessary to any lasting solution of our international maladjustments.

Our first task is to crush the military force of Germany, Japan, and their allies. The Axis, too, has plans for a new world order. Their sinister and ruthless nature should be too familiar to require elaboration. Obviously, their ambitions run no higher than to plunder and rule such areas of the world as they can conquer. We may agree, undoubtedly, that the totalitarian states' repudiation of democracy and international cooperation absolves us from any serious consideration of their war aims. It might also be well to note that Dr. Goebbels has warned the German people that "the cares and burdens that must be laid on all our shoulders in this war pale before the inferno that awaits us should we lose this war." It Germany expects such treatment from us, what may we not fear from Germany if our positions are reversed? The peace must be predicated on a victory of democracy or one thousand years of political progress will be lost.

For us, there is a peace, as well as a war, to be won. Much has been made of the blunders of the Treaty of Versailles—the pendulum of public opinion has swung from the original belief that the treaty was not severe enough to the view that it was iniquitous and largely causative of the present war, and now back again. It is not necessary to argue that point here. Suffice it to say that the intelligence with which the problems of the present war are liquidated will determine the success or failure of achieving a subsequent peace. No one can expect an unjust settlement to be maintained, and, as in the case of Versailles, a single unfortunate provision may well be exploited to discredit the just dispositions of the entire structure. Undoubtedly, we must subordinate nationalistic ambitions to the good of the whole international community. It is not too much to say that condescension to the many aspiring nationalities of Europe by the creation of many small states at the end of the last war directly weakened the entire fabric of the final settlement.

Punitive provisions against those who are the aggressors there undoubtedly must be; it will be best if they are enforced thoroughly and firmly but in as short a period as possible and in such a manner that no group or governmental regime can later be made the scapegoat for their application. If "all they that take the sword shall perish by the sword," we must still have an end to brutality and hatred. We cannot hope for a settlement that will be perfect in all eyes. It will be improved, however, if less attention is paid to territorial adjustment—which is not the end in itself that some think—and more is paid to eliminating the unhappy conditions which so frequently call for such adjustments. Our first efforts at the end of the war will of necessity be devoted to reconstruction and the alleviation of human suffering. Beyond that, it might well be preferable to leave most of the details of the peace to a gradual formulation over a period of years. Not only would this help to eliminate the effects of war-engendered passions and hatreds, but the settlement would more likely be viewed as the beginning of a new peace, and not as the liquidating of an old war. In short, we might escape cutting the suit to fit the cloth. Undoubtedly the future problems are too great to be dealt with in haste or by simply redrawing boundary lines.

A necessary concomitant of a dynamic peace settlement is an international agency to supervise its administration. This means the revitalization of the League of Nations, or the creation of something like it. But in its fashioning we must go farther than we ever have before. The League fell far short of constituting an international government; it hardly made a dent in that great barrier to international cooperation—the doctrine of national sovereignty. It is axiomatic that if problems are to be solved, they must be met on the level and within the area where they exist. Our most serious problems are no longer national ones. They plague almost every nation alike. World society is an interdependent society. We have world trade, world markets, world prices, and world depressions. Scholarship, music, art, and literature reflect a world-wide culture. Disease does not recognize national boundaries. We are, whether we would or not, citizens of the world, and we must solve our problems on that scale. There is no need here to discuss the exact nature of the new League, nor argue the merits of Union Now and the many other mechanisms that are projected. The form of the world government is much less important than the spirit behind it and the powers available to it. It must be universal. Isolation from it will be more than an uncooperative act; it will be a self-destructive one, for no nation can expect to live outside the community, willing to accept the benefits of others' cooperation and unwilling to assume responsibilities. The defeated aggressor states should be admitted to the association as rapidly as possible, so that they may share in responsibility for its decisions, but only after a clear indication of their willingness to cooperate in the general interest. Until that time they may expect to be under the supervision of the whole community.

What is to be done to remove the possibility of war? The answer to this is partly implicit in the points that will follow, but here a partial reply can be made. War has been up to now, poor though it may be, the major means of settling disputes. We must, then, offer other methods. These are to be found among the many existing means of arbitration and adjudication. The prime difference in our future order, however, must be that once decisions are reached their enforcement must be assured by the machinery of international government, and by the use of compulsion, if necessary. More important to this end, however, is that the international agency be equipped with sufficient power to provide for peaceful alterations of the status quo. There are those who view security or peace as the absolute freezing of existing conditions. But we can no more expect international life to lose its dynamic quality than we can assume an ability on the part of the physical universe to lock its mechanisms of change at some single instant in time. Such a static world would be cold, barren, and hopeless. Peace must be allied with the expenditure of energy; it cannot hope to serve as a brake against it. The greatest deficiency in previous solutions of war has been that they were directed only toward the settlement of disputes that had already arisen. The desperate need is for a means of eliminating most of these disputes before they reach impossible proportions. Recommendations for change must originate with or be approved by the international governing agency, which must be possessed of sufficient authority to enforce its decisions. Such procedures can be expected to relieve us of most of the difficulties which agitate wars today. But if some nation still persists in resorting to aggression in the advancement of its interests, it must be met by the economic and military power of the international community. With the creation of such a force, no single state will long dare to flout the will of the community. True enough, the coercion of such a state will mean the use of military power to produce peace. But that is not so paradoxical as it may sound. When we establish our domestic governments to maintain order, we do not hesitate to arm our police with guns as well as warrants. Force probably cannot be eliminated as a factor in human society; if it is to exist, it must, rather, be available only to the organized international community for use against international malefactors. Only when we can exert compulsion against states can we expect an international community based on the observance of the rules of law.

Essential likewise to world order is the equality of economic opportunity. The stability of any community rests on a universal incentive to maintain it. Revolutions occur when a substantial portion of the people no longer have a stake in the existing regime. Wars occur when states decide that their economic position will  thus be improved. So long as gross inequalities in economic satisfaction exist among nations, there will be some who would destroy the existing order as a final solution. The solution to this is not simply a matter of redividing colonies and empires. The possibility of buying peace from have-nots in such a matter is now discredited. But free trade, or at least much freer world trade, is imperative. Raw materials and manufactured goods must be generally available to those who are willing to pay for them; and to achieve easier settlements of the international balance of payments, states must be brought to realize the economic suicide in the policy of exporting without importing.

Out of sheer necessity, many nations have, in recent years, resorted to reciprocal trade agreements, negotiated tariffs, controlled currency exchange, and similar expedients. To accomplish the exchange of goods some such devices must be continued, and extended, to assure the promotion of much-needed world trade. Once the flow of commodities between states is sufficiently free, an important cause of war will be removed. Nations will prefer the benefits of that trade to the chance of war spoils, and only thus can the economic gains of our modern age be made mass gains. Without such international cooperation, we cannot assume that self-interest will lead in the desired direction of universally higher standards of living. This will require, not "share-the-wealth," not communism, not state capitalism, but cooperative planning and control beyond the national scope within which they are presently practiced. To those who would object to international regulation of economic activities, the only answer is that domestic economy has long been subject to regulation in the very same way. It is only the extension to a larger scale that is new.

Finally, an essential basis of any system of world order is a common ideology. It is a common spirit that must first move men, not a piece of machinery. The failure of the League came not because of any essential defects in its organization but from a fatal lack of common interests and ideals among its members. As Carl J. Hambro, the president of the League Assembly recently put it, "People often forget that the League is but an instrument created for the use of constructive statesmen or governments, and an instrument is not operative in and by itself. When statesmen or governments were unwilling to use that instrument, it could not function. This was not the fault of the instrument; it was the fault of those lacking moral courage and will to use it." One hardly need say that this common ideology—a universal and compelling belief in the principles of democracy—is sorely lacking. Indeed, its absence accounts for much that is wrong in the world today. There are not a few whose greatest fear for our future is that there is no longer a common ethical basis to our civilization. If the gulf between the existing ideological groupings continues, the damage may well be irreparable. How can social unity be achieved? It seems that this can be hoped for only from the extension of the political processes and concepts of democracy

to the entire world.   Only in democracy can we find those
ideals of communality, of justice, and of respect for the individual so essential to stability.   No other political system
advances such generous attitudes.

The tragedy of our present position is that mankind seems
hypnotized by its own fate.   Yet if generation after generation
is not to be futilely drawn into slaughter and poverty, rational
solutions to our problems must be found and universally
adopted.   Man's sentiment for order must be translated into
practical arrangements that will first create and then maintain
a dynamic peace.   The appalling nature of the alternatives,
should we fail in this, assures us that we dare not.


## LEAGUE SUCCESSES AND FAILURES [5]

I do not say that the League system is incapable of improvement; I agree with President Wilson's presentation of it at the
Conference in Paris: It is a "living thing," capable of growth
and decay.   For more than ten years it grew.   Since then it
has declined.   But even now it is a great improvement in
many ways on any form of peace-keeping machinery that preceded it.   What is wanted is that the decay should be arrested
and the powers of the League revived and in certain respects
intensified.   As regards sanctions, the general principle that
any attack on any of the members of the League is a matter of
concern to all of them is sound and should be retained, provided it is clearly understood that action suitable in one case
is not necessarily suitable in all.   To that I will return directly.
With respect to the other powers and duties of the League,
there is a very widespread agreement that what may be called
the politically noncontentious work of the League has been very
successful.   The industrial work of the International Labor
Office should clearly be preserved.   So should the humanitarian,
social, and cultural work of the League Committees which the

[5] From article "Peace through International Cooperation," by Edgar Algernon
Robert Cecil, 1st Viscount of Chelwood, Chancellor of Birmingham University;
winner of Nobel Peace Prize, 1937. *Annals of the American Academy.* 210:63-5.
July 1940.

Bruce Commission has proposed to strengthen and unify. For all this kind of work, a world-wide organization is almost essential.

The general framework of the League, including the Council, the Assembly and the Secretariat, and the analogous organs of the International Labor Office should therefore be maintained. That is equally true of the Permanent Court of International Justice at The Hague. It can boast of an almost unbroken record of success. Not that it has always been right; no claim of that kind can be made for any human organization. But it has built up a solid reputation for integrity and judicial spirit, and its decisions have been uniformly accepted by the parties which have come before it. The Court should continue and its jurisdiction should be extended.

Not quite so much can be truly asserted of the other and more contentious work of the League. But even there, the successes greatly exceed in number the failures. That is the case even if attention is confined to actual international disputes. In not more than half a dozen out of twenty or thirty instances brought before it, has the machinery of the League not succeeded in settling the controversies involved. There are, besides, questions like the financial restoration of Austria, Hungary, and other countries, the admirable relief and refugee operations associated with the name of Dr. Nansen, the administration of the Saar, and other activities which raised difficult political questions and have been very successfully disposed of.

Nevertheless, this does not alter the fact that in several very important cases the League has not prevented a "resort to war" in circumstances forbidden by the Covenant, of which the war in the Far East and the series of totalitarian aggressions are the gravest and most dangerous to world peace.

An examination of League history shows two things: first, that remonstrance, however general and well founded, will not alone stop an aggressive power from carrying out its policy; and second, that there has been a lack of solidarity, of *esprit de corps,* in the League powers which should have induced them, jointly and almost automatically, to resist an attack on any one of their number. That is partly due to want of imagination,

caused by geographical remoteness or other considerations, partly
to the unfamiliarity of the truth that peace is in itself the greatest
of national interests, and partly to the international looseness of
the League organization.

I believe that all these defects would be lessened if there
were inside the framework of the League, confederations of
geographically related powers with appropriate confederate organs.

The most obviously necessary of these bodies would be a
European Confederation.  And here we have an existing foundation on which to build, in the Anglo-French partnership which
the war has brought into existence.  It has already produced a
common War Council and common economic and financial
action.  That movement should be continued and developed
after the war into what might well become a definite European
Confederation, the central object of which should be the preservation of European peace.  It should be open to European members of the League who fully accept the principle that aggression
is an international crime and are prepared to use all their strength
to protect victims of it in Europe.  A European General Staff
would be needed, and possibly other organs.

The Confederation would be autonomous in the sense that
it would not be subject to the control of any other international
authority; but it would remain in close touch with the League
and notify the Council and the Assembly of its proceedings.
There must be no rivalry between the two organizations, but, on
the contrary, the closest cooperation.  The general peace-keeping
machinery of the Covenant would remain, including the duty
of all members to do what is reasonably possible to protect any
one of their number from aggression.  The creation of the
European Confederation would be no more than a closer definition of these duties in one area.

Obviously, what has been said is a mere indication of the
underlying idea.  Much else would require elaboration, with the
object of increasing and emphasizing the Confederation's corporate life.  Questions like social and economic progress, including possibly a common currency and a common tariff policy
and, it may be, a Confederation flag, would doubtless arise.  If,

as is vital for permanent peace, a scheme of international limitation of armaments is adopted, it might probably involve an international air force under the control of the European General Staff. Certainly some machinery would have to be created for dealing peaceably with international disputes unsuitable for reference to the Hague Court as depending rather on questions of general policy than on legal or logical arguments.

All this, it may be said, is only another piece of machinery. After it has been created, the fundamental difficulties will remain. No machinery can do more than facilitate the action of the peoples. Unless they and their governments really put the maintenance of peace as the first and greatest national interest, no confederation or federation can force them to do so. But I believe that confederation,—that is, the constitutional union of independent states, inside the general framework of the League —may help to make men realize that it is only by international cooperation that peace can be preserved.

## THE LEAGUE OF NATIONS [6]

At the close of the First World War, the victorious nations drew up the Covenant of the League of Nations. Established as a new international organization in 1919, the League is still technically in existence; but it is in a state of suspended animation and, for that reason, will here be referred to in the past tense. The proposal to be debated in this chapter is for a revival of the League with no essential change in its purpose, structure, or function. Before proceeding with the arguments, it will be necessary to have clearly in mind the League's characteristic features as originally planned and provided for in the Covenant.

The proposals discussed in previous chapters have one thing in common: they are limited in scope. None of them contemplates a universal organization or association. In contrast,

[6] By Arthur C. Millspaugh, Political Scientist; Member of Staff, Brookings Institution, 1929-1942. From his book *Peace Plans and American Choices*. p. 67-81. Brookings Institution. Washington, D.C. 1942. Dr. Millspaugh's negative summary is reprinted on p. 223-9.

the League of Nations, when established in 1919, was expected
to include all or nearly all nations in its membership.  This
expectation was never fulfilled; but we shall assume in the
present discussion that, if the League is revived, its membership
will be relatively universal from the beginning, including all
the great powers, victor and vanquished alike, along with most
of the small nations.

The organization provided for in the Covenant was a very
loose confederation with an Assembly, a Council, and a permanent Secretariat.  It represented governments, not peoples.  The
member states were treated as equals, each having one vote in
the Assembly.  In most matters, the Assembly or the Council
could come to a decision only by unanimous vote.  The Council
departed somewhat from the principles of equality and unanimity, since its membership was limited to certain great powers,
which were permanent members, along with a few other states
selected from time to time by the Assembly.  Nevertheless, any
nation belonging to the League was entitled to send a representative to sit as a member of the Council during the consideration
of matters especially affecting the interests of such nation.

The League as a system of collective security rested on a
broad mutual guarantee "to respect and preserve as against
external aggression the territorial integrity and existing political
independence of all members of the League."  In case of any
aggression or "any threat or danger of such aggression," the
Council was to advise upon the means of fulfilling this undertaking.

Certain provisions, however, seemed to offer opportunity
for peaceful change.  Both the Assembly and the Council were
authorized to deal with "any matter within the sphere of action
of the League or affecting the peace of the world."  It was
declared to be "the friendly right of each member of the League
to bring to the attention of the Assembly or of the Council
any circumstance whatever affecting international relations which
threatens to disturb international peace or the good understanding between nations upon which peace depends."  The
Assembly was authorized to "advise the reconsideration by
members of the League of treaties which have become inap-

plicable and the consideration of international conditions whose continuance might endanger the peace of the world."

More specific provision was made for the settlement of disputes. The members of the League agreed that any dispute between them likely to lead to a rupture would be submitted either to arbitration or to enquiry by the Council; and they further pledged themselves "in no case to resort to war until three months after the award by the arbitrators or the report by the Council." They argreed to carry out in good faith any judgment that might be rendered and not to make war against any member complying with such judgment. In case of non-execution, the Council was to propose what steps should be taken to give effect to the judgment. The Permanent Court of International Justice, later established under the Covenant, was empowered to give advisory opinions on matters referred to it by the Council or the Assembly.

Provision was therefore made for political, as well as for judicial, settlement. Serious disputes not submitted to arbitration were to be laid before the Council. If this body failed to settle the dispute, it was to make and publish a report of the facts and its recommendations; but, if the dispute referred to a matter within the "domestic jurisdiction" of one of the parties, no recommendation should be made by the Council. In case a report was unanimously agreed to by the members of the Council (other than the representatives of the parties to the dispute) all members of the League were obliged "not to go to war with any party to the dispute which complies with the recommendations of the report." If the report was not unanimous, the members could take whatever action they might "consider necessary for the maintenance of right and justice."

It was foreseen that a member of the League might resort to war without fulfilling the obligations just mentioned. Such member, the Covenant says, "shall *ipso facto* be deemed to have committed an act of war against all other members of the League." The latter were thereupon obligated to subject the offending state immediately to certain nonmilitary sanctions or means of coercion, chiefly of an economic, financial, and commercial nature, amounting in effect to a nonbelligerent blockade of the lawbreaker. In addition, the Council was to recommend "what effective military, naval or air force the members of the League shall severally contribute to the armed forces to be used to protect the covenants of the League." Each member state bound itself to help in the application of economic and financial sanctions and in resistance to counter-measures by the covenant-breaking nation, and to give passage through its territory to the forces of the cooperating members. Finally, a violator of the Covenant could be expelled from the League.

Provision was made for handling disputes involving non-members. These were to be invited to accept the obligations of membership with reference to the dispute. In case of refusal, the nonmember, if in dispute with a member, became subject to the economic, financial, and military measures just described; but, if the dispute was between two nonmembers and both refused, the Council could adopt whatever measures and recommendations might be appropriate to prevent hostilities and terminate the dispute.

Finally, the Covenant declared that any war or threat of war is "a matter of concern to the whole League," which "shall take any action that may be deemed wise and effectual to safeguard the peace of nations."

While the League was intended to be universal, it was provided that nothing in the Covenant should "affect the validity of international engagements, such as treaties of arbitration or regional understandings like the Monroe Doctrine, for securing the maintenance of peace."

With reference to disarmament, the Covenant recognized that "the maintenance of peace requires the reduction of national armaments to the lowest point consistent with national safety and the enforcement by common action of international obligations." The Council was charged with formulating plans for such reduction; and, after adoption of the plans, no government could exceed the limits fixed without the concurrence of the Council. "Grave objections" were seen to the private manufacture of munitions; and the Council was to "advise how the evil effects attendant upon such manufacture can be prevented." The members of the League undertook to interchange full and frank information on armaments, military programs, and industries adaptable to war purposes.

In addition to these features of the League as a peace instrument, the Covenant established the mandate system of colonial administration, set forth principles regarding labor, assigned social welfare activities to the League, adopted something like the principle of equality of economic opportunity, and made provision for putting under the League's direction various international bureaus and commissions.

Obviously, the nations of the world, during the twenty years of the League's active life, did not inaugurate a regime of peaceful change, settle all disputes by peaceful methods, establish security, bring about disarmament, or prevent all wars. It may be conceded that the general effort to maintain peace was a tragic failure. But whether the League was impractical, defective, or otherwise at fault is another question and one that is answered in different ways.

Acceptance of the League of Nations as the world's best hope for the future might be based on the following argument:

1. The League of Nations had its roots in past experience. The Covenant embodied those ideas and practices in the international sphere, which during the nineteenth century had come into being and had been generally accepted as wise, moral, and constructive. These had been supported and many of them initiated or exemplified by the United States. The founders of the League rejected such discredited alternatives as isolationism, imperialism, alliances, and balances of power; and they likewise stopped far short of world federation or a supergovernment. The League was a new combination of familiar parts. It enlisted the understanding and support of the public opinion of the time, appealing generally to the leaders of public thought and also to the masses. After 1920, the League was misunderstood in this country; and later in Europe it was systematically misrepresented and undermined by Hitler and Mussolini. Nevertheless, the United States did not repudiate the main principles of the League; for these were traditionally American.

2. While the League was rudimentary, it was expected to grow and was so framed as to permit evolution and adaptation.

It was, as Wilson termed it, "a vehicle of life." The most practical course of action at the end of this war will be to launch the League again under more promising auspices. Later, we may wish to make changes in the Covenant. Many alterations were proposed and thoroughly studied during the League's active life; and it is always easier to revise what has already been adopted and is understood than to create something entirely new. In Europe habits and loyalties have formed around the League; and the League has more symbolic value now than ever before, because its dictatorial arch-enemies are now discredited. The League organization will be better adapted to the work of postwar reconstruction than would be the war agencies of the United Nations.

It is possible that those who now advocate the League will be denounced, as Woodrow Wilson was, for being "idealistic," "visionary," and "utopian." If so, it may be well to compare the idealism and far-sighted vision of Wilson with, for example, the so-called and once boasted "realism" of Mussolini. Hitler and the Japanese war lords have also prided themselves on being "realists"; but, as we are now in process of proving, their schemes and methods have been shot through with illusion, delusion, and sheer blundering.

3. The machinery of the League was well adapted to its purposes and principles. It constituted, not a government, but an organization through which governments could act collectively and cooperatively. The Versailles Conference assumed that the world was not ready for a superstate. Nationalism and national sovereignty could not yet be eliminated or even greatly reduced. The League was, therefore, based on a treaty, not on a constitution; and it took the form of a confederation of governments, in which were applied, in a flexible manner, the three principles of sovereignty, equality, and unanimity.

The League possessed in embryo legislative, executive, judicial, and administrative departments.

Legislation took the form of peaceful change and settlement of disputes. Provision was properly made for political as well as judicial deliberation and action. The following opinion has been stated with considerable authority: "Clearly the international society with the greatest chance of success will be that one which will assure a dynamic peace with the minimum sacrifice of national sovereignty." Did not the League Covenant provide for that kind of a society?

4. The principle of universal membership embodied in the League was and is sound. A universal or relatively universal association is the only one able to bring to bear an overwhelming preponderance of power against an aggressor.

To operate as a system of collective security, an international organization must include the countries that are potential enemies. Accordingly, if any of the great powers are left out, the way is open for hostile alignments and undermining campaigns from the outside.

Two restricted conceptions of the League were wisely rejected by its founders. One was that it should be purely a concert of free peoples. In a federation, autocracies and democracies might make strange bedfellows; but in a loose confederation having the single purpose of maintaining order it is possible for all forms of government to cooperate. Ideological similarity may be desirable, but it is not indispensable. The second restricted conception was that the League should comprise only the great powers. While small nations might be omitted from the standpoint of military power, their inclusion is essential from other standpoints. They are most devoted to the principle of collective security; they are involved in the beginnings of war; they need to be heard; their statesmen are worth hearing; and the principle of democracy demands that they be represented.

In general, the League was adapted to an interdependent world, in which the processes of peace must be no less universal in scope than the impact of war.

5. While membership was to be universal, the principles of the League permitted regional arrangements. In fact, these were recognized and encouraged by the terms of the Covenant and by League practice. In addition, there was an appropriate concentration of authority and responsibility in the hands of the great powers, not merely because of the set up of the Council

but more for the reason that weak countries naturally follow the leadership of the strong.

6. Circumstances that will not be repeated after this war, prevented the League in actual operation from achieving even a relatively universal membership, and failure in this respect produced fatal weakness. The absence of certain great powers contributed to the feeling of insecurity, led to rearmament, and encouraged the return to alliances and balance-of-power policies. Because the League was a confederation, its most important organs were the member nations; and the actual structure, functioning, and effectiveness of the League were determined in large measure by how many and what nations were inside or outside.

If Germany, Russia, and the United States had been in from the beginning, the story of the League and of Europe would have been very different. Germany was a member only from 1926 to 1935 and Russia only from 1934 to 1939. During the first six years, when the League was getting its start, neither of these great powers was a member. Disarmament of Germany and refusal to give her the protection of League membership presented that key power with a grievance, a reason for feeling insecure, and an excuse for rearming. Lacking universality, the general tendency was for the League to become merely one combination ranged against another.

The unexpected absence of the United States altered the character of the League and substantially contributed to its final collapse. The Versailles Treaty was shaped in the belief that the United States would stand behind it. The Covenant was peculiarly an Anglo-American product. America's refusal to ratify it destroyed three possibilities: (1) of uninhibited American leadership, (2) of Anglo-American predominance, and (3) of Anglo-American cooperation. In the absence of the United States, League leadership was left to Great Britain and France; and Britain's attitude toward Germany was in the main conciliatory, while that of France was in the main repressive. On some vital matters, the two countries worked at cross purposes.

It will be recalled that a Tri-Partite Treaty of Mutual Guarantee was concluded at Paris between Great Britain, France, and the United States. Had this Treaty been ratified by the United States, France would have had reason to feel secure. Had the power and popularity of this country been added to the League, other nations too, would have felt safe. Under these circumstances, France would not have proceeded at once to encircle Germany with alliances; and Germany would have had more reason to feel secure. In such a situation, disarmament would have been possible, reducing the likelihood of aggression and making easier the application of sanctions.

The record suggests that the system of sanctions would have succeeded with American participation and Anglo-American cooperation. In the Far East, such cooperation was foreshadowed by the Washington Conference (1922); but in the case of Manchuria (1931), the United States and Britain, without the habits and common obligations that the League would have supplied, were unable to put effective pressure on Japan. In the case of Ethiopia (1935) nonmilitary sanctions were belatedly and half-heartedly applied to Italy; and their failure is largely to be attributed to the noncooperation of the United States. In the case of Spain (1937), a number of factors permitted Mussolini and Hitler to have their way; but not the least of them was the lack of understanding and coordination between the United States, Britain, France, and Russia.

7. After this war, the international association will not be identified with an unpopular peace treaty. The League was seriously handicapped by the fact that it was intertwined with the Versailles peace. The League was charged with the carrying out of numerous Treaty provisions. Treaty and Covenant were in some respects contradictory. For example, the doctrine of self-determination embodied in the Treaty encouraged a highly disintegrating kind of nationalism, broke down the Austro-Hungarian Empire, increased the number of small nations, and multiplied points of friction and sources of conflict. Self-determination and nationalistic autonomy were safe and practi-

cable only after an effective League had been established. In general, the League suffered from its association with the treaty.

8. The ideological differences that hampered the League will be absent or greatly mitigated after this war. The menace of revolutionary communism has been removed by a movement of capitalism toward communism and of communism toward capitalism, as well as by Russia's part in this war. Postwar national economies will be mixed systems, including elements of both freedom and control. Class privilege will have largely vanished. In the political sphere, the struggle will be decided in favor of democracy. Faith in popular government will have been renewed.

9. Economic conditions will also be more favorable. The turn in the fortunes of Germany and of the League came with the depression of 1929. Had the German people possessed a reasonable degree of economic, along with international security, the Republic would have been saved and with it German support of the peace structure.

10. Peoples and governments will now have the will needed to make the League work. The system set up at Geneva would have succeeded if that will had existed. The League itself was merely structure and machinery. Its motive and directive force had to come chiefly from the governments of the great powers. Nothing was wrong with the League itself. German and Italian efforts against it proved that they feared it. As members, Italy and Japan were insincere. Germany and Russia were in and out. Great Britain and France were lacking in faith and determination.

Peace in accordance with the Covenant was not the aim of all governments. In this situation, the democracies, when they should have acted at the risk of war, were paralyzed by their own pacifism. Thus, they encouraged aggression. Now, they have finally learned that appeasement is not the way to peace, and that the real risk comes from inaction, not action. In the future, we shall know much better how and when to act; and we shall prefer collective action to being destroyed one by one. Britain and France were primarily interested in preserving the existing order. They were not actively concerned with peaceful change or with the removal of causes of conflict. In the future, a different attitude may be expected, especially when the more flexible and detached American viewpoint becomes influential. The conservative and nationalist elements that distrusted and opposed the League will be weaker in all countries after this war.

It may be expected, furthermore, that peace organizations in the different countries will supply the people with real leadership. They will no longer be divided between pro-Leaguers and anti-Leaguers.

11. In spite of everything, the League came within an ace of permanent success. Before 1926, it really helped to keep the peace. Had there been a different turn of events after 1931, the League might have had time to consolidate both its strength and prestige. Thereafter, neither would have been challenged again. Even as late as the middle thirties, a strong stand against Italy and Japan might have put a stop to both fascism and aggression. At the very worst, the League lost by a narrow squeak; and it has earned a second trial under fairer conditions.

12. Some believe that the League can win the attachment of peoples only by dispensing benefits, by having positive economic and social functions, or by assuming administrative responsibilities, for example, over colonies. Friends of the League have no quarrel with such suggestions, provided they do not divert attention from the primary purpose of keeping international order. The League as originally conceived was in no way inconsistent with economic progress and social justice.


## THE NEW LEAGUE OF NATIONS [7]

There is a good deal of reluctance to give the name of League of Nations to the international body which will have to come into being after the victory of the United Nations. Should it be known as a "Community of Nations" or a "Society of States" or a "World Commonwealth" or an "International

[7] By Luigi Sturzo, Author of *Italy and Fascismo, The International Community and the Right of War*, etc. *Contemporary Review*: 163:71-7. February 1943.

Federation?" There is something curious in this quest for new names in order to express the simple fact that we wish to build a new League of Nations better than the old. Let us consider, rather, the substance of the matter, leaving aside questions of nomenclature. And, while waiting for the discovery of some fine new name, let us continue to speak of a League of Nations. We do not want all the past to be forgotten, and we are anxious to recall to life and usefulness all that was good at Geneva and The Hague. Since in this essay we seek to sketch the characteristics of the future League of Nations, we shall proceed as in every scientific or practical experiment, taking the past as something achieved and the future as something to be created, thus bringing out the features of the new structure and paving the way for the more significant changes to be sought.

All states will be able to become members of the League; but, in practice, only those will be admitted that are willing to accept both spirit and letter of the new covenant. The mistake of the past, a mistake *de facto* more than *de jure*, was that of admitting to membership of the League states that were morally or politically unable to assume the coresponsibilities of membership, and which subsequently became enemies and saboteurs of the League. This was the case with Japan, who organized the first aggression against Manchuria, and for this aggression was not expelled from the League as she should have been. Even when Japan resigned her membership, after being censured by the League, she continued to act as Mandatory power over the Marshall and Gilbert Islands and the League made no attempt to cancel this mandate. The cases of Italy and Germany were similar. At Geneva future enemies lived cheek by jowl. What was stranger still, while those who were preparing the present war worked to undermine the League, no remedial measures were taken by other states.

The new League must be formed by the United Nations who have signed the Washington Declaration, numbering thirty at the present time, with the addition of France, ultimately to be identified with the Fighting French. The United Nations have pledged themselves to fight for liberty, religious freedom, justice, the rights of man, order and international cooperation. Once victory is attained, it will be their duty to redeem their pledges.

One hears doubts expressed about Russia. Our repeatedly expressed opinion has been that the common victory will mean a new era for Russia, too. It is today legitimate to think that Russia, in her own interests, will cooperate loyally with the League and will merit help and confidence. If the opposite hypothesis should be verified, and if Russia should attempt to disturb international order by communistic propaganda or armaments in excess of the limits commonly agreed, the same League would have to make a stand and recall Russia to the fulfilment of her word, just as the old League should have done in the case of Germany when she withdrew from the Disarmament Conference and abandoned her League membership.

We should remember that Geneva was not powerless; what was lacking was a show of good will on the part now of Great Britain, now of France and often of both at once, not to mention the lack of cooperation from the United States, even as outsiders, which weakened the League from the beginning. The most perfect covenant may be drawn up, but if the will to fulfill its terms is lacking, it will never be really alive, and will remain a dead letter.

The states that have remained neutral during the present war will have to be scrutinized one by one, to ascertain whether they deserve trust and may therefore become members of the League. Those among them that have totalitarian tendencies, deny freedom to their citizens or persecute religious, racial or linguistic minorities, should be adjudged as not possessing the same spirit as the founders of the League and should be denied admission until their political system or their frame of mind be modified.

With regard to the vanquished countries, it will be necessary to wait for the formation of new governments, the establishment of new constitutions, in order to decide whether and upon what conditions they should be admitted. The League must not be envisaged as a formal body but as a living community. Just as the citizen must be loyal to his country, so the member states must be loyal to the League. After a world crisis like the present, loyalty will be presumed in the victors but not among the vanquished. The former have fought for an ideal opposed to those of the Axis and its satellites; the latter must therefore provide certain proof of having undergone a change, of having renounced their order of ideas and adopted that of the new League. Only then will they be eligible for membership.

In the Wilsonian League there was an attempt to reconcile the individualistic and the hierarchic principle. On the Council there were permanent seats held by the Great Powers and non-permanent seats filled partly by election and partly by rotation. The prevalence of the Great Powers was safeguarded. But in order to respect the sovereignty of individual states, the absurd rule was enforced that the validity of the commitments of the Assembly depended on a unanimous vote. One single vote was sufficient to paralyse the League's mechanism, and sometimes the states' delegates at Geneva were obliged to resort to the parliamentary tricks of absence or abstention or of backstage compromises. All this flowed from one fundamental mistake, then perhaps unavoidable owing to lack of experience of any kind of league, but which today would be unforgivable after twenty years of hard trials. This mistake lay in conceiving of the League as an assembly of delegates. The League as such could have no effective powers beyond those regarding its internal structure. Political and international powers were provided by each single government; hence the necessity for unanimity, since the member states had not given up a fraction of their sovereignty.

Are the United States, Great Britain, China and Russia today willing to surrender something of their sovereignty and, in international matters, to bow, with all due precautions, to the law of the majority, be it merely a two-thirds majority? If the answer is yes, then all other states will say yes, including the neutrals and the vanquished. But if the attitude of the United States, Great Britain, China and Russia is negative, the new League will have an even unhappier experience than the old and will end in failure.

Let us assume the affirmative. The consequence will be that the three or four Great Powers will want permanent seats on the executive body, and this is right; they will also seek to ascertain in all earnestness the nature of the states sharing responsibilities with them, and this is even more right. This scrutiny was never undertaken in the past by France or Great Britain where Nazi Germany or Fascist Italy were concerned, because membership of the League did not commit them in any way; Geneva, indeed, often fulfilled a useful rôle as a smokescreen. But when the League has its own powers and will be in a position to commit London, Moscow and Washington even beyond the actual will of their respective governments, then fellow members will be subject to serious scrutiny.

What must be avoided at all cost is that one group should form a bloc and dominate the League. Whatever the nature of that group, be it Moscow-London-Washington, or London-Paris-Washington, or London-Washington-Berlin, or any similar combination, its formation must be prevented. At the same time any coalition of small or medium states should be forestalled if its intent is to paralyze the functioning of the League.

No one doubts that the future League should have consultative and judicial powers like those of the Permanent Court of International Justice at The Hague. No one will wish to deprive The Hague of such a court; the changes required will mean a broadening of its jurisdiction and improvement of its structure. Nor will anyone minimize the services rendered by the International Labor Office in the social field, or by the special technical and economic commissions, which as a whole have worked well, even though sometimes hampered by a certain kind of bureaucracy which tended to slow down the activities of Geneva.

The question of the League's powers concerns the political field. Here three problems of decisive importance present themselves.

The first one is the definition of aggression, a definition which must be not theoretical but practical and statutory. The associated states will have to consider as aggression, no matter what the juridical or political motives, any and all offensive acts carried out *manu militari* against a state, any military action on foreign territory, all military preparation in furtherance of a threat of aggression. It must be the right and duty of the League to order the cessation of hostilities between states; the side refusing acceptance of the League's order within the delay fixed will be deemed an aggressor and liable to sanctions.

The Covenant of 1919 foresaw four legitimate grounds for war; the new Covenant will have to exclude the legitimacy of any war between states. The League alone should have the right of armed intervention as a police measure, as a measure of sanction and as a defense of rights in protection of the attacked state, and only the League will be entitled to call upon other states to share in the defense of the state subjected to aggression.

There are politicians, writers and pressmen who, since the failure of economic sanctions against Italy, doubt the feasibility of such a system. Others are outright opposed to it. All of these either have no clear idea of the future League or are thinking in terms of an impotent League. It would seem idle to argue with them. Let us merely remind them that the failure of sanctions against Italy must not be debited to the system itself but to the hesitancy of the London and Paris cabinets; the truth is that they never wanted to proceed further.

Leaving aside economic sanctions, for their efficacy must be ultimate rather than immediate, we shall consider military sanctions as being really adequate to nip in the bud any attempt to start a war. Either a state will be strong enough to defy the League and the states which it represents, and in such case will by itself constitute a permanent danger to world peace, . . . or else it will be wholly unable to face the power of the League and it will not then be in a position to begin a war. Only a weak and divided and powerless League can be checkmated, as the League was not only by Italy but also by the Free City of Danzig.

The view is gaining ground that the United Nations will have to assert the principle of unilateral disarmament for an unpredictable period, to enable the vanquished countries to abandon their aggressive mentality. It is not a question here of debating the length of such a period. What seems evident is that it cannot be prolonged beyond the time when a vanquished country is accepted as a member of the League of Nations. Within the League there must be no longer victors and vanquished, but only members cooperating to maintain international order. The military system to be fixed for all members of the League will be extended to the vanquished countries once they have been adjudged worthy of admission.

What the Atlantic Charter has to say on collective security is very vague. Nothing is said of it in the Declaration of Washington and it occupies a subordinate position in the Anglo-Russian treaty of alliance. Though governmental declarations on disarmament, or rather the reduction of armaments, are not lacking, we are yet in unexplored territory. But whatever the limits of a reduction of armaments to be achieved after the complete disarmament of the vanquished countries or in subsequent agreements among the United Nations, it is certain that a League of Nations cannot possibly be formed without endowing it with military powers and creating military organisms in its dependence. If we want peace in the world, we must take the decisive step and create a real and living supernational organism.

To the League we should attribute the surveillance and policing of air and seas, and direct responsibility for certain internationalized territories, like Tangiers. Plainly, not all armies nor all military aircraft will be placed under the control of the League. But there will have to be certain internationalized corps endowed with autonomy and their own sphere of action for the maintenance of security and order.

It is also possible to foresee a delegation of powers by the League to one or more individual member states for the fulfillment of special military missions, a kind of military mandate. Similarly the League should be able to organize—entrusting its operation to the states most concerned—a military cordon round the state which, in violation of pacts, is arming itself and preparing an aggression. The possible developments of a system of international security centering in the League are many, and it is easy to show the significance and the essentially peaceful nature of the new armies, a real police force of a truly new order. Time will favor mental and practical adaptations, both individual and collective. Up to the present we have had military alliances, entered upon with a view to carrying out a specific war. Tomorrow there will be a permanent alliance, also on the military plane, to guarantee a peace achieved after so many sacrifices.

Let us not delude ourselves that all this can be smoothly effected. There will be the jealousies between today's friends and mistrust of yesterday's enemies. No one likes to drop into the background and receive orders, but it is just here that the secret of statesmanship lies—to know how to command when command is necessary, to know how to cooperate with others and rely on them when that reliance guarantees the common good. If we look back to the ages of slavery and polygamy, how great has been the progress in the social machinery of mankind! Therefore we can have faith in a League of Nations endowed with political and military powers.

Every state, and not only the vanquished states, must accept the principle of international control. The vanquished states will have to accept a special control imposed by the armistice until all their obligations under it have been fulfilled. When they are deemed worthy of admission to the League, they will come under the control common to all members.

Such control is necessary to ensure that members respect pacts, in loyalty to the League and to the moral and juridical principles upon which it is founded. The cardinal point of the new League should be that its members must all be of a like mind. If there is a repudiation of the League's principles on the part of a member, that member will have to be rendered harmless. If the League had intervened in time in the cases of Japan, Italy and Germany, as soon as their armaments began to show, or, even better, when those countries began to manifest their totalitarian tendencies, the present war would have been averted. In a League endowed with political and military powers, a control will have to be created to prevent important mandates and military powers from falling into untrustworthy hands. Did not Japan retain her mandate over the Marshall and Gilbert Islands, Vichy France over Syria, Franco Spain over Tangier? Was not the Chairman of the League's Minority Commission an Italian when Fascist Italy was persecuting Slovene and German minorities?

There are Englishmen and Americans who are frightened by the revolutionary implications of such a League. But if this war is not a revolution, what other event could be? Is it still thought that China will tolerate European concessions upon her territory, or that India will continue to be ruled by the British, or that the islands of the Pacific will again become a field for capitalistic exploitation? There will also be a new revolution in Russia and great changes in England and the United States.

Every country will have the government it chooses. The League will be concerned in ensuring that the moral, legal and cultural principles for which we are fighting today, and in whose name we shall be victorious tomorrow, are at its basis—political and religious freedom, independence, rights of human personality, justice, protection of the rights of racial, religious and linguistic minorities, and the ultimate attainment by colonial peoples of political and economic personality.

The League will have the task of safeguarding the international order emerging from the new Covenant and will have to be endowed with adequate powers and rights acknowledged by all. The state that does not keep its pledged word and undermines the new order, even if only within its own territory, must be excluded from the League and subjected to sanctions.

It must be anticipated that not a few states will remain outside the League, temporarily or indefinitely. They will be small states with a special structure. Switzerland, for instance, may feel even tomorrow that neutrality is for her the best solution, and might choose to remain outside. It would be foolish to have recourse again to compromise: League and neutrality are at opposite poles. Nevertheless, between Switzerland and the League there will be established those relationships of friendship that the democratic spirit of respective institutions will make effective and cooperative. Other small states for local reasons may not be willing to introduce those freedoms that are at the basis of the new League, and will be inclined to retain a system which yesterday used to be called authoritarian and reactionary without being totalitarian. I am thinking of certain republics of Latin America where a restless general may engineer a *coup d'état*. Better for such states to stay out of the League rather than infect it with totalitarian tendencies. The time will come when they become converted; their people will react; their freedoms will be rewon, and the League will open its doors. Until such time, let us maintain diplomatic contacts and a limited measure of trust and collaboration from without. But let us bar them from association within the League.

If it is a question of Great Powers, and these could only be the members of the Berlin-Rome-Tokyo Axis, the League will remain watchful as against a potential enemy. Let us suppose that Japan after her defeat, even after acceptance of the armistice terms, were to refuse to correct her political system, which would therefore be left in the hands of militarists and ultra-nationalists, or were to refrain from applying for admission to the League. Then it would be clear that hopes of revenge were secretly being fostered; Tokyo would be acting on the basis that in twenty years all the governments of the world would have changed their personnel, and the same problems would be looked upon with different eyes; that new and convinced appeasers would not be lacking, and critics of the past, which is our present, would perhaps be very bitter against our Churchills and Roosevelts. The Japanese might think that by means of a subtle policy they could find a backing and render revenge possible. A country secretly nourishing such sentiments, aimed against the orderly processes of the community of nations, is more dangerous as a member of the League, helped perhaps by the indulgence of London or Washington or Moscow, than as an outsider under close control. The old slogan, "I accept freedom in order to have freedom to deny it," cannot be accepted in the new order. The League must have the power both to refuse admission to a state which does not inspire confidence and to expel a state that fails in the keeping of its pledged word.

Since it is a question of vanquished states it is obvious that they will be granted parity of rights (also in regard to armaments in the measure which has been agreed) if they become members of the League. But if they will not become members, either because they do not wish to do so or because they have not fulfilled the conditions of the armistice or because they do not comply with the League's pacts, they will also have to be deprived of all rights to proportional and relative parity in armaments.

To build a new edifice on Christian ethical principles and on the principles of international law is the aim of the war now being fought by the United Nations. The instrument will be a League of Nations, created upon these very principles and made effective by political and military powers which no future coalition will be able to destroy.

One of the most acute remarks of Mr. T. V. Soong, the Minister for Foreign Affairs of the Chinese Republic, is that the old League of Nations was born too late. Instead of being set up during the war (when the urgencies of the struggle bring the constant effort to overcome obstacles in the way of unity), it was formed at a time when the Allies felt secure each on its own account. The peril had passed and the future was not visible.

The same may be said today. The League should be reborn during the war, and not wait for it to end. Now is the time to come to a decision on what should be the system of the future, and the position of the separate states in the new order that is being forged with the sacrifices and lives of the young of all countries.

What is lacking is a sound political conception. That Britain and the United States with their immense potentialities will be at the center of economic reconstruction is beyond all doubt. But there is a great danger—that of a political monopoly of two or three or four big powers (America, Britain, China, Russia), of improvization where what may be considered minor national problems are concerned, of compromizes with classes or cliques of the various neutral and enemy countries, and, above all, of the sowing of new discords (as happened at Versailles) liable to ripen into a Third World War.

Mr. Soong's idea should be considered. The League of Nations, which today functions in a marginal fashion, for the study of economic and labor problems, should have its Political Commission, made up of representatives of the thirty United Nations and possibly those neutrals that wish to cooperate. This commission, assisted by experts, could draft the constitution of the new League, and discuss, now, its possible working and the improvements to be made to the Covenant. Here are theoretical and practical problems not easy of solution, but which cannot be solved in a day or a night after the war.

When this preliminary work has been done, an assembly of states should be called to approve the text, and the new League should begin to function. To it should be entrusted little by little those postwar tasks that must be carried out in common by the states, while each separate government should get to work on that part of organization that will be entrusted to it. Thus centralized coordination and decentralization, a single heart and a manifold activity: today, not tomorrow *incipit vita nova.*

## EXCERPTS

Now, we have accumulated a vast store of experience in international administration and cooperation since 1919, and it would be a grave mistake not to utilize that experience, which is the result of the international activities built up by the League of Nations, the International Labor Organization, and the Permanent Court of International Justice.

Fortunately we do not start at scratch, and it is sometimes quite peculiar to look at the rather ghastly dance of peace executed by passionate ideologists who seem to think that we have to start from nothing at all and build up an entirely new world without remembering anything that has happened. As the French philosopher said, who translated John Stuart Mill's *Liberty* into French, "What distinguishes man from the animal is continuity, and my right as man is my right to have the feeling of continuity." In the international community we can build on this feeling when we are planning the future world organization.

The international difficulties will be exactly the same whether we speak of a World Organization, a Federation, a Confederation, a Union Now, or a Revitalized League of Nations. Nomenclature is of absolutely minor importance.—*C. J. Hambro, President, Parliament of Norway (the Storting); President, League of Nations Assembly. Annals of the American Academy. Jl. '42. p.* 110.

Fully agreeing with Don Sturzo's proposal, I want to state here not my ideal reasons, which are evident, but a few immediate practical reasons. I am for a revived League of Nations now:

a. Because, as the Italian proverb goes, "il meglio è nemico del bene" (The better is the enemy of the good), and since the League of Nations of the 1919 Covenant is still alive, it is better to begin by using it in spite of too many errors attached to its name.

b. Because, the Fascist regime being unnatural and artificial, and the Nazi regime being in danger of being ousted by the German General Staff, as happened with the Kaiser, it is most important that when they disappear—and they may do so sooner than we think—a supreme international organization should be ready for certain urgent delicate tasks, like the administration of ports and centers of an international character.

c. Because the immediate resurrection of the League would give the lie to dangerous anti-United-Nations slogans and therefore might hasten the creation of a healthy European mentality where this mentality has become morbid.

d. Because, with a League active again it will be easier to proceed rapidly to necessary reforms in it. These in my opinion are:

1. Outlawry of any sort of war;
2. Supression of the unanimity rule; and
3. Admission to the League only of reliable, honest members, as was envisaged in an article in the first draft of the

Covenant, eliminated later in order to please the "realists," who in every country have been the most responsible accomplices of the war schemers.—*Count Carlo Sforza, Italian Statesman, Educator and Author. People and Freedom. (London). Jl. '43. p.* 1

It is not so important *when* the League is renewed but it is important *how.*

A long acquaintance with the work of the League convinces me that its failure was due to the work of so many experts and to the scourge of a laborious research for a "formula" by which to express its mind and to give shape to its action.

As a matter of fact, the real mind and its translation into action was barred under the heavy weight of legislative niceties. "Formulas" became bandages gradually devitalizing and mummifying the body of the League.

Experts, painfully sweating to invent and prepare "formulas," brooding hesitations and uncertainties, camouflaging dissensions and concealing evasions, were not in agreement between themselves.  The highest authority at the League, when I approached him with a question concerning Greece, shrugged his shoulders and said in despair: "I consulted five of the experts; each of them expressed a different opinion." One would think that experts were created not to disentangle, but to muddle the threads of problems.

The Covenant of the League was as wise and as complete an achievement as a human work of this kind can be. It was killed by finesse and insincerity.

If an opinion such as mine may have any value, I would venture to suggest a League without so many experts, with fewer diplomats, and with a number of delegates elected direct by the people, or by the respective Parliaments.  The responsibility of final decision will, of course, lie with the governments; but the contribution of a group representing popular feelings would be a valuable asset in the work of a future League, which should be founded on more solid bases and with a spirit of absolute fidelity to the conception of "collective security."—*Demetrius Caclamanos, Greek Minister in London, 1918-1935; Repre-*

*sented Greece in the League of Nations and at the Lausanne
Peace Conference 1923-24. People and Freedom (London). Mr.
'43. p. 1.*

The fate of the League of Nations indicates that it might be
wise not only to provide machinery for changing the peace structure, but also to make it mandatory that all nations reconsider
the treaties at definite intervals.   This was the intention of
Lord Robert Cecil who, on behalf of the British delegation to
the last Peace Conference, proposed that Article 19 of the
Covenant of the League should state that "the Body of Delegates shall make provision for the periodic revision of treaties
which have become obsolete, . . . the continuance of which may
endanger the peace of the world."

Under this clause the members of the League would have
been obligated at specific periods to survey legal, economic and
social factors—such factors as helped produce this war.   They
would have been obligated to consider in orderly manner and in
reasonable atmosphere such questions as those of the mandates
and colonies, of the Sudetenland, of Austria and Danzig.   But
the wording of Article 19 was changed so that instead of providing that the Assembly "must consider grievances," it read
"may consider grievances."   Then, when Bolivia and Chile
sought to have the League settle their boundary dispute at the
Second Assembly, it was eventually ruled that the League could
not "of itself modify any treaty."

This time it should be recognized that the primary business
of a peace system is to modify treaties when the necessity arises.
More should be done than has ever been attempted heretofore
to watch the development of disputes, grievances, conditions
of any kind that are likely to cause trouble, if not dealt with in
time.  To this end a permanent commission charged to study and
report on the early symptoms of war might well be as organic a
part of a peace structure as the international health section of the
league.  The Chile-Bolivia boundary case suggests that regional
councils, if set up within an over-all world organization, might
form a first court of appeal for disputes within the region.

The main difficulty will be in making governments accept revisions and modifications of the *status quo* in the interest of world peace. Therefore I suggest that the United States (which played an important part in changing the wording of Article 19 from must to may) should accept its full responsibility and join with other nations in helping to solve these international problems, and that this time we support Lord Robert Cecil's vital proposal.—*Arthur Hays Sulzberger, President and Publisher, The New York Times. New York Times. Je. 6, '43. p. 32.*

It is unlikely that the international organization of the future will follow exactly the pattern of the first League of Nations. We must take full account of the weaknesses of that pattern and of the ways in which it failed. Nevertheless, any new international system must contain many elements of the League.

Any new system will need a general Assembly to provide a forum for the discussion of international problems. It will need some sort of Council to provide a smaller administrative body which can be summoned easily and frequently. It will certainly need an international civil service very similar to the League Secretariat. The powers and functions of any new Assembly and Council may be different; their membership may be differently selected; the fields of work for a new Secretariat may be differently organized. Nevertheless, the framework of the new organization is likely to be much the same.

Moreover, many of the still existing nonpolitical sections of the League could well be taken over by any new international system. Perhaps the splendid buildings in Geneva will again serve as the home of at least a large part of any such system. The World Court must resume its administration of international justice. We have today in the International Labor Office a body which continues in its working center in Montreal its all-important work for social justice and which must continue to do so in an expanded way under any new system.

No one can say man's first attempt to organize his world for peace failed completely. From it there remains much that can be utilized in newer and better plans. Those who frame a new international covenant will have 25 years of historical experience which was denied to those who drafted the Treaty of Versailles.

We have said that the League lacked power of its own. In planning for the future many believe that any new system must have the power to enforce its decisions, or those of its World Court, through an international police force. Only thus, perhaps, can aggression be prevented. This might mean the sacrifice of part of its sovereignty in the political field by each nation in order that force may be behind international law. Perhaps several regional groups of nations should be organized to deal with regional problems but this is desirable only within the framework of a general international system.

Then, too, the League did not do enough to promote change by peaceful agreement. Some feel, therefore, that in any new system there must be some means that will require the frequent and regular consideration of any situation that might endanger peace. Thus only can the causes of war be gradually removed. This might mean, for example, the surrender of some of its sovereignty in the economic field by each nation, giving the new international system some control over its tariffs and trade.

A new international system should also see to it that certain basic human rights such as freedom of speech and assembly are secured for all men. If certain nations deny these rights to their citizens, the peace of the world is in danger.

But the best plans will not succeed unless enough people everywhere realize that security and prosperity, freedom and dignity, depend now upon the organization of an international system.

Certainly, in any case, the people of the United States must see before this war is over that no international system can succeed without full cooperation by our country. That realization should result in a public opinion prepared to support the acceptance of those obligations to win the peace as well as the war which we refused after 1918—*The League of Nations— Today and Tomorrow. League of Nations Association. New York. N. '42. p. 7-8.*

*Whatever safety measures the peace treaties may contain, they will not be sufficient to guarantee permanent peace and cooperation.* Unilateral disarmament of the aggressor nations is a political necessity for a transitional period, during which the victors, especially Great Britain and the United States, will have to exercise international police power.

At the same time, however, the basis for an international organization, a new League of Nations, must be laid. We refrain from discussing details of its form, but some basic principles and functions can be presented.

The League must have executive power, backed by armed force. To this end, the constitution of the new League will have to differ from that of the old League of Nations.

The absolute sovereignty of each state was primarily responsible for the failure of the League of Nations, as formed in 1919. Some elements of national sovereignty must be relinquished, especially in two respects.

The armaments of each state and the production and trade in arms must be controlled by the League. As the new international order is strengthened, it will be possible gradually to supplant the police power of the English-speaking nations by an international sea and air force. Finally, when international cooperation is fully established, the way will be open for gradual, general, and controlled disarmament.

Furthermore, the League should admit only nations in which the people possess certain fundamental rights, such as *habeas corpus,* free elections, right to form parties and trade unions, freedom of speech, press, assembly, association, and religion. The League must guarantee these fundamental rights to the people of its member states against force that would destroy their free institutions. Measures adopted by a democratic state, to protect itself against those who set out to undermine the democratic system, are in no way inconsistent with democracy and cannot be considered as grounds for appeal to the League.

As an organ of the League, a World Court should be established, to which disputes between states must be referred for arbitral settlement or adjudication. In either case the verdict must be enforced by the League, and the refusal by any state to submit a dispute for arbitration or adjudication should be considered as an act of aggression calling for immediate action by the League.

The new League of Nations should give full attention to the problem of cultural *rapprochement* and collaboration among the nations. The League must stimulate moral disarmament and especially help to overcome the disastrous consequences of the totalitarian ideologies of cruelty, inhumanity, and race hatred, by which the younger generations have been poisoned.

*Europe must be organized in some form within the framework of the League of Nations.* Great Britain and also Russia, once she has been freed from totalitarian rule, will necessarily be included in the European grouping. Whether or not this will take the form of a "United States of Europe" is a question to be determined by the states immediately concerned, but it must be strong enough to deal effectively in the first instance with specifically European problems, and to insure the mutual collaboration which the common interests of the European peoples require.

*Participation of the United States is essential.* Just as the United States cannot be isolationist in war, it must not be so in peace. America must not repeat the error of 1919, which weakened the League of Nations from the start and thus contributed to its failure to preserve peace.

Twenty-five years ago, and again now, America's security has been threatened by events in Europe. In her own interest, the United States must collaborate with the other nations of the world to maintain peace.

The Pan American Union is desirable, but it can be no substitute for the participation of the American nations in the World League. The existence of a Pan American Union not connected with the League of Nations might easily lead to conflicts between the two.—*War Aims, Peace Terms, and the World After the War.* Rand School Press. New York. '41. p.7-9.

# ALTERNATIVE PLANS

## POWER IN INTERNATIONAL GOVERNMENT [1]

Among those fighting totalitarian aggression no dissenting voice can be heard as to the necessity for a new effort in the direction of international organization. Even among the Tory refugees, the conservative politicians in exile, no group or outstanding individual can be found advocating a return to the pre-1914 policies of alliance and power alignment. This is, however, about all on which agreement is general.

As soon as one proceeds from generalities to the concrete questions, the cleavage appears. There are those who still believe that a kind of League of Nations without any coercive attributes is about the best arrangement men can hope for. There are those who advocate an improved League, leaving, however, its essential characteristics untouched. This body of opinion has the most impressive rostrum of adherents and advocates; most of the former League officials belong to it and the great majority of the teachers of international law and international affairs at American universities. Moreover, there are theoretical regionalists or *de facto* regionalists, like the adherents of Federal Union. Most of the federalists are regionalists, but not all regionalists are federalists. There exists an infinite number of variations and combinations of opinion. A serious attempt must be made first to clarify fundamentals and then to find a common ground if possible. For we must realize that our speculations may have a considerable influence upon the concrete shape of the future international order, as similar speculations in the years 1916-17 had upon the shaping of the League of Nations Covenant.

An obstacle to the clarification of the fundamental questions is to be found in a false sentimentality for the League of Na-

[1] By Egon F. Ranshofen-Wertheimer, former member of the League of Nations Secretariat; Professor of International Affairs, American University. *Free World*. 3:78-82. June 1942.

tions.   Exaggerated importance is attached by some of the
most genuine adherents of a stable international order to the
legal survival of the League of Nations, to the continuity of
international organization.   We are told that so and so many
people are still employed by the League, that so and so many
countries retain their membership, that certain League services
are still functioning, certain studies still being continued.   No
possible objection could be taken to such statements were they
not accompanied by a kind of pathetic pride that the League
was still operative and its machinery ready for the major tasks
of international administration.

The League has failed, and it has not failed only because of
the ill will of the countries and the weakness and lack of
courage of the majority of the statesmen.   It has failed also
because of some constitutional defects inherent in the League
of Nations Covenant.   If we seriously wish to prepare the
ground for a workable international machine, we must get away
from the patterns of the recent past.   We must begin thinking
and arguing from scratch.

The Covenant is the typical product of Protestant Anglo-
Saxon psychology as applied to international affairs.   This has
more fatally determined the fate of the first great experiment
in international government than is usually recognized.   It has
decisively influenced the role assigned to power in the international organization of 1920 and with this the most important
single factor in the success of international government.   It
has sometimes been asserted that the League Covenant suffered
from an undervaluation of the power factor in international
affairs.   This is not quite correct.   The tragic defect lies not
in an underestimation of power as such, but in a pathetic belief
in the effectiveness of a certain type of power; not in a mis-
interpretation of the role of power used, but of the place to
which it should be strategically applied in international government.

The Covenant is based upon the axiomatic belief that moral
forces would prevail in any future international crisis.   It is
this overemphasis on the decisive character of moral sanctions
against technical organization of collective security which con-

stitutes the fatal weakness of the Geneva system. Those responsible for the drafting of the Covenant believed that aggression had been so utterly compromised by the World War 1914-18 that no country would possibly revert again to it in our era. If contrary to all rational probability, any country were to embark again upon a policy of aggression, public opinion would so violently react against the statesmen responsible for such policies that the intended aggression could not be consummated. If, nevertheless, a country were to revert to aggression, public opinion of all the other countries would automatically line up against the aggressor. There would inevitably be a common front of all peace loving humanity; the aggression would be overwhelmingly crushed. The whole group of articles of the Covenant, 10-16, dealing with this contingency, rests upon such hypotheses. It explains the comparatively slight importance which men like Wilson and Cecil (to take the two chief exponents of the psychology of Geneva) attributed to the question of sovereignty, to hard and fast advance rules governing the League in a crisis, to the automatism of sanctions. Since they believed in a common endeavor to crush the would-be aggressor, they saw no primordial necessity of any advance cession of sovereignty.

The Anglo-Saxon group of statesmen in Paris, having desperately fought for the creation of the League, having overcome seemingly insurmountable obstacles, naturally assumed that the people of the world would enthusiastically and gratefully hail the new peace machinery. They simply could not understand the lukewarm reception which the new creation encountered. They had believed that they were implementing the dreams of the anonymous millions in all the countries and they found France cynical, though appreciative; Italy friendly in a noncommittal way; most of the other Allies politely complimentary; but hardly anyone enthusiastic, with the sole exception, perhaps, of Czechoslovakia which considered itself dutybound to salute the League in gratitude to Wilson. Moreover, the statesmen resented the fact that the League was greeted with thinly veiled enmity on the part of the Germans, even by those passionately devoted to the idea of a future peaceful collaboration of the nations. They had naively assumed that Germany would consider the League as the chief extenuating factor of the peace settlement. A Gallup poll, undertaken in the first postwar years, would have shown a most puzzling indifference to the League.

What was the reason for such scepticism? It was by no means due to a dislike of international cooperation or to an unwillingness to participate in international government. It was due rather to the instinctive feeling that the League somehow would not work. The eudaemonism underlying the Covenant, its lack of clearcut prescriptions for action and for sanctions in case of noncooperation was contrary, not only to the instincts, but to all individual and collective experience of the European nations, and not the European nations alone. The psychology of the Covenant was alien and even puzzling to those who were to be the majority of its members. By its underlying confidence in moral sanctions it presupposed a public opinion active and decisive in international affairs. This hardly existed in England and was nonexistent in the majority of countries, including the European democracies. Even in an indisputably democratic country like France, public opinion in international affairs was far more a correlative of governmental action than in any Anglo-Saxon country. In the majority of countries, however, public opinion was directed from above to an extent that neither Cecil nor Wilson could possibly conceive, for their own political experiences at home afforded them no means whereby this could be gauged. For most nations the League was like a well-meant gift, the giver of which is convinced that it is ardently desired by the recipient, the latter unwilling and unable to show his disappointment to the influential donor.

The attitude, therefore, was one of wait-and-see. Success or failure would obviously depend upon the degree to which the two Anglo-Saxon world powers would identify their policies with the League. The early abstention of America was the first blow. It soon became evident that Great Britain was not prepared to direct or determine the actions of the League except in a negative sense. This passive attitude of expectation

on the part of the majority of the League members must by
no means be confounded with active antagonism. Most
countries, including the Germany of 1925-30 were resolved
to make the best of it. The League having been created,
no possible hope for a radical recasting could be entertained
as even minor amendments were practically excluded by a
cumbersome procedure of revision. All the good will existing,
therefore, was bound to flow in the direction of the new
agency. This potential good will was tremendous and it had
to find an outlet. No wonder that it crystallized around the
only body created for this special purpose. These were the
days when Geneva leaped into a bewildering variety of activities
in the political, social, economic, and health fields. Instead
of interpreting this as a proof of the existence of an accumula-
tion of good will, the League crusaders saw in it a proof of
the excellence of the League itself.

At least part of the peace failure of 1919-39 is attributable
to the League itself. I am taking as example the episode
gravest in consequences, the Ethiopian tragedy. Here was a
clear case of aggression, committed by a regime, a country as
nearly morally isolated as any can and ever will be. All,
or nearly all the prerequistites of successful action on behalf of
the League were assembled in rare completeness. The Covenant
contained in Article 16 stipulations for such a case. The
sanctions machinery actually was set into action. It failed.
Not because of the unwillingness of the British to apply oil
sanctions and the noncommittal attitude of America, not even
because of Laval's thinly veiled treachery, much as this had to
do with the final outcome. It failed chiefly because of the
inadequacy of the stipulations of the Covenant. In spite of
hesitations by London, Paris, and Washington, the smaller
countries, especially Italy's neighbors and satraps, overwhelmingly desired to stop Italy in Ethiopia. This was not
because of Ethiopia by any means. The country meant little
or nothing to most of the nations eager to thwart Italy. Its
territorial integrity was Hecuba to them. Its sovereignty did
not worry the man in the street in Bucharest, Madrid, Sofia,
and Belgrade. But there was a violent antagonism against the

Fascist spirit of aggression. What they feared was the possibility of successful aggression leading to an unwanted increase in the prestige and power of the aggressor. The whole
existence of these states was at stake if any aggression were
to be successful in Europe.

These countries were, therefore, ready for a collective action,
including if need be, military sanctions, but they were not prepared to take any individual responsibility. The Covenant,
unfortunately, left each country a free agent in its decision.
They simply could not afford to be individually responsible
to the aggressor; moreover, the necessity of individual decision
made them subject to blackmail, or opened up vistas of profits
from individual bargaining. A system of automatic collective
sanctions would have saved them all these troubles. They
would have been protected by their collectivity. They would
not have faced Rome; Rome would have faced the League.
The stipulations of the Covenant reflected the inability of
those responsible for its constitution to envisage in practical
terms the mechanism of international psychology in a critical
situation.

The above is based on the assumption that Italy would have
fought, even if the net of sanctions had been more closely woven.
In all probability this would not have been the case. Stipulations of automatic, progressively stringent sanctions would,
in practice, act in themselves as a formidable deterrent to aggression. The other alternative, that the powers would not
have declared Italy an aggressor if this committed them to
compulsory sanctions, would have been extremely regrettable,
but it would not have been half as disastrous as sanctions
which peter out. It would have implied the cynical abandonment of Ethiopia; it would have shown that the guarantee
of territorial integrity contained in Article 10 of the League
was highly problematic; but it would not have shaken to the
ground the whole concept of collective security.

Where, then, is a way out of the vicious circle constituted
by potential aggression, potential collective defense, and failure
of collective security? Certainly not in a mere revision of the
Covenant, consisting in the suppression of the unanimity rule,
in the creation of an international police force, in an amend-

ment of the revision clause embodied in the famous Article
19, in the compulsory intervention of a Court of International
Justice. Whatever improvement this may constitute, it would
not any more safeguard peace than did the old League. The
essential weakness, the placing of confidence in moral sanctions
when the functioning of public opinion remains uncertain,
would not be abolished. Such a League would still be an
attempt to compromise between "resistance and non-resistance."
The much-advocated plan of "putting teeth" into the League
would invite a new disaster. Force would still be placed in an
ex-centric position and not in the center of the future machinery,
and thus it would likely be wasted.

The way out is to recognize that international organization
must be transformed into international government. An international agency, in order to function in an emergency, must have
a power of its own, in advance delegated by the component
parts for this purpose and in itself sufficient to crush, if necessary, a maximum of ill will on the part of the greatest
number of its members. This can only be achieved if the
universal machine is split up in regional bodies. International
government can only succeed if its territorial range is limited
to such region or regions as can be effectively controlled by
the permanent power at its disposal. This is impossible in
a federation, if the whole military power is pooled and vested
in a central agency. Any agency whose states retain their
military sovereignty and their liberty of action, and only promise
*ad hoc* contingents is uncertain in its efficiency. The international agency's size must, therefore, be directly proportionate
to the number and size of the countries who are prepared
to invest it with full military power. It is, under present
circumstances, out of the question, that all the important states
of the globe would be prepared to make such sacrifice, even
if the United States should come out of the present conflict
sufficiently shaken to participate in such a body. But who
would be bold enough to assume that the U.S.S.R. would
forego its military autonomy in favor of a majority of capitalist
states? That the Latin American countries would voluntarily
bind themselves in such a manner? A universal agency cannot
at present be also a coercive body. World anarchy will

certainly not, in the political and diplomatic field, disappear tomorrow even if this war is fought and won on a planetary basis. The world is not ripe for planetary action in the political field.

What can be controlled are regions, sectors, continents, and territories bound together by some sort of geographical, economic, national, social, spiritual bonds. Europe is one of these regions. It is still the key to the pacification of the world. Europe, not Russia and not Asia, has twice plunged the world into world-wide conflicts within one generation. If Europe can be successfully pacified, one of the chief permanent sources of wars will automatically disappear.

The first question is, of course, why Europe should be considered a unity. It is neither so in an ethnological nor an economic sense. Moreover, it seems psychologically disunited beyond repair. Yet, in spite of the permanent divisions, Europe is essentially one, over and above its violent antagonisms. It is one in its outlook and what the Germans call "Lebensgefühl." There is a deep cleavage between the Germans and the majority of the other European nations, but this cleavage is offset by deeper spiritual common traits. If the end of the present conflict brings about the expected collapse of totalitarianism, the common denominator for all things European will reassert itself.

Unable to create a universal enforcement machine, the victors will be forced into organizing Europe as a unit, if for no other reason, in order to escape the necessity of occupying great parts of Europe for an indefinite period. There are a thousand reasons why the Europeans will never be able to undertake this for themselves. There are a thousand equally valid reasons to believe that, once this step has been enforced upon them, the inhabitants of Europe will do everything to make it work. It is the kind of step they want to have forced upon them from the outside, preferably by America.

Such a European federation, which is the only practical way to neutralize German aggressiveness and to divert the great German qualities to positive endeavors, would imply a central authority with military and economic power. Europe is not too large to make an effective control by its own forces impossible.

Once established, the common bonds will assert themselves so overwhelmingly that no power inside or outside will be in a position to destroy the new status. Into the creation of a European federation and perhaps of similar regional organizations in other parts of the world should go the major portion of the creative efforts aiming at pacification of the world.

A world organization will certainly be created after this war. It would, however, be dangerous to attempt, as far as political affairs are concerned, anything more ambitious than a purely consultative body. Such universal machinery will not be able to safeguard or guarantee peace. There must be no guarantees of territorial integrity; there must be no sanction paragraphs, as there will be no possibilities to enforce sanctions on a world plane; there must be no compulsory jurisdiction, as there would be no policeman to compel the execution. Never must there be again a steep, downward grade of the kind which led from the Manchurian aggression, to the Ethiopian debacle, and to the World War. There must never be belief in security where there is no security, paper guarantees where there are no ready sanctions, hope where all the odds are against its consummation. There is one mortal sin in international organization—the creation of a false sense of security. Better nothing than make-believe. The world will be in a better position to defend itself against dangers it knows, it expects, and it fears, than against the dangers of self-deception created by an agency based purely on moral sanctions. The world must never again tread on the thin ice of illusion.

## THE LEAGUE OF NATIONS [2]

Rejection of the League as a means of maintaining world order might rest on the arguments sketched below.

1. The League of Nations was an unrealistic conception in the first place, since it assumed a morality, an interest in

[2] By Arthur C. Millspaugh, Political Scientist; Member of Staff, Brookings Institution, 1929-1942. From his book *Peace Plans and American Choices*. p. 81-8. Brookings Institution. Washington, D.C. 1942. Dr. Millspaugh's affirmative summary is reprinted on p. 185-95.

peace, and an understanding of peace that governments did not have. It was the result of an abnormal situation and was accepted by the Paris Conference largely because of Woodrow Wilson's persistence and because of Clemenceau's hope that French security would be guaranteed by Great Britain and the United States.

The League, it is true, was misrepresented and undermined; it had hard luck, but it would have failed anyway. It went either too far or not far enough. No intermediate position can be taken between anarchy and government.

2. It is possible that after this war the League might be better understood and supported by public opinion; but no great change can be expected in feelings and attitudes unless or until a real change is made in world organization. So long as nations remain independent and sovereign, men will feel and function nationally, not internationally. To catch the imagination and win the loyalty of peoples, the League must be as revolutionary in constitution and in action as it was in theory. Unfortunately, some of the psychological factors may now be changing for the worse. In some quarters, the feeling of nationalism may be growing stronger. Why should the spirit of appeasement be any weaker? As a matter of fact, the League itself, instead of stimulating internationalism, accentuated nationalism (1) by continually emphasizing the independence and equality of nations, and (2) by making governments more "touchy."

3. Since the League's basic and determining principle was that each nation remained independent and sovereign, Geneva became merely a front for the old nationalistic power-system. The League functioned as a meeting of diplomats. Neither the Assembly nor the Council had any real authority or initiative. Decisions were made "backstage" by the old-fashioned process of bargaining. In the major and critical matters, action depended almost wholly on the position taken by the great powers. Accordingly, what went on in the League was not very different from what went on outside it. What the League accomplished could have been accomplished by ordinary diplomatic negotiations or conferences.

4. Since the League made no essential change in the international system, the natural tendency was for it to become a combination of members facing a hostile combination of nonmembers. Thus, the League became in the end nothing much but an association of peace-loving "have" nations, with practically all the warlike "have-not" nations on the outside. Under the circumstances, the association could have maintained peace only by recognizing the requirements of a balance-of-power system and developing aggressive policies in the interest of defense, that is, by becoming an armed alliance or federation with a single diplomatic and military command.

5. The League could not ensure peace because it left untouched the root-cause of war. For this reason, the new organization did not bring security; and without security nations would not disarm.

It was necessary for the success of the League that it should give security to both France and Germany. At the very beginning France proceeded to build up a system of alliances. It is true that she might not have done so if she had the guarantees of Britain and America provided in the unratified Tri-Partite Treaty; but that such a treaty appeared necessary proves the inadequacy of the League. In the Locarno Pact (1925) Great Britain and Italy joined in a four-power renunciation of war and in a guarantee of the Rhine Frontier. This treaty introduced a measure of security and stability in the relations of Germany and France; but the "spirit of Locarno" had little relation to the League Covenant, except to demonstrate the latter's futility.

Aside from French policy and general economic conditions, the most important factors in the security of Germany were general disarmament and peaceful change. Germany had been disarmed; but, since the League failed to provide security, Britain and France had not kept their implied promise to disarm.

The League left the solution of domestic problems to the individual states, disregarding the fact that most wars are caused by conditions or politics that can be construed as "domestic."

6. The League came near enough to universal membership to demonstrate that such a principle is unworkable in connection with the other principles on which the League was based. A unanimous agreement is often possible among a few powers. It becomes extremely difficult or impossible when the parties are numerous, are widely separated geographically, and possess divergent interests. In the settlement of European questions, Siam, Persia, or Haiti had the same voting power as Great Britain or France and in many important cases could veto a proposal approved by all the other nations. In practice, near-universality, along with unanimity, produced delay and paralysis.

The fact that modern wars tend to be world wars does not prove that all nations are equally involved in the causing of war or that a system of preventing war should be universal.

The Covenant contains a vague recognition of regionalism; but no machinery was set up to decentralize decisions or action, or could be set up without a radical alteration of the League. On the other hand, in its actual functioning the League tended to break up into regional blocs.

7. Much of the time and energy of those who gathered at Geneva went to the discussion of ways to strengthen the League; for neither its constitution nor its machinery was well adapted to the purpose of maintaining peace. The whole structure rested on a shifting contractual foundation. Some provisions of the Covenant were so vague as to have little specific meaning. Functions appeared only in a shadowy form. The major organs of the League had no life or power of their own. Certain serious deficiencies proved impossible to correct; for example, the failure to provide for compulsory arbitration, the lack of a definition of aggression, and the fact that war under certain circumstances was recognized as legal.

8. The League in Woodrow Wilson's mind was a democratic conception; but the men who represented their governments at Geneva were in most cases not popularly elected and could not speak for the groups whose pressures gave life and meaning to the domestic policies of the democracies. Since the League statesmen were not accountable to the people for their actions at

Geneva, it was not possible to subject the League to control by public opinion or to create the public opinion necessary for control.

9. Peaceful change is the function of legislation; but the League retarded, rather than promoted, peaceful change. The mandate system did provide for adjustments in a few backward areas; but, in general, the mutual guarantee of independence and territorial integrity and the exclusion of domestic affairs from the jurisdiction of the League tended to freeze the international situation as of 1919. Since the Covenant was chiefly concerned with preventing war, its purposes were to be achieved in the main by repression. A dynamic peace, on the contrary, implies a continuous process of liberation, of relieving tension and pressure by adjustments, in a manner similar to the legislative process in domestic affairs. Furthermore, the Covenant embodied an inadequate view of the meaning of international disputes. If no dispute is dealt with until it threatens war, the difficulty of settling it becomes well-nigh insurmountable. In international as in domestic affairs, differences must be removed or compromised in the early stages before they arouse emotions and become irreconcilable.

The setting up of a new system of negotiation at Geneva and a supposedly complete plan of international control made it more difficult to adapt procedures to special and limited situations.

The Covenant provided a means to revise treaties and to bring up for discussion any condition in the world that might lead to war. But how in an assembly of diplomats representing proud and sensitive sovereignties could such subjects be discussed?

10. Judicially, the system was inadequate. It is true that, in international as in domestic affairs, the most serious conflicts are political rather than legal, and they call for settlements by the political organ—the legislature. Nevertheless, it is possible for courts, in deciding disputes brought before them, to make adjustments in human relations and within limits to develop law. The establishment of the Permanent Court of International Justice was a real advance; but the Covenant did

not compel the submission of all disputes to arbitral or judicial settlement; and the Permanent Court of International Justice is not a court of equity and does not decide political questions. International law, therefore, is left in a static condition.

11. On its executive side, the deficiencies of the League were demonstrated by the failure of sanctions.

The major and critical aggressions were by Japan in Manchuria (1931), Italy in Ethiopia (1935), Germany in the Rhineland (1936), and Germany and Italy in Spain (1936-37). The failure of the League in these cases was good evidence of its impotence; and Hitler, Mussolini, and the Japanese warlords were accordingly encouraged to proceed with their plans for future and greater aggressions.

The failure of sanctions may be attributed in part to the prior failure of disarmament and perhaps also to the difficulty of defining aggression and recognizing the aggressor. But the real reason for the breakdown of the League's executive power lay in the fact that Britain and France, the nations that bore the primary responsibility, were acting as independent powers, independent of the League and independent of each other. They consulted their special and separate interests. They were not always in agreement. Each vacillated and procrastinated. They were told that sanctions meant war; and one or the other or both shrank from war. The League had no will of its own. For means of coercion it had to depend on the member states. It had no military or economic general staff and no plans. Sanctions have their inherent limitations and difficulties; but these were not the determining factors. The real trouble was the lack of will and singleness of purpose.

How can we say that the League "almost" succeeded? It is idle to speculate on "what might have been." As a matter of fact, before 1926, when the League is supposed to have been at the peak of its power, Poland had seized Vilna with impunity and Italy had bombarded Corfu.

12. The League might well be preserved, but not as an instrument for maintaining peace. Stripped of its political functions, the League can be put to good use as a reconstruction agency after this war, as an international research institution

and clearing-house, as an administrative organization, or as a means of economic and social cooperation. It must not be thought, however, that expanding or strengthening the League along these lines would materially improve its prospects or effectiveness in the field of policing. To keep order one must govern; and the League of Nations was not a government.

## UNITED NATIONS—PHRASE OR REALITY? [3]

Phrases gain reality through moral or legal acceptance by people or governments as a basis for future action, through clarification of their meanings in relation to actual situations, through organization and action in accord with these meanings, and through the functioning of institutions which they have initiated and continue to guide.

The United Nations is a reality in the first or subjective sense. It designates certain legal and moral commitments made by thirty-two nations. The declaration of January 1, 1942 is in the form of a treaty of alliance, and has been concluded under authority of the executives of the states as is customary of alliances. It also makes reference to certain general principles for which the nations are struggling, including the Atlantic Charter. Furthermore, the peoples of these nations have approved the phrase, United Nations, as indicating their desire to maintain the coalition to defeat their enemies and more vaguely to continue cooperation after the fighting is over.

The United Nations is becoming a reality in the second or intellectual sense. Through expositions by statesmen and writers, the words of the Atlantic Charter, the Four Freedoms, the United Nations Declaration, the lend-lease master agreements, and other commitments of all or some of the United Nations are acquiring concrete meanings.

In the third or volitional sense, the reality of the United Nations is less certain. There are bilateral, trilateral, and multilateral organizations among several of the United Nations,

[3] By Quincy Wright, Professor of International Law, University of Chicago; author of books and articles on international law and relations. *Annals of the American Academy.* 228:1-10. July 1943.

but there is no organization of the United Nations as a whole. It cannot be said that any action, military or political, has been in any genuine sense an action of the United Nations.

In the final sense, that of realization in the objective world of social behavior, the United Nations is not yet a reality. No permanent institution has been established which can be designated by this name.

It must be understood that these different phases of progress from phrase to reality cannot be sharply distinguished. Emotional faith may move by imperceptible degrees to intellectual comprehension, efficient action, and institutional functioning. If the peoples continue to have faith in the United Nations as the symbol of their hope for a better world after the war, that faith may move mountains of entrenched special interests and crystallized traditional ideas. The United Nations may emerge as a permanent institution.

Two factors in the contemporary world lend support to such a possibility. Certain entrenched special interests are not in reality mountains obstructing the path of the United Nations, but rivers which if utilized can carry it to the promised land of reality. Alexander Hamilton believed that projects of social and political organization might best be realized by linking them with special interests. He put the bond-holding class behind the United States by the Federal assumption of state debts. He put manufacturing interests behind the Federal Government by a mildly protective tariff. The pioneering interests were put behind the United States by the cession of western claims of the states to the Federal Government. It is true that the process of winning some of these interests to federalism alienated other interests favoring inflation, confiscation of British debts, and confiscation of western land titles. Perhaps in the long run, Jefferson's technique, which emphasized the general interest in equality of opportunity and increasing freedom for all, did more for the Federal Union than did the Hamiltonian appeal to special interests.

If the United Nations is to become a reality, special interests must not be permitted to frustrate the development of a world public opinion which associates peace, security, prosperity, and broader opportunities for mankind with the symbols of the United Nations. However, advocates of the United Nations need not overlook the possibilities which an effective world order has for serving not only the general interests of mankind and the national interests of governments and patriots in winning the war, but also certain special interests. Among these are the interest of manufacturers in expanding markets, the interest of farmers in higher general nutritional standards which will increase the demand for agricultural products, the interest of investors in more stable currencies and more secure opportunities for the profitable use of capital in backward areas, and the interest of men of adventurous spirit in organizing a world police and in pioneering in undeveloped areas. Interests as well as ideals can be marshaled behind the United Nations.

Many of the crystallized traditional ideas which have influenced world politics have become ill adapted to civilization with the progress of invention. It seems probable that the idea of a United Nations of the World is better adapted to the new conditions of technology and economy than is the idea of sovereign national states. As the United States was confronted by claims of states' rights, so the United Nations is confronted by claims of national sovereignty. States' rights began to become obsolete with the progress of canals and railways, with the development of the West and the growth of national parties, with the increase of population and of interstate trade, long before the Civil War. The latter event, however, indicates that crystallized ideas can offer substantial resistance to the conditions which doom them. In this case the resistance nearly destroyed the nation.

The ideal of national sovereignty, as expounded by patriotic nationalists and conservative jurists, is becoming obsolete under the impact of the airplane and the radio; but its power of resistance has been manifested in two world wars.

Gunpowder and the printing press destroyed the sovereignty of two thousand barons in fifteenth-, sixteenth-, and seventeenth-century Europe. They also destroyed the theory of a hierarchal order of Christendom. These inventions contributed to the establishment of a score of national states, with armies disciplined in firearms and with peoples conscious of the distinctiveness of their language, customs, and traditions.

The bombing airplane and the radio are manifesting an equally destructive influence on the claims of national states to absolute sovereignty. When one considers the general anxiety of the democracies to avoid war and to maintain policies of economic self-sufficiency during the 1930's, their present condition seems anything but a manifestation of sovereign free will. Absolute sovereignty in the present state of international contract has meant a condition of anarchy in which the freedom of all is frustrated.

As the eotechnic age ruined feudalism, so the neotechnic age is making national sovereignty a sham. In doing so, it has made a United Nations of the world possible, though it cannot guarantee that such an institution will be realized. Men and nations may satisfactorily adjust their ideas and institutions to new conditions, or they may not. If they fail, their civilization will collapse. The idea of the United Nations of the world seems better adapted to the conditions of economy, communication, and military technology in our world than is the traditional idea of national sovereignty. It is, perhaps, not an unreasonable expectation that men with the experience of this war behind them will accept the ideas which promise to be superior.

It would be interesting to trace the progress of the United Nations in world opinion. Gallup polls and other indices suggest that more people are for this symbol and the idea which it represents than against it. President Roosevelt, Vice President Wallace, Governor Stassen, Prime Minister Churchill, Foreign Secretary Eden, and Madame Chiang Kai-shek have recently won applause when they referred to it. Organizations such as the Commission to Study the Organization of Peace, the Citizens Committee for the United Nations, and the Office of War Information have been publicizing the idea and describing its potentialities.

It would also be interesting to elucidate the meaning of the documents stating the principles and policies of the United Nations. It is probably true that many of those who contribute to the favorable opinion towards the symbol do not comprehend its meaning and would object to many of its concrete implications. Efforts have been made to remedy this situation. Speeches, broadcasts, pamphlets, and books have been devoted to the task, and the United Nations is beginning to present a concrete meaning. The provisions of the Atlantic Charter, the Four Freedoms, the United Nations Declaration, the lend-lease master agreements, and the official comments of statesmen upon them outline a new social, political, economic, and legal ordering of the world.

From the social point of view, the Atlantic Charter emphasizes improved labor standards, social security, peace, and the Four Freedoms as desirable goals. Ideals of liberalism, humanism, toleration, and social justice which have spread throughout the world since the Renaissance are accepted as the standards of world civilization.

These ideals are in marked contrast to the ideals of racial superiority, national dominance, ideological intolerance, and military virtue espoused by the Axis powers. The "savage and brutal forces seeking to subjugate the world," says the United Nations Declaration, must be defeated if "life, liberty, independence and religious freedom" are to be defended and "human rights and justice" are to be preserved in their own and other lands.

The social goals appear to be the object of all the other pledges of the charter. Political, economic, and legal reforms of the world order are insisted upon because they are believed to further the social aims. The other pledges should therefore be interpreted in the spirit of these social objectives.

Politically, the United Nations contemplate the end of political aggrandizement and of power politics. They foresee self-governing national states within "a wider and permanent system of general security."

Certain doubts concerning the applicability of these principles in the Orient arose from the term "Atlantic Charter" and from Prime Minister Churchill's statement of September 9, 1941, declaring that this document "does not qualify in any way the various statements of policy which have been made from time to time about development of constitutional government in India,

Burma or other parts of the British Empire." It is now clear, however, that these principles are intended to apply universally. India, China, the Philippines, and Iraq are among the United Nations pledged to the Atlantic Charter. President Roosevelt said on February 23, 1942, "The Atlantic Charter applies not only to the parts of the world that border the Atlantic but to the whole world." Great Britain has pledged itself to extend Dominion status to India after the war and has recognized the restoration of Ethiopia. The independence of Syria and the Lebanon has been recognized by Free France and Great Britain. Extraterritorialty has been abolished in China.

The implications of these pledges for colonial areas have been discussed but no detailed agreement has been reached. On May 30, 1942, Under Secretary of State Sumner Welles said:

> If this war is in fact a war for the liberation of peoples it must assure the sovereign equality of peoples throughout the world, as well as in the world of the Americas. Our victory must bring in its train the liberation of all peoples. Discrimination between peoples because of their race, creed or color must be abolished. The age of imperialism is ended. The right of a people to their freedom must be recognized as the civilized world long since recognized the right of an individual to his personal freedom. The principles of the Atlantic Charter must be guaranteed to the world as a whole—in all oceans and in all continents.

Power politics is not explicitly mentioned in the Atlantic Charter, but its eventual elimination is implied by the expression of belief "that all of the nations of the world for realistic as well as spiritual reasons must come to the abandonment of the use of force."

A balance of military power has been the principal factor in preserving the independence of states in the modern state system established in the sixteenth century. This system has rested on the assumption that sovereign states were primarily motivated by the desires for security and for predominance. If any state with the latter motivation sought to subordinate its neighbor, the others, acting for their own security, would combine to thwart it by diplomacy if possible, by force if necessary. In a world where periodic efforts at conquest by aggressive states was to be expected, the willingness of all states to use force in self-defense and to preserve the balance of power was therefore the essential basis of such stability as existed. If under such conditions important states abandoned the use of force, there would be a grave danger that the aggressively minded would be able to augment their power by destroying others one at a time until the balance of power could no longer be restored, and the entire world could be subordinated by one state, as was the Mediterranean world by Rome in antiquity.

Since there can be no assurance that every state will forever renounce the will to dominate, the abandonment of force by states is not compatible with the continuance of a system of many nations in close contact with one another unless all have subordinated themselves to a constitution which provides a power able to prevent nullification of the constitution by any of them. It must therefore be assumed that in looking forward to "the abandonment of the use of force" by all the nations, the United Nations contemplate the substitution of such a constitution for the system of balance of power.

It has long been recognized by philosophers and religious leaders that war tends to corrode many of the finer aspects of human personality and of civilization. But it has also been recognized that under a balance-of-power system occasional war to stop aggression has been the price of national independence. The Atlantic Charter, however, declares that today the use of force must be abandoned "for realistic as well as spiritual reasons." This seems to recognize that the balance of power can no longer yield real security.

The Atlantic Charter does not emphasize national self-determination, but it asserts "the right of all peoples to choose the form of government under which they will live," the "restoration" of "sovereign rights and self-government" to those "who have been forcibly deprived of them," and a "peace which will afford to all nations the means of dwelling in safety within their own boundaries." The pledges for abandonment of aggrandizement already referred to also imply a further development of the autonomy of nations now under imperial rule.

While the words "sovereign rights" and "self-government" are used, it is clear that they are not to be taken in an absolute sense. The recognition of certain human rights and of a "permanent system of general security" in other paragraphs of the charter makes it clear that sovereignty is to be limited by an effective law. Peoples are to have freedom for national self-expression and development, but not for persecution of their populations and aggression against their neighbors.

What is to be the nature of the wider and "permanent system of general security"? The Atlantic Charter does not say in detail, though it implies that it must be sufficiently powerful and reliable to warrant nations in abandoning the use of force and disarming, and also that it must have such a relation to the individual that he can be assured certain basic human rights, even when they are threatened by his own state.

Economically, the United Nations contemplate access by all states on equal terms to the trade and raw materials of the world, collaboration of all nations for economic advancement, and a peace assuring freedom from want and freedom to traverse the seas.

The fourth paragraph of the Atlantic Charter looks toward reduced barriers to trade and toward economies devoted to the increase of prosperity rather than to the increase of political or military power, but it is full of qualifications.

"Access on equal terms" does not necessarily mean freedom of trade. It may mean only that each state must not discriminate among other states in its commercial regulations. On the other hand, taken literally it might mean that each state, having within its borders some of the trade and raw materials of the world, must give the peoples of other states access to these advantages on terms equal to those enjoyed by its own people. The fact that equality is offered to "states," not to individuals, suggests the former interpretation. This interpretation would permit a nation to governmentalize its external trade, thus making the trading units not individual firms, but states themselves.

The expression "equal terms" clearly cannot be taken in an absolute sense. It does not forbid reasonable classifications. The notion of a "permanent system of general security" suggests that aggressors may be subjected to commercial discriminations and other economic sanctions.

The United Nations recognize that in their endeavors to equalize access to trade and raw materials they should have "due respect for their existing obligations." The network of preferential treaties is such that this qualification could be applied to destroy much of the equality of economic opportunity provided.

There are regrettable possibilities of interpreting all meaning out of Article 4 of the charter. Fortunately the article has been elaborated in the master agreements made by the United States with the countries to which lend-lease aid is being given. These look toward "the elimination of all forms of discriminatory treatment in international commerce and to the reduction of tariffs and other trade barriers."

It is important that public opinion insist upon realization of the spirit of these pledges. That spirit prohibits trade discriminations against any people because it is politically weak or because it is politically disliked or because it is an economic competitor. That spirit demands that all states not guilty of aggression have reasonable access to both raw materials and markets throughout the world. The restoration of economies aimed at prosperity rather than at power requires no less. Only an application of the Atlantic Charter in this spirit will prevent a distinction from arising between "have" and "have-not" powers. This distinction, inevitably hostile both to general prosperity and to general peace, was little heard of during the relatively free conditions of trade in the nineteenth century. It is a consequence of the compartmentalizing of the world by trade barriers.

The pledge for collaboration among all nations in the economic field suggests that the purposes stated cannot be achieved by one nation alone. "Improved labor standards, economic advancement and social security" can be achieved only by international collaboration. This proposition appears to accept the classical economic doctrine that trade beneficial to one state tends to benefit the others, and to repudiate the mercantile theory that one nation's economic gain is necessarily another's economic loss.

The use of the word "collaboration," however, suggests international planning rather than freedom of international trade regulated only by the market. During the depression of the

1930's it was often suggested that nations might meet economic problems by national planning or by international planning. The former, generally resorted to at that time, led to efforts at national economic self-sufficiency and further economic and political tensions. This paragraph of the Atlantic Charter implies that the objectives set forth can be achieved only by international collaboration on many matters. The same conclusion can be drawn from the commitments of the lend-lease master agreements. They provide for collaboration by "all countries of like mind, directed to the expansion, by appropriate international and domestic measures, of production, employment, and the exchange and consumption of goods, which are the material foundations of the liberty and welfare of all peoples."

While these commitments unequivocally support economic internationalism, they leave it open whether, in a given instance, international action should plan production and consumption directly, or should merely define conditions under which free enterprise can proceed. Socialistic, free, and mixed economies are all open to the United Nations. Their present commitments leave it to the economists to decide what form of international collaboration, whether more control or more free enterprise, will in different areas best achieve the aims desired.

Freedom from want has been one of the most discussed paragraphs of the Atlantic Charter and of the Four Freedoms. President Roosevelt (January 7, 1943), Prime Minister Churchill (March 21, 1943), Vice President Wallace (May 8, 1943), and Foreign Secretary Anthony Eden (May 29, 1941) have dealt with it in general, while Sir William Beveridge and the National Resources Planning Board have attempted to show in detail how it can be realized in Great Britain and the United States respectively. All agree that while modern technology makes possible an economy of abundance, the tasks of avoiding violent economic fluctuations and assuring equity in distribution are enormous. Clearly, this, like other pledges, implies that the nations must devote their economies to human welfare rather than to political power. They must maintain national and international organizations to assure minimum living standards. Only with a peace assured by a proper political organization of the world can the efforts to free all men from want be really begun.

Freedom of the seas was among the earliest demands of those who initiated the spirit of liberty after the Middle Ages. It meant first the recognition that the high seas beyond moderate territorial waters were a great common insusceptible of appropriation by any state. It meant also common effort to free the seas of pirates. More recently it has referred to trading rights in time of war. Experience has amply demonstrated that in modern war belligerents will not respect any "rights" of trade directly or indirectly benefiting the enemy. The Atlantic Charter properly recognizes that freedom to traverse the seas can exist only with "peace." The article does not refer specifically to limitations of freedom of the seas which might be imposed by the world community as a sanction against aggression. This qualification, explicitly stated in the third of President Wilson's Fourteen Points, may be implied from the charter's assumption that "a permanent system of general security" will be established.

The Atlantic Charter does not mention freedom of the air, but such freedom was extended with certain qualifications among the parties to the Paris, Madrid, and Habana air navigation conventions of the 1920's. Freedom of the air for the commercial navigation of peaceful states accords with the spirit of the Atlantic Charter far more than do the proposals recently made for the use of national sovereignty to gain national predominance in aerial navigation.

The United Nations have by implication committed themselves to the modification of international law so as to protect certain universal human rights, to prevent aggression and other crimes against the world community, to subject states to peaceful procedures for settling international disputes, and to permit modifications of international law without unanimous consent.

The preservation of "human rights" is referred to as a war aim in the United Nations Declaration. The Atlantic Charter and the Four Freedoms include commitments to the following human rights: freedom of speech and expression; freedom of religion and worship; freedom to travel on the high seas; freedom to trade; freedom to exercise influence against transfers of the territory on which one lives; freedom to influence the form of government to which one is subject; freedom from fear, including freedom from invasion, from excessive armament burdens, and from tyrannical government; and freedom from want, involving improved labor standards, economic advancement, and social security. The latter freedoms were particularly emphasized in the list of human rights proposed by the National Resources Planning Board in 1942.

While the first two of the freedoms mentioned are not explicitly stated in the Atlantic Charter, they were included in President Roosevelt's speech of January 6, 1941, setting forth the Four Freedoms. Both President Roosevelt (August 21, 1941) and Foreign Secretary Eden (May 29, 1941) have assumed that these freedoms are included among the war aims for which the United Nations are striving. Such an assumption may be implied from Premier Stalin's statement on October 7, 1942, recognizing "the restoration of democratic liberties" as a war aim.

The commitments of the United Nations suggest that international law must also be developed so as to define aggression and other international crimes, whether committed by governments or by individuals, and to provide procedures for their suppression. The problem of punishing "war criminals" has been discussed and declarations have been made by several of the United Nations, but there appears to have been no agreement upon the legal theory or the tribunal to be utilized. The Atlantic Charter also suggests a development of international procedures for settling all international disputes peacefully and for adapting the law to changing conditions. The "wider and permanent system of general security" which is contemplated seems to imply that in international relations each state should no longer be competent to judge its own case and to enforce its own decisions. Nor should each state be entitled to exercise a *liberum veto* over changes in the law demanded by a consensus of world opinion.

Social, political, economic, and legal changes are suggested by the pledges of the United Nations, but they are not specified in detail. Furthermore, no machinery exists for working out the details.

The United Nations as a whole remains unorganized. We cannot here examine the organizations which some of the United Nations have developed for dealing with problems of strategy and supply, such as the Combined Chiefs of Staff in Washington, the Pacific War Council, and the various commodity and shipping boards and committees. These organizations are soon to be supplemented by United Nations conferences on food, relief, and economic problems. By improving their organization, the United Nations can win the war more rapidly and less expensively.

Important as is more intensive organization of the United Nations during the war, such organization will be even more important during the transitional period. Activities during that period will determine whether or not the United Nations is to become a permanent reality. The tasks of the transitional period are dynamic. With the solution of immediate problems of restoring order must go a development of military occupation into permanent peace. The nature and the duration of each of the stages in the progressive realization of the conditions permitting the withdrawal of military occupations must be foreseen in broad outline. Planning for these tasks of the transitional period must be undertaken by the United Nations while the war is in progress. Many of these nations are now planning individually and training personnel for such activities. The schools at Charlottesville and Columbia University and the Lehman commission are cases in point. The danger of duplication, rivalry, and misunderstanding will, however, be great unless these plans are coordinated by the United Nations as a whole before the time of execution begins. In some areas responsibility for administration may well be assumed by a particular nation; in others, by a regional organization of the United Nations; and in others, by the United Nations as a whole. If such allocations of authority over a territory are given to single states, they will be difficult to change. They must be made with care after due consideration of the principles to which the United Nations are committed and with authority of the United Nations as a whole.

What would be the nature of the institution in which the United Nations might be permanently and objectively realized? It appears to be the function of the United Nations to give the universal community of nations, known to international lawyers since the time of Suárez and Grotius, a more perfect organization. Its aim is not to be realized by a limited association or a contractual league to which states are admitted and from which they may resign. The community of nations, if it is to preserve peace, must be, as the Supreme Court said of the United States, a "permanent union of permanent states." The states must automatically become members when they are recognized as states, and they must continue to be members as long as they exist as states. Governments in revolt must be temporarily denied the privileges of the community, but the states must remain members entitled to continue cooperation when they have reestablished governments ready to observe the fundamental law.

A world community has existed, but it has been organized only through the highly decentralized diplomatic and consular systems and various contractual unions, leagues, and associations. Major improvements in organization are required. These include a police authority to prevent aggression, a legislative authority to prevent excessive barriers to trade, and investigatory, advisory, and judicial authorities to assure the protection of fundamental human rights.

The question has been raised whether the war is conservative or revolutionary. The answer must be that it is both. The United Nations are struggling to conserve principles of democracy and of liberty for which the leaders of civilization have stood since the Renaissance and to which governments have increasingly committed themselves since the British revolution of the seventeenth century, the American and French revolutions of the eighteenth century, and the Russian and Chinese revolutions of the twentieth century.

The United Nations believe that the declarations of individual and social rights figuring in the constitutions of nearly every state of the world, including those of Germany, the Soviet Union, and Japan, indicate a fundamental acceptance by world public opinion of these principles. They look upon the repudiation of these principles by a few governments and the failure properly to implement them by others as faults of evil intention or of negligence contrary to the general will of mankind. They consequently believe that they are entitled to assume leadership and authority in establishing a world political order which will conserve these precious heritages of mankind.

The United Nations realize, however, that in our shrinking and interdependent world these principles cannot be conserved unless the system of power politics and certain assumptions of international law upon which that system rests are radically changed. The concepts of nationality and sovereignty have been pushed to extremes which threaten the values they were designed to protect. The Nazis, the Fascists, and the Japanese militarists, in their exaggerated interpretations of these ideas and their assertions of rights of conquest and oppression, are in revolt against the world community established by international law and developed in the principles of the League of Nations Covenant, the Statute of the Permanent Court of International Justice, the Constitution of the International Labor Organization, the Pact of Paris, and the Atlantic Charter.

The United Nations are, therefore, engaged in the dual task of suppressing this revolt and of improving the constitution of the world community so that it can better conserve the principles of liberal civilization. This campaign of world proportions is conservative in that it rests upon principles as old as the Magna Charta, the Mayflower Compact, the Bill of Rights, the Declaration of Independence, and the Declaration of the Rights of Man and Citizen; but it is revolutionary in that it realizes the need of important innovations in the organization of the world community if these ancient principles, now embodied in the Atlantic Charter, are to be realized in the modern, shrinking, interdependent, and dynamic world.

## THE STATUS OF THE UNION: INTERNATIONAL OR SUPRA-NATIONAL? [4]

The League is discredited. Therefore, when it is revived in a new form, it would be a psychologic mistake to retain the name of the discredited institution. The new start should be made under a new name.

[4] By Edward J. Byng, author of *Of the Meek and the Mighty;* Member, U.S. Delegation, International Press Conference, Geneva, 1926, 1927. *Five-Year Peace Plan.* p. 150-3. Coward-McCann. New York. 1943.

President Roosevelt has coined the highly expressive and symbolic term, "United Nations," to describe the community of nations fighting for liberty, democracy, and progress. But that fight will continue after its military phase is over. And if the Axis countries become sincerely and truly democratic after their present regimes have been liquidated, they should be proud to be received in the fold of the United Nations.

For both these reasons, I suggest that the joint, permanent postwar organization of the United Nations for the preservation of peace be known as the Union of Nations. (In French: *Union des Nations.* In German: *Völkerverein.*)

The well-known reasons why the League failed are:

1. The League was strictly *inter*-national, i.e., it had no actual *supra*-national authority.

2. A provision in the League Covenant prescribed unanimity for the decisions of the League Council. This was a standing invitation to sabotage of every important decision by any one of the nations represented on the council.

3. The delegates to the League assemblies, the members of the League Council, and, actually, though not officially, even the more important employees of the League Secretariat, *were expected to act primarily as the representatives of their respective countries.* This meant of necessity that the interests of their countries were expected to transcend all considerations of justice and fair play whenever there was a conflict between the two.

Almost always there was a conflict between the two.

If the new permanent democratic organization for the preservation of peace, to which I will henceforth refer as the *Union of Nations*, is given *unrestricted supra-national* authority, many countries, especially the big ones, will probably defy its authority and thereby render its machinery ineffective.

On the other hand, if the Union of Nations is merely *international* in character, with no authority over individual nations, its machinery will be just as ineffective as was the League's.

Well then, how is the problem to be solved?

*The Union of Nations must have supra-national authority. Its status must transcend the national sovereignty of its members. At the same time, however, the supra-national authority, the supra-sovereignty of the Union must not be of a general, sweeping nature but must be positively restricted to clearly defined specific fields.*

These fields are political, economic, and spiritual in character. They derive directly from the political, economic, and spiritual aspects of the postwar era. They are clearly indicated in the previous chapters devoted to these three aspects of the Five-Year Peace Plan.

Subsequent extension of the Union's supra-national authority to other fields must then be left to human wisdom, "if any." A big tree grows gradually round a healthy core. And in the last analysis, human institutions have just as much or just as little prestige and authority as have the men who run them.

What poisons relations between nations as between individuals is fear. This truth is the key to the understanding of world affairs.

Fear breeds suspicion. Suspicion breeds hate. Hate breeds war.

Conversely, absence of fear creates confidence. Like fear, confidence also can become a habit. But great historical institutions grow and are shaped primarily by habit.

Of course we must police the postwar world. Of course the Union must have "teeth." But if it is run with impartiality and wisdom, it will probably never have to bare them. Let the men who run the institution create the habit of trusting the Union of Nations. Then, as world-wide confidence in the Union's integrity grows, it will become possible to extend its supra-national authority by stages to more and more new fields.

In my opinion "Union of Nations" is a much more suitable name for the permanent postwar institution for the preservation of peace than "United Nations Council" or "Council of the United Nations." In the first place, as I have said, "Union of Nations" is a logical derivative of the term "United Nations." It clearly conveys the idea that the institution is the continuation in permanent form of the wartime association of peoples known as the United Nations. In addition, I believe that the word "Union" carries more weight than "Council" because it implies an association of states with supra-national authority over the individual states of which it is made up. For example, the United States are often referred to as the "Union," as in the Presidential reports "on the state of the Union." The federation of Russian Socialist Soviet Republics is known as the Soviet Union. Let us recall that the Union of Nations, as described in these pages, would have supra-national authority over its members, although that authority would be restricted to special fields.

The term "United Nations Council" automatically conjures up the picture of an association of states merely *inter*-national in character, with no authority over its members. In other words, "council" smacks of the spirit of the defunct League of Nations.

## THE FUNCTIONING OF THE UNITED NATIONS SYSTEM [5]

The fact that the United Nations now function primarily as a war machine has a certain number of consequences both restrictive and creative which must be clearly understood.

I. Those limiting the Allied effort in organization are the following:

A. The legal basis of the present collaboration among the United Nations is as simple as possible. They are bound together by the Declaration of January 1, 1942, which constitutes their only charter. The Declaration pledges all of them to a common ideal as expressed in the Eight Points of the Atlantic Charter. But, the Declaration by United Nations is essentially a pledge of full cooperation against the enemies and a promise not to make a separate armistice or peace with them.

There are no detailed conditions for admission stipulated in the Declaration. The final phrase runs, "the foregoing Declaration may be adhered to by other nations which are or may be rendering material assistance or contributions in the struggle for victory over Hitlerism." At first sight, it would seem that even a nation merely having severed diplomatic relations with any of the Axis Powers could, therefore, ask to join the coalition. Such,

[5] By Henri Bonnet, Director International Institute for Intellectual Cooperation. From his pamphlet "Outlines of the Future." p. 19-26. World Citizens Association. Chicago. 1943.

however, is not the case. Each signatory government is pledged to "employ its full resources military or economic" against one or all of the Axis powers, and that pledge eventually and inevitably means war.

The thirty-two United Nations are those at war. Any additional country which formally declares war against one of the members of the Tripartite Pact can automatically become a member of the Association if it signs the Declaration. Iraq, Abyssinia and Bolivia recently did so as soon as they became belligerents. There is no other condition for admission; there is no vote taken on admission by the other United Nations.

There was even a question for some months as to whether or not some of the Allies would not remain outside the group of the United Nations. Brazil, which declared war against Germany and Italy on August 22, 1942 did not immediately sign the Declaration. It was rumored at that time that its government did not wish to join an organization of which Soviet Russia was a member. Such a refusal to join, if actually caused by such a reason, could have endangered the frail legal structure of the whole body. Russia, however, has been as emphatic as any of her associates in declaring her adherence to the principles of the Atlantic Charter and her devotion to the high ideals of the United Nations. That particular threat of possible discord and abstention, moreover, was dispelled on February 6, 1943, when, after the visit of President Roosevelt on his way back from Casablanca, Brazil became officially a member of the United Nations. They now include all nations which are at war on the side of the Allies. There could not be a stronger bond. It is so strong, in fact, that legal ties for the purpose of strengthening the United Nations solidarity can, at first sight, be omitted.

B. The very simplicity of this legal structure has resulted in the lack of legal procedures for the regular functioning of the United Nations. There was no provision made for periodical meetings of United Nations representatives at the time of the signing of the Declaration. The initiative in such a matter would have to be taken by some one of them, very likely the United States Government—as Depositary for the Declaration. In such a case, the Depositary Government will probably seek previous agreement with Great Britain, Russia and China. The agenda would have to be established after negotiations by officials of the government which takes the initiative in calling the gathering together.

There is no secretariat of the United Nations. There are no councils or committees entitled to act in the name of all of them, even for simple matters or in an advisory capacity.

C. The principal machineries of the United Nations are controlled by those countries which have been able to meet the common needs, notably in matters of production.

The most outstanding of such bodies are the Combined Chiefs of Staff in Washington which plans the strategy for the United States and Great Britain, and the five Combined Boards which, under the Chiefs of Staff, deal with all the questions of raw materials, food, industrial production, assignments of ammunition and weapons, and adjust the available shipping to the requirements of the various Allied countries and different theaters of war. Other combined committees of less importance have recently been created to deal with questions of limited scope, such as ensuring supplies to North Africa, or with problems which are not urgent, for example, a combined committee for export trade.

All of these bodies, as is quite well known, are British-American. They must consider the needs of the other United Nations as well, and must work in the interest of all of them. But the contacts between the combined centers in Washington and the rest of the United Nations have been maintained partly through negotiations with other allied countries in London or in Washington, and partly through exchanging permanent or temporary technical missions between various capitals. That may work as a war system and an efficient one indeed, but must also be considered as of a provisional character.

II. In spite of such limitations, there are also constructive forces at work within the United Nations system:

A. Such combined collaboration as that represented by the bodies established in Washington and London has begun to spread all over the world. In fact, the needs resulting from the vast extent of the war have led to consideration of regional demands.

The need for such arrangements in the military field is obvious and, from the beginning, regional commands were created to meet it. But production and organized administration are also vitally important in the present war. No system of military command can be separated from the civilian effort supporting it. Organizations which deal with such matters on the various battle fronts are indispensable to the united effort and will continue to be so in greater degree. Important combined centers have already been established in the Middle East at Cairo, and in North Africa. There is other regional collaboration in the field of production such as the Allied Supply Council functioning in Australia in conjunction with the United States, and the Eastern Group Supply Council created by the British following the Economic Conference which met at New Delhi in October 1940. Such cooperation among several United Nations in given areas will gradually extend to the liberated lands during the war itself.

B. The needs and forces which have led to the establishment of an already intricate network of collaboration continue to make their pressure felt. They will necessitate constant additions of new parts in the existing machinery. Certain problems could have been avoided some months ago, but an increasing number will surely have to be faced and settled as the ring tightens around the Axis forces and the end of war draws near. Striking examples of such a process are now taking shape. There are, for instance, the negotiations for creating a United Nations Relief Agency; the convoking of a Food and Agriculture Conference by the United States; the negotiations between the American and British Treasuries on future steps necessary to stabilize currencies and to devise some sort of organization capable of dealing with the various aspects of these technical and political problems; the arrangements which have been concluded between wheat-producing countries; tomorrow perhaps, negotiations will start that will result in necessary agreements concerning civilian aviation after the war. The solution of many other questions waiting to be settled must come about before the end of the war if there is to be a real peace.

C. Development of the war also makes necessary various decisions of an entirely new character. Some of the difficulties which will have to be understood and controlled were shown in the North African experience. They are of a political nature. All the United Nations will have to see that the seeds of dissension planted by Naziism and Fascism will have to be torn from the earth's soil if the benefits gained from the struggle against international tyranny are to be fully enjoyed and of lasting endurance.

"It is one of our aims as expressed in the Atlantic Charter," said President Roosevelt in his radio address of February 12, 1943, speaking of North Africa and the future of France, "that the conquered peoples of today will again be the masters of their destiny." That will mean the adoption of a well and clearly defined policy to be applied in connection with the liberated countries. The military authorities of occupation must be protected against improvization. Methods and procedures must be defined in advance so as to allow the people who have been freed from tyranny to restore the legislation they want and to establish provisional—and as soon as possible definite—governments deriving their authority from popular will.

Many other political problems will become urgent and will require preparations, as the end of the war approaches.

D. Even though certain of the bodies and procedures set up for war purposes alone will vanish, it is evident that the need which forced many of those new steps will be of a lasting nature. The facilities which now exist for coping with such permanent needs should render increasing services and should be retained for that purpose after the war.

It would be a great and mistaken illusion to believe that, this time, there will be a clear-cut line of demarcation between war and peace—that on one day all the effects of war will vanish and a liberated and joyful world will proceed triumphantly towards a new destiny. That was supposed to be the glorious outlook for the League of Nations in 1919. That organization was thrust into a position where it had to start building everything—to construct something strong and permanent on shifting, and sometimes, treacherous soil. It struggled hard and successfully for years, in order to fulfill its tremendous duty, to develop by means of persuasion and negotiation the necessary power for such a great task. The history of the League, and the mistakes committed by the nations in the League, must not be repeated. Whatever has so far been used to save the world from the most deadly perils it has faced in modern times, and which can be turned to good purpose for the future, must be kept to form the solid foundations of a world community.

## FEDERALISM [6]

Support for a federation of world states grows out of the belief on the part of many students of international affairs that a *confederation,* like the League of Nations, cannot assure permanent peace. A confederation is a league of sovereign states each of which retains final independence of action. The central authority has no financial independence, no independent military power, no control over individual persons within the national states, and consequently no adequate means, they say, of curtailing international anarchy.

A *federation,* on the other hand, is a system of government in which a central authority prevails in matters of interest to all, while the local authorities have control over matters only of local interest. For example, under the American federal system we have a central government chosen by and responsible to the people of the entire nation, financially independent of any of the states, with a monopoly of military power, and with complete control over interstate affairs. Each state may make any laws it likes, institute any reforms it wishes, so long as it does not exercise powers of an interstate nature or interfere with the rights of other states or act against the common good.

The plan for federation most widely discussed is the one offered by Clarence Streit. His ultimate idea is a federation of all democratic nations. The governmental structure of this federation is to be like that of the United States. The federal legislature is to consist of two popularly elected houses similar to the American Congress. The number of representatives in

[6] From pamphlet "Toward Greater Freedom; Problems of War and Peace." p. 45-8. Commission to Study the Organization of Peace. New York. August 1943.

one house is to be based entirely on population.  The second house will allow smaller states almost as much representation as the larger ones.  The executive department is to consist of a five-man board, three chosen directly by the people of the union and the other two by the federal legislature.  The board shall name one of its members as premier and he, together with a cabinet of his own choosing, shall do the executive work.  The premier and cabinet shall be responsible to the legislature.  The judicial department of the new union is to be modeled after the American Supreme Court and have similar powers.

This central government of the federation is to have control over currency, tariffs, immigration and settlement of international disputes.  The constitution of the proposed federation is to include a bill of rights guaranteeing the basic freedoms to all citizens.

Since the entire plan is based on the popular will, there is no place in it for totalitarian states.  To permit totalitarian nations to join the federation would mean that citizens in these nations would be playing a part in guiding the destinies of the international government while they would have no power over their own national governments, an obviously dangerous situation.  After the war the plan is that the victorious democracies will begin a campaign of education in countries where democracy has never really taken root, to prepare these peoples for self-government and eventual admission into the union.

Of the many questions that present themselves in considering this plan, two are outstanding.  What place shall be made for colonies?  You will remember that the same question was raised with reference to the western territories of some of the thirteen states that organized our own federal union.  The problem was solved by the decision to cede all these territories to the federal union.  It is proposed that the identical procedure be followed here.  All participating nations shall hand over their colonies to the federation.  Just as our own United States eventually admitted these outlying territories into the union, so shall these colonies be trained in the art of self-government, and, when ready, be accepted as equals in the federal union.

Secondly, can the great masses of India and China be prepared within a reasonable time to take that position in the new federation to which their vast numbers and their war sacrifices entitle them? Obviously no genuine world federation whose ideals are justice and equality can exist without China and India. To keep them out would mean perpetuating the Nazi idea of different grades of citizens. People who favor the union idea feel that both China and India have already made giant strides along democratic lines. Furthermore, they point to the transformation brought about in Russia in less than a generation as proof that the task of preparing China and India for membership can be accomplished within a reasonable time.

Since the outbreak of the war, the original plan is altered. Instead of an immediate union of all democracies, the suggestion now is union of the United States and "peoples with whom we have compelling natural ties." A democratic federal union of all nations is still the ideal.

Those who favor a world federation of nations point to the economic advantages which would result. They claim that the removal of trade barriers, the cheapening and speeding up of communication and transportation, the maintenance of a common stable currency and a raised standard of living throughout the world would open boundless opportunities for trade and work. Such was the case when internal tariffs were removed in France at the time of the French Revolution. In the United States those who support union compare the difficulties of trade under the Articles of Confederation, which permitted interstate trade barriers, to the limitless economic opportunities when a new federal union wiped out these barriers.

Of course, many practical difficulties present themselves. Those who propose this idea point out, however, that the American federal union was recognized when it was first organized to be far from perfect, but it was a working start and difficulties were overcome as the union progressed. They claim that the obstacles to world union can also be surmounted.

## WHAT ARE THE CHANCES THAT THE WORLD FEDERATION PLAN WILL BE ACCEPTED? [7]

A system of world settlement, however desirable, is of little value unless it has a chance of being adopted. Psychologically, that plan or system is most likely to be adopted which not only fulfills a long-felt need, but which does so with the minimum amount of opposition within the nations and among them. On this basis the World Federation Plan, in spite of its new approach and great scope, has a remarkably good chance of being adopted. It was expressly designed to be approved by practically all the nations of the world. To illustrate this, let us consider the position of the powers which will play the leading roles in the world settlement after the Axis defeat.

*Great Britain*: It has become evident, even to many Englishmen, that the British Empire as constituted today cannot long survive. The sprawling empire is threatened on every side by vast blocs of industrialized nations, and the dangers, far from decreasing after this war, will increase—there will be threats from revived Europe and from new industrial giants such as China and the Middle East, or even India.

England tried the balance-of-power policy, and it failed. She tried the League of Nations, and that failed also. After this war, England might attempt a domination of Europe by establishing, under some high-sounding name (such as "European Planning Authority") an economic and military dictatorship of a "New Europe"—a la Hitler, but in reverse English. Such an attempt would also fail; for, aligned against her, England would find Russia, most of Europe, and eventually the United States, probably with some of the British Dominions.

England cannot simultaneously maintain the largest navy, the largest air force and the largest army; nor can she at the same time defend her overseas Empire, engage in world-wide trade to maintain the high standard of living in her overpopulated island, and hold off the continental powers of Europe and Asia.

[7] Ely Culbertson, Bridge expert, creator of the Plan for a World Settlement. *Summary of the World Federation Plan.* Garden City Publishing Company. Garden City, N.Y. 1943. p. 61-4.

A permanent partnership with the United States may be the best solution to Britain's postwar problems. But there are certain obstacles to this. There are, for instance, millions of Americans who suspect the motives of the British "Ruling Class," fearing that after this war England will once again emerge with a bigger, if not better, British Empire, leaving the United States holding the lend-lease bag. The World Federation Plan removes this American objection to postwar support of Britain and makes a true co-union of the English speaking commonwealths practicable.

The World Federation guarantees the existence of the British Empire substantially as it is except for India, offering Britain a unique opportunity to resolve her inner contradictions without danger of future aggression.

*Russia*: To Russia, the World Federation Plan offers a guarantee of collective security against aggression from Europe or Asia. Within her own strategic zone . . . protected by her own quota of armed forces, Russia is free to continue her great experiment unmolested, and yet is welcomed into the family of nations on a basis of absolute equality. There is no other way in which Russia can feel lastingly secure in the postwar world against the threat of a coalition of capitalist powers. The government of Soviet Russia is too realistic to trust the good intentions of the Anglo-Americans after their common enemy has been defeated. Unless Russia obtains *effective guarantees* of postwar security (as she will under the World Federation Plan) she too, in self-defense, will have to resort to power politics, seeking to profit by every disorder or war among her neighbors. Thus, Russia might be a constant threat to the nations of Europe and Asia.

The World Federation Plan offers Russia and her neighbors irrevocable guarantees of security. Such a solution of the Russian problem would do more (even during the war) to unite Russia with her allies than a hundred solemn treaties.

*China*: The World Federation Plan assures the termination of a national nightmare which began with the Boxer Rebellion— the partition of China. The Plan enables her to reassemble her severed parts and become a whole and prosperous nation, with a vast strategic zone of her own. . . It permanently guarantees her sovereignty and finally liberates her from the threat of white domination—economically and militarily. Furthermore, the World Federation enables China to develop industrially without exciting the fears of other great nations. Without the World Federation, power politics might dictate that other nations should sooner or later strike at China, to prevent her five hundred million people from becoming too powerful industrially, and therefore militarily. For China, as well as for other nations, the World Federation, with its Quota Force Principle, is the only practical and lasting substitute for power politics.

*Other Nations*: It is not necessary to enumerate in detail the equally great advantages offered to other nations. Turkey will once more become the central state of the ancient Arabian Empire, now revived in the Middle Eastern Federation. Poland, squeezed from the west and the east by the Germans and the Russians, will realize the dream she has treasured since medieval times. But instead of trying to hack her way by force to the Baltic and the Black seas, she will find the way open through voluntary cooperation with her sister nations in the Middle European Federation. France, Italy and Spain, separately, would be doomed to vassalage under the Germans or the Anglo-Americans. Reunited in a powerful Latin bloc, they will resume their historic civilizing role. France, with her vast possessions and nonincreasing population, will gain by taking her natural allies into partnership and giving them a common stake to defend.

As for the smaller nations of the world, the enormous advantages of the World Federation have been discussed elsewhere. Without the World Federation, each small nation would either have to seek a powerful protector (and pay heavily for that protection) or eventually perish. Under the Quota Force Principle, the weak individual nations can become the strongest collective power on earth—an impregnable bulwark of lasting freedom and peace.

*United States*: American public opinion is of great importance to the adoption of the World Federation Plan. Accordingly, the Plan was designed to fit the psychological structure of the American mass mind.

Few nations in the world are as idealistic as the American nation, and none is so successfully materialistic. Almost any American mind is a battlefield for these opposing tendencies.

There are millions of Americans, materialistically inclined, who have little interest or faith in saving the world. History has convinced them that force is paramount and permanent, and that there is no substitute for power politics. They want to know what their own country will get out of this war for its greater security and power.

There are millions of other Americans, idealistically inclined, grateful to God for the blessings He has bestowed upon the nation, or inspired by the spiritual might of their country, who wish to give from its plenitude to tortured humanity.

The American materialists are determined that *this time* America's own military security and power shall be perpetuated; the idealists are determined that *this time* a better and more just world order shall emerge from the war. The materialists do not want the rest of the world to cheat America; the idealists do not want America to cheat the rest of the world.

No plan of world settlement can succeed unless it satisfies the demands of both these basic groups of Americans. A middle way will not do; for in our democracy each side is strong enough to prevent the other side from realizing its postwar plans. This fundamental and traditional cleavage, which cuts across political lines, will continue, for it corresponds to the two different solutions of the fundamental problem of security for the United States. There is a similar traditional cleavage between the isolationists (some of whom are idealists) and the internationalists (some of whom are materialists).

Assuming that the Axis is defeated, the United States can defend itself against future aggression in one of two ways:

1. The United States can make itself militarily powerful enough to be practically independent of the rest of the world. This it can achieve by creating a vast strategic zone.

2. The United States can save itself by saving the world. This it can achieve by using its tremendous power to help establish a new world order in which effective aggression will be impossible.

Internationalists will object that the first solution resolves nothing; that it will not eliminate or even reduce the incidence of war. Isolationists will object that any plan for lasting peace is but a dream, and that "to be prepared for war is the best way of preserving peace." There is many a slip, they insist, between the lip service of the politicians and the Cup of Peace.

The true solution is *both* solutions. Any plan which excludes either solution has very little chance of adoption by the American nation.

Nothing is as important to the American nation as *unity*, not only during but after the war. The only way to maintain that unity long enough to win the peace is by establishing a positive ideal wherein both the materialists and the idealists will have an equally vital stake. The materialists may scoff at the pound-foolishness of the idealists' proposed world order; but they will be paid off in the materialistic coin of the American strategic zone. The idealists may scorn the penny-wiseness of the materialists; but they will be paid off in the idealistic coin of the World Federation.

To the materialists, and to the incurable cynics about world peace, it may be pointed out that the World Federation Plan avoids Wilson's tragic error: it does not put all the eggs into one idealistic basket. In entrusting its destiny to the World Federation Plan, the United States runs no risk whatsoever. If the promise of lasting peace is betrayed, the American nation will still have the "insurance" of the American strategic zone. Together with her neighbors—400 million strong—America will be powerful enough to remain isolated or to throw a decisive weight against future aggressors. But if it becomes clear that the World Federation and its Quota Force Principle are operating smoothly, then even the most hardened cynic must admit that there will no longer be the precautionary need for the American strategic zone.

There will be some who may object to the World Federation Plan, not on any specific grounds, but with the general argument that the whole system is too new and untested by history. Let them be reminded that in the year 1291 the selectmen of three tiny Swiss Cantons met in a field and took an oath of Perpetual

Alliance against the war lords who threatened their peace and freedom. The Alliance grew and endured for more than six centuries, in spite of wide differences in language, religion and economic structure. This was because each Canton retained its full freedom but created a special organism—the Federation—to carry on the common defense. What the Swiss did on a microscopic scale, the United Nations can now do on a world scale.

## A UNITED AND UNIVERSAL SOCIETY OF NATIONS [8]

The Society of Nations is and for many years has been, a political entity. It had—long prior to 1919—its own governmental institutions including scattered judicial tribunals, a crude legislative system, a body of law, and even a few executive officials. It owns several buildings in various cities throughout the world, in which it functions. As a system of world government it is pitifully inadequate. But it exists, and it deals with very practical realities.

The Society of Nations has, however, always been a complete pauper in its own right. It has been obliged to pass the hat among the nations to feed even the meager crumbs of government which it has supplied to a hungry world.

Saddest of all, this mother of the family of political institutions, has repeatedly been disowned and denied. So fearful have our scholars and statesmen been of offending national pride, that they have told us over and over again that there is no sovereign power superior to that of the nations.

They are wrong. Countless examples will occur to you in which the modern world has acted upon the principle that national sovereignty has its limits. We are giving our all for that principle now. In the name of international justice we propose to enforce the rights of the peoples of the world, which surpass the will of any single nation.

Dr. Philip Jessup, who addressed you last night and this morning, and whom I regard as the outstanding young leader

[8] By Amos J. Peaslee, Lawyer and author, Clarksboro, N.J. From "Some Financial Problems of World Government," address before the Institute of Foreign Affairs, Earlham College, May 15, 1942.

among the authorities in the field of International Law, in his able treatise published in 1935 entitled "International Security—the American Role in Effective Action for Peace," refers in one place to the conception of a super state as a "ghostly specter." He took issue with one of President Harding's observations that the League of Nations was an organization with "super-powers." I would like to raise the question with Dr. Jessup, whether he still thinks it wise to refer to "super-powers" as a "ghostly specter." Perhaps that was one of the times when President Harding was right.

Isolationists have been wrong in their fear to strengthen the sovereign powers of the Society of Nations. But they have been completely right in recognizing that the attributes of a "super-state" exist and will exist in any effective international organization. The creators of the confederate League of Nations in 1919 denied the sovereign existence of any super-state, yet they actually sought to strengthen it. Their opponents recognized that they were dealing with a super-national organism, but they feared that it would become too strong.

It is desirable now, both to admit honestly that the Society of Nations is a super-sovereignty, and then to confer upon it sufficient powers to do its job.

If any of you has followed my thesis so far to the extent of agreeing with it—or any of it—you will ask the question:

How can a united, universal and sovereign Society of Nations be made financially self-supporting?

There are possible approaches to that problem which will occur at once to you as they do to me:

1. The functions of the super-sovereign government of the Society of Nations should be defined and restricted to those which affect the world as a whole, and which interfere in the least possible way with the domestic economy and system of government of any particular nation. But there is an ample field within which a super-government should operate and where indirect taxes could be applied and collected in support of very valuable governmental institutions. A substantial volume of revenue could be obtained, for example, through the administration of fair rules of international trade, travel and com-

munication. If the right to harass travelers and traders across national boundaries by the levying of multiple tribute and trouble by each of the sixty-five nations could be struck down, and power to regulate international commerce could be vested exclusively in the sovereign Society of Nations, we would have unlocked a secret which perhaps more than any other factor accounts for the tremendous prosperity of the United States of America. The benefits, if internationally applied, would be incomparably greater than the cost of the service rendered.

2. One of the greatest boons which could be conferred upon a harried and almost prostrate commercial world, would be the establishment of a sound system of world currency. Gresham's law that "bad money drives out good money" defines a difficulty which cannot be overcome without a surrender of national powers which most governments will resist and unless a very concrete workable scheme can be offered. The best minds of the world have not yet been able to produce an acceptable project for a universal currency. But it may come, and, if it does, the resulting value would be worth a substantial service charge. The United States, with its present immense holding of gold, has an opportunity to influence the course of world action in this respect. Let us fervently hope that if it attempts to do so, it will do it with wisdom and discretion.

Since I have tossed around various other projects so freely, you will probably demand to know more concretely how I propose to finance the organs of government which the Society of Nations should provide.

Unfortunately I cannot give you the complete answer; but I do believe that whatever man or men, woman or women, can successfully solve that problem will have contributed as much to the welfare of mankind as has ever been done before by any single act. When and if the international organism of government is made financially self-suporting, other problems may gradually solve themselves.

A discussion at this time of world government is justified, if at all, only because of its relation to possible enhanced human happiness. Men are giving their lives now as they did twenty-five years ago, not because they like war but because they abhor it. For the sake of future generations they desire above all else to supplant international anarchy with international justice, freedom and fair dealing.

## SHALL THE NEXT PEACE ALSO FAIL? [9]

The history of the last twenty years in Europe and Asia proves that the tragic errors which brought the nations of the world to their present pass have been due, not to the fact that such plan or blueprint as they had (as, for instance, in the League) was in itself defective, but that governments and peoples refused, when it came to the point, to fulfill obligations which were necessary if any constitution, any league, any federation, was to work. They refused because certain primary questions of principle had (and have) remained unanswered.

I recall so vividly how, during the last war, some of us in Europe (and the United States) labored weeks, months, years, over the details of a League Constitution, so as to get them "just right." And when it failed, as it did, it was not because those details were defective (though they may have been), but because large sections of the public, and so of vote-seeking governments in Britain and France, did not really want any league at all, however good; did not see the need of it, did not want, as they put it, to "interfere in quarrels that did not concern them," to be mixed up in the affairs of others. For years in Britain great popular newspapers maintained such slogans as "Let Us Mind Our Own Business," "Keep Out of the Continent."

In other words, the fundamental convictions necessary for any form of international cooperation had not been established had too often been overlooked in the discussion of detail.

Since what is to happen in the future, the kind of peace and the kind of world which are to follow this war, all depend on the degree to which that one truth is recognized (first of all by the British and American peoples), it is worth a little effort to get it clear, though it is so little obscure as to be self-evident. If

[9] By Sir Norman Angell, Nobel Peace Prize Winner, 1933. *Rotarian.* 60: 8-12. March 1942.

we cannot be sure of this one principle as the core of our future policy, nothing else is worth discussion.

What is the primary "right" of all upon which all others, quite obviously and self-evidently, depend?

It is, of course, the right to life, existence, the right not to be killed, tortured, wiped out, destroyed. It applies to nations as to persons. If that right is not assured, no others have any value. To tell a man that he will have freedom of speech, security in his possessions, but that any neighbor who differs from him and desires his property may kill him and nothing will be done to prevent it, sounds very like a bad joke. For nations solemnly to confer about right of access to raw materials and markets, so that all nations may be assured "freedom from want" (one of the four freedoms), but for all to refuse to take any action whatever to defend a nation threatened with simple extinction by a ruthless neighbor, is to reduce any proclamation of right so conditioned to simple nonsense.

First things first, and the first right is the right to life. Without that, none other can have any reality.

Now there are certain features about that right which we should recognize as self-evident. The first is that unless it is defended collectively, by a considerable number acting against attack on the principle that all stand for each, it cannot be defended at all. For if those threatened by violence and aggression do *not* act collectively, helping each other in mutual defense, then some strong attacker can pick them off one by one, knowing that he will not have to face the combined strength of those he would subdue. The only effective reply to "one by one" attack is "all together defense."

There is a second fact about this right: It must be defended on behalf of good and bad alike, unless the badness takes the form of attack upon others.

There is a third fact about this right: If it is known beforehand that collective force will defend it, the use of that force will very seldom be necessary, because the prospective aggressor will know that he is up against more than he can tackle.

Lloyd George was once asked whether the First World War could have been prevented, and replied instantly, without hesitation, "Yes. If Germany had known beforehand that the result of following the policy she was following would be to bring against her the vast array of power she finally confronted, she would not have followed that policy and there would have been no war."

Yet so little was that tragic lesson, the most outstanding of all the lessons of the Great War, learned that it was the selfsame blindness which produced this war. If Britain, even Britain alone, had been prepared to say ten years ago that she would do exactly what she is now doing, she would never have had to do it; the world would not now be at war.

Today, in the hour of her peril, and out of her own dire needs, Britain extends aid to China and to Russia. Yet ten years ago, before Germany was rearmed, Britain flatly refused the aid to China she now gives.

Recently, British armies were fighting and British ships were being sunk in the defense of Ethiopia. Yet in 1935 the British Foreign Minister declared he would not risk a single ship for Ethiopia, and his colleagues made it plain that they regarded any interference with Mussolini as gratuitous war mongering.

It is obviously impossible to answer the question, What is the price of peace? What must we do to be saved? without stressing the truths just indicated. For those truths are the first condition of peace. And if we reject them, no plan, no scheme, no blueprint, no constitution, however cunningly devised, can possibly succeed.

We in Europe have attempted in the past to evade this primary obligation to do our share in the defense of the victim of violence on the ground that no nation would be guilty of violence or aggression if it were fairly treated, if its just grievances were remedied, its needs met. But the greatest grievance of a nation is insecurity, its greatest need defense.

Again and again at the Peace Conference in Paris this sort of situation arose: A nation would claim territory which obviously did not belong to it. On behalf of justice, and so of peace, it was asked to forego the claim. The claimant would then point out that by including this alien territory it got things necessary for defense—an easily defended frontier, raw materials—adding in effect this: "If we make the frontier you—the Conference, the Big Four—desire, we shall be weak, open to attack. If we accede to your request, and then, as the result of our consequent weakness, we are attacked, will you defend us?" The answer was usually a mumble of a decisive "No." "In that case," in effect replied the claimant in question, "we shall stick to this territory and this strategic frontier, even if it does strain the principle of nationality. Survival comes first; self-preservation is the law of life."

*The precondition of peace or justice is security.*

Given that one primordial condition, many of the other difficulties which haunt us may become soluble. Take tariffs. Americans ask, "Does international cooperation and peace involve the disappearance of economic independence, the surrender of tariffs?" That some surrender of independence will have to be made is certain, but the example of the nations of the British Commonwealth reveals how great a measure of economic and political independence can be retained if once the principle of cooperation for defense is assured.

Nine states within the ring of the British Commonwealth have now tariff-making rights. Britain has been ready enough to accept the right of Canada or Australia or South Africa to erect tariffs even against herself, to allow those states complete fiscal independence as long as their cooperation in defense is secured. Once that is assured, reciprocal economic arrangements become much easier, because Britain knows that in fact she will have access to, say, Canadian nickel for defensive purposes, even though authority over it is vested in the Canadian, and not in the British, Parliament.

The respective chance of success for two differing approaches to peace may be indicated thus: Suppose you were to draw up the best possible plan of federation or confederation for fifteen or twenty—or fifty—nations, providing in its many and intricate clauses for every possible contingency, and were to take that draft constitution to the Congress of the United States and the Parliaments of Britain, Ireland, Canada, Australia, South Africa, New Zealand, the Scandinavian States, The Netherlands, Czechoslovakia, a dozen other countries. You would have long and bitter parliamentary debates.

The end might be rejection.

But note what a different method of approach to increasing cooperation was actually achieved before December 7, 1941. Mere defense—that is to say, security and peace—demanded a certain step like the occupation by American forces of British territory. It was an extremely radical step, and it had never happened before that a great nation should say to a neighbor, "Come and establish your power on our territory, within our lines." But the British took this radical step readily and willingly.

Then the United States just as willingly did something just as radical: it assumed a large part of the defense budget of neighboring nations. The United States, Canada, Britain, thus had made a beginning of pooling their defense costs; there is a United States-Canadian Board of Defense.

We shall not retrace those steps; America will not withdraw from British territory; Britain won't ask her to. Other similar unretraceable steps have been taken, will be taken. And one day some half dozen, it may be a dozen or two dozen, countries will wake up to the fact that, without any very bitter discussion, they have brought about a defensive confederation upon which peace can be founded.

The road to a system of peace is to accelerate those separate steps, to prove by experience that each separate measure is workable and serves the ultimate purpose of security and peace.

## EXCERPTS

The League of Nations, the last of these noble experiments, was a failure. Its failure has been blamed on the United States, because we did not join it. Our refusal to become a party to that military alliance had nothing whatever to do with its failure. The League's failure was inherent in the League itself.

Not once did the United States refuse to cooperate with the League. In every crisis, we threw our weight behind the League. But, on the other hand, the League failed us. On the really critical occasion, the occasion that led directly to this war, the League and all of its member nations, refused to cooperate with us. . . It is a false hope, and a cruel one, to assume that the only thing necessary 'to maintain world peace is to recreate the League of Nations, perhaps call it by another name, and this time have the United States as a participating member.

Such a conclusion, so popular right now, is based upon the assumption that the United States will underwrite the stability and peace of the world. That is the only deduction possible, and why not? We have bailed the world out of two world revolutions within one generation.—*Melvin A. Maas, United States Representative from Minnesota. Congressional Record. S. 21, '43. p. A4203-4.*

Now to consider another basic fallacy in Mr. Culbertson's fanciful concoction. One of the chief structural weaknesses of the League of Nations (the first practical attempt at world organization) was the lack of direct popular control. The unwieldly and unworkable system of nation-by-nation agreement defeated League attempts to maintain peace and to prevent war. Mr. Culbertson does a remarkable thing with this problem if, indeed, he gave it any consideration whatever: he makes certain that there is even less chance of even the remotest control over his Peace Trust or Pool. He achieves this by rearing a complex structure of regional federations (11 of these, and the way the combinations are evolved would need a critical analysis by itself). To these regional federations, the respective *national* governments (not the people, mind you) send regional senators. Then each regional superstructure appoints the World Senators who sit in the Peace Pool, whose only constitutional function is to punish aggression.

By comparison with this unwieldly colossus, the League of Nations appears almost a stream-lined instrument of popular control.—*Edith Wynner. World Federation—Now. Je. '43. p. 4.*

When Mr. Churchill declared at Harvard that the League of Nations had failed because it was abandoned and betrayed—

abandoned by the United States and betrayed by the "futile pacifism" of Britain and France—he gave further emphasis to the need for postwar unity and the maintenance of force to keep the peace. His proposal to continue the Joint Chiefs of Staff Committee embodies both ideas. But it seems clear that he envisaged this body as only the nucleus of postwar collaboration among the United Nations. And it may be assumed that he would favor also the continuance of wartime agencies, such as the Combined Raw Materials Board and the Combined Food Board, to provide for the economic as well as the security needs of the postwar world. United Nations collaboration could then become the prelude to a genuine world order.—*Howard P. Whidden, Jr., Research Associate, Foreign Policy Association. Foreign Policy Bulletin. S. 10, '43. p. 3-4.*

On the possibility that the Genevan League may be revived we need waste few words. It was the invention of jurists, who ignored economics and misunderstood military power. They believed that sovereign states, which retained all their independence, would none the less obey a lawyer's contract that bound them to assist each other in their hour of need. They built their flimsy structure on a contradiction. A power which arms, as Britain and France did, on the assumption that its own fleet and army must suffice to insure its own safety, will not suddenly behave as if it were its brother's keeper. A power which adjusts its tariffs and administers its empire for its own advantage alone, will not act, even in a crisis, on the principle of mutual aid.

Collective security is a possible rule of life only if considerations of the common interest penetrate the entire relationship between states. When men trade and tax, invest and plan for the general good of a group of states, it will seem axiomatic that they should defend its safety as they defend their own. This enlargement of the political and economic unit may be a slow growth, but the League's constitution, so far from promoting it, forbade it. It began by affirming the absolute sovereignty of all its members, and so, logically enough, it required for action or legislation the consent of each and all. The result was that it acted feebly and legislated only on minor details. The outward sign of any effective international society will be the adoption in some form of a procedure by majority vote.—*H. N. Brailsford, British Journalist, Editor and Author. American Mercury. Jl. '40. p. 279.*

We might well begin now to think through the governmental structure by which our common purposes with the other United Nations will be preserved and through which nations now neutral and those now our enemies may ultimately be added.

A legislative or parliamentary body as the key unit for such a United Nations government might best safeguard human rights. The executives might well spring from the parliamentary body in a manner similar to the Canadian and British systems.

Obviously, such a United Nations government, as it gradually develops over a period of time, should have very limited powers, with the member nations maintaining their own domestic sovereignty.

Such a United Nations government should enact a very elementary code of justice world-wide in scope, based upon, not nations' rights but human rights. It should include provisions for abolishing slavery, for the protection of minorities wherever they may be, and for preventing religious persecution.

A United Nations court would be needed to administer the code of justice.

Realistically recognizing man's weaknesses, should we not contemplate establishing a United Nations legion or police force to keep the Axis nations and other outlaw territories disarmed, to enforce the basic code of justice and to support the administrative functions?

No orderly government on any level in all of history has ever been successful without a police force. This was one of the three fatal weaknesses of the League of Nations. . . I do not suggest that we place all of our eggs in the international basket, but we should definitely place some of our eggs in continuing United Nations government. They might at least hatch something better than recurring wars, each of increasing tragedy and horror.—*Harold E. Stassen, Governor of Minnesota. Address, March 11, 1943. Congressional Record. Mr. 16, '43. p. A1299.*

When I hear league advocates argue in favor of another League of Nations instead of a Federal Union, I keep thinking of Alexander Hamilton's oft-repeated reference to a league as an imbecility. Understand, of course, I do not refer to the League advocates as imbeciles. It is more becoming in me to let Hamilton do that.

Hamilton had good reason for such a statement. A league is a government of nations instead of a government of men. Of this system he wrote in the *Federalist* No. 15:

> Government implies the power of making laws. It is essential to the idea of a law, that it be attended with a sanction; or, in other words, a penalty or punishment for disobedience. If there be no penalty annexed to disobedience, the resolution or commands which pretend to be laws will, in fact, amount to nothing more than advice or recommendation. This penalty, whatever it may be, can only be inflicted in two ways: by the agency of the courts and ministers of justice, or by military force; by the coercion of the magistracy, or by the coercion of arms. The first kind can evidently apply only to men; the last kind must of necessity, be employed against bodies politic, or communities, or states. It is evident that there is no process of a court by which the observance of the laws can, in the last resort, be enforced. Sentences may be denounced against them for violations of their duty; but these sentences can only be carried into execution by the sword. In an association where the general authority is confined to the collective bodies of the communities that compose it, every breach of the laws must involve a state of war; and military execution must become the only instrument of civil obedience. Such a state of things can certainly not deserve the name of government, nor would any prudent man choose to commit his happiness to it.

And at the end of the *Federalist* No. 20:

> A sovereignty over sovereigns, a government over governments, a legislation for communities, as contradistinguished from individuals, as it is a solecism in theory, so in practice it is subversive of the order and ends of civil polity, by substituting violence in place of law, or the destructive coercion of the sword in place of the mild and salutary coercion of the magistracy.

—*John F. Schmidt, Arlington, Va.  Congressional Record. Jl. 7,* '43. *p.* A3830.

Organized international cooperation can be successful only to the extent to which the nations of the world are willing to accept certain fundamental propositions.

First, each nation should maintain a stable government. Each nation should be free to decide for itself the forms and details of its governmental organization—so long as it conducts its affairs in such a way as not to menace the peace and security of other nations.

Second, each nation should conduct its economic affairs in such a way as to promote the most effective utilization of its human and material resources and the greatest practicable measure of economic welfare and social security for all of its citizens. Each nation should be free to decide for itself the forms of its internal economic and social organization—but it should conduct its affairs in such a way as to respect the rights of others and to play its necessary part in a system of sound international economic relations.

Third, each nation should be willing to submit differences arising between it and other nations to processes of peaceful settlement, and should be prepared to carry out other obligations that may devolve upon it in an effective system of organized peace.

All of this calls for the creation of a system of international relations based on rules of morality, law and justice as distinguished from the anarchy of unbridled and discordant nationalisms, economic and political. The outstanding characteristic of such a system is liberty under law for nations as well as individuals. Its method is peaceful cooperation.

The form and functions of the international agencies of the future, the extent to which the existing court of international justice may or may not need to be remodeled, the scope and character of the means for making international action effective in the maintenance of peace, the nature of international economic institutions and arrangements that may be desirable and feasible —all these are among the problems which are receiving attention and which will need to be determined by agreement among governments, subject of course to approval by their respective peoples. They are being studied intensively by this government and by other governments. They are gradually being made subjects of consultation between and among governments. They are being studied and discussed by the people of this country and the peoples of other countries. In the final analysis, it is the will of the peoples of the world that decides the all-embracing issues of peace and of human welfare.—*Secretary of State Cordell Hull. Radio broadcast September* 12, 1943. *Congressional Record. S.* 14, '43. *p.* A4065.

This writer is a humble disciple of Woodrow Wilson. But acceptance of his ideal of a World Covenant of Nations does not imply a blind adherence to the antiquated machinery of the League of Nations, which was no more than a hastily modernized revival of the plans of the sixteenth- and seventeenth-century French pacifists.

The League of Nations was a beautiful child, with a big heart beating spasmodically, a cloudy head, and a puny muscular system. It was doomed from the start, not so much by world events as by the defects of its own constitution.

The authors of the League of Nations sought to reconcile two incompatible principles: the principle of *unlimited* sovereignty of nations, and the principle of a sovereign law of nations. As a result, the League of Nations fast became a Babelian assembly of ambassadorial puppets.

The argument that the present world tragedy could have been prevented if America had fulfilled her obligations toward the League of Nations, is misleading. For many years Britain and France were the leading members of the League. They were all-powerful as against Germany without arms and Russia in turmoil. Back of Britain and France was mobilized the good will of the peaceful nations of the world, including the United States which, as in the case of the Japanese aggression against Manchuria, was ready to take an active hand. Time and again the League could have stopped the aggressor nations in their tracks. And yet the League of Nations collapsed like a house of cards. The main reason for this collapse was that the Articles of the League's Covenant were not rooted in a strong body politic of a true World League, independent of the power politics and intrigues of the sovereign states composing it. The League was a creature of its makers, the victorious powers; and when the Anglo-French alliance was shaken by suspicion and rivalry (which never fail to arise among victorious allies) the League itself became paralyzed.

If the American people come to look upon the fallacy of American "betrayal" as truth, the only logical conclusion after this war will be to reestablish the League of Nations with American participation. Strong groups here are already agitating for this, as though the new Battle of Peace can be won with the same broken weapons which lost the last one.

There is no question of the sincerity of the supporters of the League of Nations. But they would be horrified to think that, if they gain their point, they will merely be leading in through the back door that same old war horse of power politics, only this time with a shiny blue ribbon on its tail, gold lettered "The League of *United* Nations."

The true solution of the world's problems does not lie in futile attempts to resurrect the League of Nations (which has already been buried with military honors) but in trying to build a new House of Nations on the imperishable foundations of Wilson's great ideal. The toil and sacrifice contributed to the cause of the League of Nations by men and women of good will has not been in vain. Wilson and his co-workers for the League have awakened a world consciousness that will never die. For the first time, humanity has beheld a world center around which the civilized forces of peace and freedom might crystalize against the primeval forces of war. The League of Nations collapsed because of its unsound structure, but its defeat was only temporary. Its essential spirit will be reborn, and will triumph, in another world federation that embodies its principle—the supremacy of a law of nations over the anarchy of individual nations. Here is the meaning of the titanic struggle between the eternal Wilsons and the perennial Hitlers.—*Ely Culbertson, Authority on Contract Bridge. Summary of the World Federation Plan. Garden City Pub. Co., Garden City, N.Y. '43. p. 6-7.*

Many candid supporters of Wilson admitted the faults of the peace treaties, but argued that we should join the League anyway, and exert our influence to correct them through the League machinery. In time, war bitterness would pass, older generations of soldiers and statesmen would retire from the scene, and reconciliation would be possible. The European victors, given a feeling of security by our acceptance of the obligations of the Covenant, would eventually be more willing to make concessions. This was a persuasive argument, but it was not good enough.

The answers were cogent and, I still believe, correct. By joining the League, we should have assumed a blanket obligation to support the *status quo* even if it were not modified. Knowledge that we had assumed this obligation would deprive the victors of incentive to make the necessary changes, since we should under all conditions be guaranteeing their safety from any future attack by the vanquished. Far better to remain outside in the hope that concern for their future by Europeans themselves would bring about the necessary changes. We could not impose upon Europe a democratic unity that its ruling powers did not want.

Even more basic than this position was a prophetic intuition that neither the nations of Europe nor the United States had undergone the internal changes which would be necessary as a basis for a cooperative and peaceful world. The dark forces that really controlled affairs had revealed themselves in the peace conference and in the reaction to the war in this country. Wilson's idealism was artificial, or at least premature. You could not build a real federation of the world on balance-of-power politics, or on imperialism in Europe plus isolationism in the United States. There was not only no assurance that Europe would wish to go in the right direction under its old national regimes, but no prospect that the United States would push it in that direction. The ensuing period of reaction in this country, with its high tariffs and obdurate attitude toward collection of war debts, fulfilled this gloomy expectation.

The League, in any event, became more and more a hollow shell, except for its nonpolitical constructive work such as was carried on by the International Labor Organization. It was chiefly a mask for the power politics of the great nations controlling it. They failed to disarm, and made a mess of reparations for many years. Though Germany was finally admitted to membership, little of the damage of the treaties was undone. Fascism appeared in Italy and was welcomed by the conservatives in power in Britain and France (as well as by those in the United States). Japanese aggression against China went unrestricted.

After Hitler gained power in Germany it was worse than useless to make concessions. But then the League powers underwent a curious change of heart. They failed to apply the sanctions against breaches of the Covenant which might have checked the rise of military aggression in Italy and Germany. Instead, they offered the Nazi dictatorship the appeasement which they should earlier have given to liberal, republican Germany. All through this period, the ruling powers were more afraid of the leftward revolutionary forces in Europe than they were of aggressive, nationalist war-makers. They sacrificed the League and eventually their own national security on the altar of imperialist capitalism, just as it had been feared that they would.—*George Soule. New Republic. F. 2, '42. Pt. 2, p.* 165-6.

# BIBLIOGRAPHY

An asterisk (*) preceding a reference indicates that the article or a part of it has been reprinted in this book.

## BIBLIOGRAPHIES

Aufricht, Hans. World organization; an annotated bibliography. 16p. Woodrow Wilson Memorial Library. 8 W. 40th St. New York. Jl. '43.

Aufricht, Hans. War, peace and reconstruction; a classified bibliography. 56p. Commission to Study the Organization of Peace. 8 W. 4th St. New York. (In press.)

Breycha-Vauthier, A. C. de. Sources of information: a handbook on the publications of the League of Nations. 118p. Columbia University Press. New York. '39.

Cam, Gilbert A. comp. Preparing for the post-war world; a bibliography. 10p. mim. American Library Association. 520 N. Michigan Ave. Chicago. F. '43. o.p.

Commission to Study the Organization of Peace. Bulletin. 2, no. 5-6: 1-28. My-Je. '42. General bibliography on international organization and post-war reconstruction. Hans Aufricht.

National Education Association of the United States. Research Division. Bibliography on postwar planning. 47p. mim. The Association. 1201 16th St. N.W. Washington, D.C. Jl. '43.

United Nations Information Office. Section for Information on Studies for Postwar Planning. Research and postwar planning; bibliography. Pt. 9. p. 150-89. mim. The Office. 610 5th Ave. New York. Ag. '43.

United States. Library of Congress. League of Nations: a selected list of recent references. Ellen Fay Chamberlin, comp. 46p. mim. Washington, D.C. '33.

## GENERAL REFERENCES

### Books, Pamphlets and Documents

Alguy, Jeremiah S. Permanent world peace. 304p. Standard Publication Co. New York. '43.

Aly, Bower, ed. American war and peace aims; seventeenth annual debate handbook, 1943-1944. (Committee on Debate Materials and Interstate Cooperation. National University Extension Association) Lucas Bros. Columbia, Mo. (In press.)

Aly, Bower, ed. World organization; sixteenth annual debate handbook, 1942-1943. (Committee on Debate Materials and Interstate Cooperation. National University Extension Association) 2 vols. Lucas Bros. Columbia, Mo. '42.
Reading list, selected and annotated, vol. 2, p. 211-19.

American Society of International Law. Proceedings, 1940:104-15. Post-war international organization. J. Eugene Harley.

American Society of International Law. Proceedings, 1940:115-24. Pacific settlement of international disputes: recent trends. H. Duncan Hall.

American Society of International Law. Proceedings, 1941:70-98. Essential conditions of international justice; with discussion. Hans Kelsen.

Armstrong, George Gilbert. Why another world war; how we missed collective security. 224p. George Allen & Unwin. London. '41.

Bingham, Alfred. United States of Europe. 336p. Duell, Sloan & Pearce. New York. '40.

Birdsall, Paul. Versailles twenty years after. 350p. Reynal & Hitchcock. New York. '41.

Bourquin, Maurice. Dynamism and the machinery of international institutions. (Geneva Studies, Vol. 11, no. 5) 62p. Geneva Research Centre, Geneva; Columbia University Press. New York. S. '40.

Brown, Francis James; Hodges, Charles; and Roucek, Joseph Slabey, eds. Contemporary world politics. 718p. John Wiley & Sons. New York. '39.

*Brunaer, Esther Caukin. Building the new world order. (International Relations Series) 44p. American Association of University Women. 1634 I St. N.W. Washington, D.C. D. '39.

Buell, Raymond Leslie. Isolated America. 257p. Alfred A. Knopf. New York. '40.

Burton, Margaret E. Assembly of the League of Nations. 441p. University of Chicago Press. Chicago. '41.

Burton, Margaret E. Toward international organization. 74p. Womans Press. New York. '40.
Bibliography, p. 71-4.

Butler, Geoffrey. Handbook of the League of Nations; with a chronological record of its achievement brought down to April 1928. 239p. Longmans, Green & Co. New York. '28.

Butler, Harold. Lost peace. 246p. Harcourt, Brace & Co. New York. '42.

Butler, Nicholas M. Why war? Essays and addresses on war and peace. 323p. Charles Scribner's Sons. New York. '40.

Calderwood, Howard B. Higher direction of the League Secretariat. (Arnold Foundation Studies in Public Affairs. Vol. 5, no. 3) 31p. George F. and Ora Nixon Arnold Foundation. Southern Methodist University. Dallas, Tex. Winter '37.

Carter, Gwendolen M. Consider the record; Canada and the League of Nations. (Behind the Headlines. Vol. 2, no. 6) Canadian Institute of International Affairs. 3 Willcocks St. Toronto. My. 1, '42.

Clinchy, Everett R. World we want to live in. (Human Relations pam. no. 4) 98p. National Conference of Christians and Jews. 381 4th Ave. New York. '43.

Commission to Study the Organization of Peace. Third report; the United Nations and the organization of peace. 36p. The Commission. 8 W. 40th St. New York. F. '43.

*Commission to Study the Organization of Peace. Toward greater freedom; problems of war and peace. rev. ed. 80p. The Commission. 8 W. 40th St. New York. Ag. '43.
  *Federalism, p. 45-8; Bibliography, p. 74-80.

Commission to Study the Organization of Peace. Your stake in the peace; a study course on the problems of the future peace. 32p. The Commission. 8 W. 40th St. New York. '43.
  Includes suggested readings.

Conwell-Evans, Thomas P. League Council in action. 292p. Oxford University Press. London. '29.

Corbett, P. E. Post-war worlds. (Institute of Pacific Relations Inquiry series) 208p. Farrar & Rinehart. New York. '42.
  Bibliography, p. 197-9.

Crossman. Richard H. S. Failure of the League. *In his* Government and the governed. p. 246-53. G. P. Putnam's Sons. New York. '40.

Davies, David Davies, 1st Baron. Federated Europe. 141p. Victor Gollancz. London. '40.

Davies, David Davies, 1st Baron. It need not have happened. 144p. Staples & Staples. London. '42.

Dell, Robert. Geneva racket, 1920-1939. 375p. Robert Hale. London. ['41.]

Eagan, James M. Pope's peace program and the U.S. (Christian Democracy series no. 4) 32p. Paulist Press. 401 W. 59th St. New York. '40.

Einstein, Albert. A farewell. *In his* World as I see it. p. 201-2. Covici Friede Pubs. New York. '34

*Engel, S. League reform; an analysis of official proposals and discussions, 1936-1939. 282p. (Geneva Studies, Vol. 11, no. 3-4) 282p. Geneva Research Centre. Geneva, Switzerland; Columbia University Press. New York. Ag. '40.
Bibliography, p. 271-82.

Fry, Varian. Bricks without mortar; the story of international cooperation. (Headline Books no. 16) Foreign Policy Association. 8 W. 40th St. New York. '38.

Garnett, Maxwell and Koeppler, H. F. Lasting peace. 288p. George Allen & Unwin. London. '40.

Gathorne-Hardy, G. M. Short history of international affairs, 1920-1938. rev. & enl. 487p. Oxford University Press. London. Issued under the auspices of the Royal Institute of International Affairs. '39.

Geneva Institute of International Relations. Problems of peace; lectures delivered at the Institute. 13 series. Ser. 1-5. Oxford University Press. London; Ser. 6-10. Oxford University Press. New York; Ser. 11-12. George Allen & Unwin. London; Ser. 13. Peace Book Co. London. '27-'38.
The entire series is valuable. The last five bear the titles: Pacifism is not enough; Anarchy or world order; The League and the future of the collective system; Geneva and the drift to war; and, War is not inevitable.

Geneva Research Centre. League of Nations and raw materials, 1919-1939. Karl W. Kapp. (Geneva Studies, Vol. 12, no. 3) 64p. Columbia University Press. New York. S '41.

Geneva Research Centre. League of Nations, International Labour Organisation and the United States. (Geneva Studies, Vol. 10, no. 1) 66p. The Centre. Geneva; Columbia University Press. New York. Mr. '39.

Geneva Research Centre. United States and the League, the Labour Organisation, and the World Court during 1940. Arthur Sweetser. (Geneva Studies, Vol. 11, no. 8) 19p. Geneva; Columbia University Press. New York. D. '40.
*Same.* International Conciliation. 372:603-13. S. '41.

Geneva Research Centre. United States and the League, the Labour Organisation, and the World Court in 1939. (Geneva Studies, Vol. 11, no. 1) 67p. Geneva; Columbia University Press. New York. F. '40.
*Same.* International Conciliation. 361:207-57. Je. '40.

Godshall, Wilson Leon. Labyrinth of peace efforts, 1919-1930. *In* Contemporary Europe; a study of national, international, economic, and cultural trends; symposium. p. 40-65. D. Van Ostrand Co. New York. '41.
Bibliography, p. 64-5.

Graduate Institute of International Studies, Geneva. World Crisis. 385p. Longmans, Green & Co. New York. '38.
Mantoux, Paul. Contribution to the history of the lost opportunities of the League of Nations. p. 3-35; Rappard, William E. What is the League of Nations? p. 36-59; Potter, Pitman B. Present crisis in international organization. p. 98-130; Kelsen, Hans. Separation of the covenant of the League of Nations from the peace treaties. p. 133-59; Guggenheim, Paul. Legal and political conflicts in the League of Nations; a contribution to the reform of the League. p. 200-26.

Graham, Malbone W. Problem of world organization. *In* Problems of war and peace in the society of nations; lectures arranged by the University of California Committee on International Relations. p. 103-28. University of California. Berkeley. '37.

Greaves, H. R. G. League committees and world order; a study of the permanent expert committees of the League of Nations as an instrument of international government. 266p. Oxford University Press. London. '31.

Greene, Jerome D. League: its weakness and a possible remedy. 17p. Fletcher School of Law and Diplomacy. New York. '35.

Gunther, John. Half a League onward. *In his* Inside Europe. p. 394-403. Harper & Bros. New York. '36.

Haines, Charles Grove and Hoffman, Ross J. S. Origins and background of the Second World War. 659p. Oxford University Press. New York. '43.

Hambro, C. J. How to win the peace. 384p. J. B. Lippincott Co. New York. '42.

Hemleben, Sylvester John. Plans for world peace through six centuries. 227p. University of Chicago Press. Chicago. '43.
Bibliography, p. 195-222.

Hoffman, Ross. Great republic; a historical view of the international community and the organization of peace. 167p. Sheed & Ward. London. '42.

*Hoover, Herbert and Gibson, Hugh. Problems of lasting peace. 291p. Doubleday, Doran & Co. New York. '42.

Howard-Ellis, Charles. Origin, structure and working of the League of Nations. 528p. Houghton Mifflin Co. Boston. '28.

Hudson, Manley O. Pacific settlement through the League of Nations. *In his* By pacific means. p. 21-46. Yale University Press. New Haven. '35.

Institute for Advanced Study. World organization, 1920-1940; the technical and non-political activities of the League of Nations, the Permanent Court of International Justice, and the International Labor Organization described with particular reference to the future. 39p. The Institute. Princeton, N.J. '41.
*Same.* International Conciliation. 372:614-43. S. '41.

Institute of World Affairs. Proceedings, sixteenth session, December 11-16, 1938. Postwar quest for collective security. Edith Dobie and others. p. 131-63. University of Southern California. Los Angeles. '39.

Institute of World Affairs. War and society; proceedings of the eighteenth session, December 8 to 12, 1940. 299p. University of Southern California. Los Angeles. '41.
*Sweetser, Arthur H. Our future international society. p. 271-84.

Institute on World Organization. World organization; a balance sheet of the first great experiment; a symposium. 426p. American Council on Public Affairs. Washington, D.C. '42.
*Reprint.* Sweetser, Arthur. League of Nations in world politics. 22p.; Castendyck, Elsa. Social questions and world organization. 11p. The Council. Washington, D.C. '42.

Jennings, William Ivor. Federation for western Europe. 208p. Macmillan Co. New York. '40.

Jerrold, Douglas. Christianity and the League of Nations. *In his* Future of freedom. p. 190-215. Sheed & Ward. New York. '38.

Jerrold, Douglas. They that take the sword; the future of the League of Nations. 247p. John Lane, the Bodley Head. London. '36.

Johnsen, Julia E. comp. "Eight points" of post-war world reorganization. 126p. (Reference Shelf. Vol. 15, no. 5) H. W. Wilson Co. New York. Mr. '42.
Bibliography, p. 103-26.

Johnsen, Julia E. comp. International federation of democracies (proposed). 263p. (Reference Shelf. Vol. 14, no. 8) H. W. Wilson Co. New York. Ap. '41.
Bibliography, p. 239-65.

Johnsen, Julia E. comp. Plans for a post-war world. 238p. (Reference Shelf. Vol. 16, no. 22) H. W. Wilson Co. New York. S. '42.
Bibliography, p. 213-38.

Johnsen, Julia E. comp. World peace plans. 281p. (Reference Shelf. Vol. 16, no. 5) H. W. Wilson Co. New York. Ag. '43.
Bibliography, p. 250-81.

Johnson, T. F. International tramps; from chaos to permanent world peace. 399p. Hutchinson & Co. London '38

Jones, Shepard S.   Scandinavian states and the League of Nations.
298p.   Princeton University Press.   Princeton, N.J.; American
Scandinavian Foundation.   New York. '39.
Bibliography, p. 279-91.

Kalijarvi, Thorsten V. and Associates.   Modern world politics.   843p.
Thomas Y. Crowell Co.   New York. '42.
Chap. 6, World organizations.   William Lonsdale Taylor and Thorsten V.
Kalijarvi; Chap. 27, Plans for a new world order.   Joseph Hanc.   Bibliographies,
p. 165-7, 279-91.

Keeton, George W.   National sovereignty and international order.   (New
Commonwealth Institute Monographs)   191p.   Peace Book Co.
London. '40.

Keith, Arthur Berriesdale.   Causes of the war.   554p.   Thomas Nelson
& Sons.   New York. '40.

Kelsen, Hans.   Conditions of international justice.   In Anshen, Ruth
Nanda, ed.   Science and man.   p. 375-97.   Harcourt, Brace & Co.
New York. '42.

Kelsen, Hans.   International administration or international court?   In
his Law and peace in international relations.   181p.   Harvard University Press.   Cambridge. '42.

Kelsen, Hans.   Legal technique in international law; a textual critique
of the League Covenant.   (Geneva Studies, Vol. 10, no. 6)   178p.
Geneva Research Centre.   Geneva; Columbia University Press.   New
York.   D. '39.
A study of possible reform or revision of the Covenant.

Knudson, John I.   History of the League of Nations.   445p.   Turner
E. Smith & Co.   Atlanta, Ga. '38.
Bibliography, p. 437-9.

Landone, Brown.   Which road to permanent peace.   48p.   Landone
Foundation.   Orlando, Fla. '40.
Same condensed.   Johnsen, J. E., comp.   International federation of democ-
racies (proposed).   (Reference Shelf.   Vol. 14, no. 8) p. 148-63.   H. W. Wilson
Co. New York. '41.

Langsam, Walter Consuelo.   World since 1914.   837, 107p.   5th ed.
Macmillan Co.   New York. '43.

League of Nations.   Report on the work of the League, 1938-1939.
(1939 General 2).   194p.   Columbia University Press. '39.

League of Nations.   Report on the work of the League, 1941-1942.
(1942 General 1) 94p.   International Documents Service.   Columbia University Press; Woodrow Wilson Foundation.   8 W. 40th
St.   New York. '42.

League of Nations.   Secretariat.   Aims, methods and activity of the
League of Nations.   rev. ed.   221p.   The Secretariat.   Geneva;
Columbia University Press.   New York. '38.

League of Nations. Secretariat. Information Section. Council of the League of Nations; composition, competence, procedure. 141p. The League. Geneva; Columbia University Press. New York. '38.

League of Nations. Secretariat. Information Section. Essential facts about the League of Nations. 10th ed. rev. 359p. Columbia University Press. New York. '39.

League of Nations. Secretariat. Information Section. League from year to year (1938). 214p. Columbia University Press. New York. '39.

League of Nations Association. Essential facts underlying world organization. 47p. The Association. 8 W. 40th St. New York. N. '41.

League of Nations Association. League of Nations—today and tomorrow. 8p. The Association. 8 W. 40th St. New York. N. '42.

League of Nations Association. Twenty questions on the League of Nations. 4p. The Association. 8 W. 40th St. New York. My. '41.

League of Nations Society in Canada. What about the future? 6p. The Society. 124 Wellington St. Ottawa. '43.

League of Nations Union. Peaceful change; a memorandum on pacific remedies for international grievances. (No. 420) 12p. The Union. 11 Maiden Lane. London, W.C.2. Ja. '42.

Lerner, Max; Lerner, Edna and Abraham, Herbert J. International organization after the war. (Problems in American Life, unit no. 15) 56p. National Association of Secondary School Principals. 1201 16th St. N.W. Washington, D.C. '43.

Libby, Frederick J. Which is your favorite peace plan? 19p. National Council for Prevention of War. 1013 18th St. N.W. Washington, D.C. '43.
*Reprint* from Peace Action. Ja-Mr. '43

Lippmann, Walter. U.S. foreign policy: shield of the republic. 177p. Little, Brown & Co. Boston. '43.
*Condensed.* Reader's Digest. 43:119-44. Jl. '43.

Lodge, Henry Cabot. Senate and the League of Nations. 424p. Charles Scribner's Sons. New York. '25.

Mackinder, Halford J. Democratic ideals and reality; a study of the politics of reconstruction. reissue. 219p. Henry Holt & Co. New York. '42.

Madariaga, Salvador de. World's design. 291p. George Allen & Unwin. London. '38.

Maddox, William P. European plans for world order. (James-Patten-Rowe pamphlet series no. 8) 44p. American Academy of Political and Social Science. Philadelphia. Mr. '40.

Marburg, Theodore. Development of the League of Nations idea; documents and correspondence. ed. by John H. Latane. 2 vols. Macmillan. New York. '32.

Margueritte, Victor. League fiasco (1920-1936), tr. by Mrs. N. Farlane. 284p. William Hodge & Co. London. '36.

*Martin, Charles E. World peace: practical ways and means. *In* Institute of World Affairs. Proceedings, fourteenth session, December 13 to 18, 1936. p. 190-205. University of Southern California. Los Angeles. '37.

Middlebush, Frederick A. and Hill, Chesney. Elements of international relations. Chap. 9. McGraw-Hill Book Co. New York. '40.
Bibliography, p. 205-7.

*Millspaugh, Arthur C. Peace plans and American choices; the pros and cons of world order. 114p. Brookings Institution. Washington, D.C. '42.

Morley, Felix. Society of nations; its organization and constitutional development. 678p. Brookings Institution. Washington, D.C. '32.

Motherwell, Hiram. The peace we fight for. 281p. Harper. New York. '43.

Myers, Denys P. Handbook of the League of Nations; a comprehensive account of its structure, operation and activities. 411p. World Peace Foundation. Boston. '35.

Nevins, Allan and Hacker, Louis M. eds. United States and its place in world affairs, 1918-1943. 612p. D. C. Heath & Co. Boston. '43.

Newfang, Oscar. United States of the world; a comparison between the League of Nations and the United States of America. 284p. G. P. Putnam's Sons. New York. '30.

Newfang, Oscar. World government. 227p. Barnes & Noble. New York. '42.

Owen, Ruth Bryan. Look forward, warrior. 108p. Dodd, Mead & Co. New York. '42.

Peaslee, Amos J. Permanent United Nations. 146p. G. P. Putnam's Sons. New York. '42.

*Peaslee, Amos J. Some financial problems of world government; address before the Institute of Foreign Affairs, Earlham College, May 15, 1942. 14p. The Author. Clarksboro, N.J.

Permanent Court of International Justice at the Hague. 137p. Columbia University Press. New York. '39.

Phelps, Edith M. ed. American league of nations. *In* University Debaters' Annual, 1937-1938:149-95. H. W. Wilson Co. New York. '38.
Bibliography, p. 184-95.

Phelps, Edith M. ed. League of Nations. *In* University Debaters' Annual, 1941-1942. p. 51-100. H. W. Wilson Co. New York. '42.
Briefs, p. 52-60; Bibliography, p. 92-100.

Phelps, Edith M. ed. Federation of democracies based on the Churchill-Roosevelt principles. *In* University Debaters' Annual, 1941-1942: 203-30. H. W. Wilson Co. New York. '42.
Bibliography, p. 223-30.

Phelps, Edith M. ed. Blueprints for a better world; the Burton-Ball-Hatch-Hill resolution. *In* University Debaters' Annual, 1942-1943: 273-319. H. W. Wilson Co. New York. '43.
Bibliography, p. 314-19.

Phelps, Edith M. ed. Federal world government. *In* University Debaters' Annual, 1942-1943:193-240. H. W. Wilson Co. New York. '43.
Bibliography, p. 232-40.

Phelps, Edith M. ed. Permanent federal union of all nations. *In* University Debaters' Annual, 1942-1943:241-70. H. W. Wilson Co. New York. '43.

Pickard, Bertram. Geneva institutions to-day; some account of present activities of the League of Nations and the International Labor Organization. 13p. mim. Peace Section. American Friends Service Committee. 20 S. 12th St. Philadelphia. My. '42.

Potter, Pitman B. Article XIX of the Covenant of the League of Nations. (Geneva Studies, Vol. 12, no. 2) 98p. Geneva Research Centre. Geneva; Columbia University Press. New York. Ag. '41.
Bibliographical note, p. 97-8.

Ranshofen-Wertheimer, Egon. Victory is not enough; the strategy for a lasting peace. 322p. W. W. Norton & Co. New York. '42.

Rappard, William E. Geneva experiment. 115p. Oxford University Press. London. '31.

Rappard, William E. Quest for peace since the World war. 516p. Harvard University Press. Cambridge. '40.

Reynolds, E. E. League experiment. 163p. Thomas Nelson & Sons. New York. '39.
Bibliography, p. 140-2.

Riches, Cromwell A. Unanimity rule and the League of Nations. (Johns Hopkins University Studies in Historical and Political Science. Extra Vol. n.s. no. 20) 224p. Johns Hopkins Press. Baltimore. '33.
Bibliography, p. 218-20.

Robinson, Howard. Hitherto. *In* Toward international organization; a series of lectures at Oberlin College. p. 1-30. Harper & Bros. New York. '42.

Roelofs, Henrietta. Toward world government. 23p. Womans Press. New York. ['42.]

Rowan-Robinson, H. Sanctions begone! a plea and a plan for the reform of the League. 244p. William Clowes. London. '36.

Royal Institute of International Affairs. Future of the League of Nations; the record of a series of discussions held at Chatham House. 188p. Oxford University Press. London. '36.

Rugg, Harold O. Now is the moment. p. 133-79. Duell, Sloan and Pearce. New York. '43.

Salter, Sir James Arthur. United States of Europe. 303p. Reynal & Hitchcock. New York. '33.

Sarolea, Charles. Policy of sanctions and the failure of the League of Nations. 63p. International Publishing Co. London. '35.

Schwarzenberger, Georg. League of Nations and world order; a treatise on the principle of universality in the theory and practice of the League of Nations. (New Commonwealth Institute Monographs) 191p. Constable & Co. London. '36.

Shaw, George Bernard. League of Nations. (Fabian Tracts, no. 226) 11p. Fabian Society. London. Ja. '29.

Shotwell, James T. On the rim of the abyss. p. 289-355. Macmillan Co. New York. '36.

Slocombe, George E. Mirror to Geneva; its growth, grandeur and decay. 338p. Henry Holt & Co. New York. '38.

Smuts, Jan C. Address before British Parliament, October 21, 1942. *In* Proposals for a free world; toward new horizons no. 2. p. 18-19. Office of War Information. Wash. D.C.

Spykman, Nicholas John. America's strategy in world politics; the United States and the balance of power. 500p. Harcourt, Brace & Co. New York. '42.

Steiner, H. Arthur. Principles and problems of international relations. 835p. Harper & Bros. New York. '40.

Stephens, Waldo E. Revisions of the Treaty of Versailles. 285p. Columbia University Press. New York. '39.
Bibliography, p. 263-71.

Swanwick, H. M. Collective insecurity. 285p. Jonathan Cape. London. '37.

Sweetser, Arthur. America seen from abroad. *In* Kern, John D. and Griggs, Irwin. This America. p. 115-30. Macmillan Co. New York. '42.

Temperley, A. C. Whispering gallery of Europe. 359p. Collins. London. '38.

United Nations conference organized as the seventeenth session of the Middle Atlantic model assembly of the League of Nations. March 18-20, 1943. 22p. Hamilton College. Clinton, New York. '43.

Webster, Charles K. and Herbert, Sydney. League of Nations in theory and practice. 320p. Houghton Mifflin Co. Boston. '33.
Bibliography: suggestions for further study, p. 309-13.

Williams, Ernest T. Lasting peace and a better world; a plan to achieve them. 142p. Victory Fellowship. 1 Overlinks Dr., Parkstone, Dorset, England. '43.

Willoughby, Westel W. Sino-Japanese controversy and the League of Nations. 733p. Johns Hopkins Press. Baltimore. '35.

Wilson, Florence I. Origins of the League Covenant; documentary history of its drafting. 260p. Published by Leonard and Virginia Woolf at the Hogart Press. London. '28.

Woodrow Wilson Foundation. Unity of nations; recent statements by the foremost authorities. 4p. The Foundation. 8 W. 40th St. New York. ['42].

Woodrow Wilson Foundation. World we want to live in; lessons from the past, plans for the future; symposium at Institute for Advanced Study, Princeton. 8p. The Foundation. 8 W. 40th St. New York.
*Reprint* from Changing World. Ja. '42.

World Citizens Association. World's destiny and the United States, a conference of experts in international relations. 309p. The Association. 84-86 E. Randolph St. Chicago. '41.

Wright, Quincy. In search of peace. 16p. Columbia University Press. New York. '39.

Wright, Quincy. International law and the world order. *In* Foundations of a more stable world order. Walter H. C. Laves, ed. p. 107-34. University of Chicago Press. Chicago. '41.

Wright, Quincy. Study of war. 2 vols. University of Chicago Press. Chicago. '42.

Young, Sir George. Federalism and Freedom, or Plan the peace to win the war. 204p. Oxford University Press. New York. '41.

Zilliacus, Konni (Vigilantes, pseud.) Why the League has failed. New People's Library. Vol. 11. 96p. Victor Gollancz. London. '38.

Zimmern, Alfred. League of Nations and the rule of law, 1918-1935. 2d ed. 542p. Macmillan & Co. London. '39.

## PERIODICALS

Academy of Political Science. Proceedings. 17:287-95. My. '37. Mechanism for peace in Europe. James T. Shotwell.

Agenda. 1:59-72. Ja. '42. Failure of the League of Nations. C. A. W. Manning.

*American Association of University Professors. Bulletin. 28:318-26. Je. '42. Literature for defense. Charlton G. Laird.

American Historical Review. 47:545-51. Ap. '42. American sectionalism and world organization; ed. with introduction by William Diamond. Frederick Jackson Terner.

American Journal of International Law. 30:506-9. Jl. '36. Failure of the League of Nations. C. G. Fenwick.

American Journal of International Law. 31:614-41. O. '37. Italian-Ethiopian dispute and the League of Nations. John H. Spencer.

American Journal of International Law. 33:138-46. Ja. '39. Amendment of the Covenant of the League of Nations with a view to its separation from the treaties of peace. Manley O. Hudson.

American Journal of Sociology. 46:571-81. Ja. '41. International peace, by court or government? tr. by Aaron Bell. Hans Kelsen.

American Mercury. 47:56-61. My. '39. Requiem for the League of Nations. Reginald Wright Kauffman.

American Political Science Review. 20:847-52. N. '26. League of Nations: a corporation, not a superstate. Dayton Voorhees.

American Political Science Review. 22:706-11. Ag. '28. What is the League of Nations? Herbert Brown Ames.

American Political Science Review. 23:17-31. F. '29. America's role in the League of Nations. Manley O. Hudson.

American Political Science Review. 25:406-24. My. '31. Some problems of Article XXIV of the covenant. S. H. Bailey.

American Political Science Review. 27:721-37. O. '33. Nationalism and the League of Nations today. William E. Rappard.

American Political Science Review. 31:455-72. Je. '37. Reform of the covenant of the League of Nations. Clyde Eagleton.

American Political Science Review. 33:193-218. Ap. '39. League of Nations covenant—1939 model. Denys P. Myers.

American Political Science Review. 33:473-86. Je. '39. Resurrection of neutrality in Europe. Hans J. Morgenthau.

American Political Science Review. 35:1120-7. D. '41. Political basis of federation. William P. Maddox.

American Political Science Review. 36:1039-52. D. '42. Power politics and world organization. John H. Herz.

American Political Science Review. 36:1136-41. D. '42. Democracy and international organization: the experience of the League of Nations. James T. Watkins, IV.

American Scholar. 11, no. 1:261-74. [Jl.] '42. Myths about the peace treaties of 1919-1920. Clarence A. Berdahl.

Annals of the American Academy. 198:65-72. Jl. '38. League of Nations and the Spanish Civil war. Frances O. Wilcox.

Annals of the American Academy. 210:1-144. Jl. '40. When war ends. Ernest Minor Patterson, ed.

Annals of the American Academy. 216:140-9. Jl. '41. America seen from abroad. Arthur Sweetser.

Annals of the American Academy. 218:132-40. N. '41. Prospect for a union of democracies. W. Menzies Whitelaw.

Annals of the American Academy. 218:153-61. N. '41. Future of nationalism and the nation-state. Percy E. Corbett.

Annals of the American Academy. 222:109-16. Jl. '42. Postwar political organization of the world. C. J. Hambro.

Annals of the American Academy. 228:1-107. Jl. '43. United Nations and the future. ed. by Ernest Minor Patterson.
　　*Wright, Quincy. United Nations—Phrase or reality? p. 1-10.

Aryan Path (Bombay). 11:180-4. Ap. '40. Future of the League; Asiatic liberations. Norman Angell.

Bulletin of League of Nations Teaching. No. 4:74-107. D. '37. Reform of the League of Nations: application of the principles of the covenant.

Calcutta Review. 82:208-16. Mr. '42. League of Nations as an inter-human pattern. Benoykumar Sarkar.

Calcutta Review. 85:27-35. O. '42. League of Nations and the future world order. Naresh Chandra Roy.

Canadian Forum. 19:207-9. O. '39. Peace aims. Frank H. Underhill.

Catholic World. 150:288-93. D. '39. Next peace. Seumas Cawley.

Catholic World. 151:651-9. S. '40. Christendom and the organization of peace. Ross J. S. Hoffman.

Christian Science Monitor Magazine. p. 2. F. 24, '40. Hurdles before world federation. Hugh Dalton.

Christian Science Monitor Magazine. p. 12. O. 26, '40. Will the League idea survive? Peter Lyne.

Christian Science Monitor Magazine. p. 3+. Ag. 21, '43. Deterrents to peace. Roscoe Drummond.

Collier's. 110:84+. D. 19, '42. League lives on. C. J. Hambro.

Collier's. 111:33-6. Je. 26, '43. New approaches to lasting peace. Herbert Hoover and Hugh Gibson.
*Also separate, condensed.* Further new approaches to lasting peace. 56p. Vanderbilt-Jackson Typography, Inc. New York. '43.

Commercial and Financial Chronicle. 149:3790. D. 16, '39. Russia expelled from League of Nations.

Commercial and Financial Chronicle. 150:3587. Je. 8, '40. President Roosevelt favors carrying out of humanitarian and non-political aims.

Commercial and Financial Chronicle. 158:119. Jl. 8, '43. League of Nations post-war program for world trade and stable economy in all nations.

Commercial Law Journal. 48:123-5. Je. '43. United Nations and the future. Morris Weisman.

Commission to Study the Organization of Peace. Bulletin. 3, no. 3-4: 1-24. Mr.-Ap. '43. United Nations and the organization of peace; proceedings of the February 27th, 1943 conference of the Commission to Study the Organization of Peace.

Congressional Digest. 21:225-56. O. '42. United States and post-war world organization; with pro and con discussion.

Congressional Digest. 22:193-224. Ag.-S. '43. Should the United States join in reconstituting the League of Nations? pro and con.

Congressional Record. 89:A2308-9. My. 4, '43. Backs Federal Union proposal; address, May 1, 1943. Owen Roberts.

Congressional Record. 89:A4063-5. S. 14, '43. Our foreign policy in the framework of our national interests; radio address, September 13, 1943. Cordell Hull.

Congressional Record. 89:A4071-4. S. 14, '43. Peace or politics. Robert A. Taft.

Congressional Record. 89:7790-813. S. 21, '43. Participation in world peace; House debate on the Fulbright resolution.

Congressional Record. 89:A4199-201. S. 21, '43. New approaches to peace; address, September 3, 1943. Herbert Hoover.

Congressional Record. 89:A4382-3. S. 29, '43. Post-war plans. John Biggs, jr.

Contemporary Review. 153:402-10. Ap. '38. Future of the League. Maxwell Garnett.

Contemporary Review. 154:582-90. N. '38. Geneva reconsidered. Robert Sencourt.

Contemporary Review. 156:160-7. Ag '39. Rebuilding world order. Maxwell Garnett.

Contemporary Review. 159:349-51. Mr. '41. Great experiment of organised peace. F. W. Pick.

Contemporary Review. 161:129-33. Mr. '42. League or union? George Young.

Contemporary Review. 162:268-73. N. '42. Unused war weapon: federalisation. V. V. Tilea.

Current History. 44:71-6. Je '36. Has the League failed? William Seaver Woods.

Current History. 45:51-5. D. '36. Reforming the League; a review of proposals to rejuvenate the old young man of Geneva. Curt L. Heymann.

Current History. 51:11. Ja. '40. League expels Russia.

Current History. n.s.2:81-6. Ap. '42. Our leadership for peace. Richard V. Burks.

Economist (London) 138:199-200. F. 3, '40. Bruce report; economic and social work of the League to be separated from political activities.

Editorial Research Reports. p. 283-302. O. 30, '41. Enforcement of world peace. Buel W. Patch.

Editorial Research Reports. p. 147-64. S. 2, '43. United States and world organization. F. M. Brewer.

Ethics. 53:110-14. Ja. '43. Keeping the peace; review of The Problems of Lasting Peace by Herbert Hoover and Hugh Gibson. Quincy Wright.

Foreign Affairs. 18:13-28. O. '39. Europe without the League. Marcel Hoden.

*Foreign Affairs. 19:179-92. O. '40. Non-political achievements of the League. Arthur Sweetser.
*Also separate.* 16p. Council on Foreign Relations. 45 E. 65th St. New York.

*Foreign Policy Reports. 19:38-48. My. 1, '43. Geneva institutions in wartime. Ernest S. Hediger.

Fortnightly. 149 (n.s. 143):129-36. F. '38. Rule of fear; ineffective measures of attaining peace. Guglielmo Ferrero.
*Same.* International Conciliation. 339:149-55. Ap. '38.

Fortnightly. 155 (n.s. 149):209-18. Mr. '41. Lord Cecil and the League. Marquess of Crewe.

Fortune. 25:110-11. Ap. '42. Fortune survey; postwar world.

Fortune. 25:sup. 1-21. My. '42. United States in a new world; I. Relations with Britain.

Fortune. 25:106-11+. Je. '42. Greatest man in Canada; John Wesley Dafoe, prairie editor. Bruce Hutchison.

*Fortune. 27:128-9+. F. '43. Draftsmen of the new world. Raymond Leslie Buell.

Free World. 5:35-41. Ja. '43. Responsibilities of the United States in the post-war world. Quincy Wright.

Free World. 5:246-70. Mr. '43. Staff of the world organization: round table.

Free World. 5:433-9. Mr. '43. Pioneers of the League ideal. Leonard Reed.

Harper's Magazine. 183:1-9. Je. '41. Ghost of Woodrow Wilson. Gerald W. Johnson.
*Same abridged.* Reader's Digest. 39:81-4. Ag. '41.

Harper's Magazine. 186:525-9. Ap. '43. Once again, the 1919 dilemma; what kind of peace will Americans accept? Elmer P. Peterson.

Harvard Educational Review. 12:234-43. My. '42. America's stake in a world settlement, past and present. Paul Birdsall.

Harvard Law Review. 55:561-94. F. '42. European federation—the democratic alternative. Arnold Brecht.

Historical Outlook. 23:410-12. D. '32. Attitude of the United States toward the League of Nations. Henry Noble Sherwood.

International Affairs. 17:187-210. Mr. '38. Great Britain and the League. John Fischer Williams.

International Conciliation. 325:587-639. D. '36. New League or no League. Lord Lothian; Alexander Hamilton and the reform of the League. L. P. Jacks; Demilitarized League of Nations. L. P. Jacks; Collective public opinion. Robert Borden.

International Conciliation. 339:123-42, 149-55. Ap. '38. What is the League of Nations? William E. Rappard; Rule of fear. Guglielmo Ferrero.

International Conciliation. 352:381-408; 361:216-47. S. '39, Je. '40. United States and world organization during 1938-1939.

International Conciliation. 363:333-69. O. '40. Causes of the peace failure, 1919-1939, by the International Consultative Group of Geneva.

International Conciliation. 369:193-531. Ap. '41. Commission to Study the Organization of Peace; preliminary report and monographs.
  *Gerig, Benjamin. Appraisal of the League of Nations. p. 303-16. *Also separate.* Carnegie Endowment for International Peace. 405 W. 117th St. New York.

International Conciliation. 375:715-20. D. '41. Next armistice—and after. Douglas Johnson.

International Conciliation. 384:429-51. N. '42. Typical plans for postwar world peace. Otto Tod Mallery.

International Conciliation. 389:201-385. Ap. '43. Commission to Study the Organization of Peace; third report—the United Nations and the organization of peace, with papers presented to the Commission.

Library Quarterly. 12:752-61. Jl. '42. Subsoil of peace. Henry M. Wriston.

Living Age. 359:343-4. D. '40. Embers of an ideal.

Nature. 146:277-8. Ag 31, '40. Social and economic reconstruction.

Nature. 146:787-9. D. 21, '40. Tradition in a new world order.

Nature. 147:245-7. Mr. 1, '41. Basis of international co-operation.

Nature. 148:233-5. Ag. 30, '41. International collaboration.

Nature. 150:354. S. 19, '42. League of Nations; abstract of report for 1941-1942.

Nature. 151:679-82. Je. 19, '43. Aspects of international collaboration.

New Commonwealth Quarterly. 2:111-215. S. '36. Proposals for the reform of the covenant of the League of Nations. Paul De Auer.

New Commonwealth Quarterly. 4:119-30. S. '38. Conditions of international order. Earl of Lytton.

New Commonwealth Quarterly. 4:131-43. S. '38. Observations on the de facto revision of the Covenant. Josef L. Kunz.

New Republic. 37:33-4. My. 20, '36. Can the League survive?

New Republic. 102:16-17. Ja. 1, '40. League of little nations. Genevieve Tabouis.

New Republic. 106, pt. 2:163-84. F. 2, '42. Lessons of last time. George Soule.

New York Times. p. 12E. Ap. 18; p. 22. Ap. 22, '43. Strong collective security system held way to peace. Sarah Wambaugh; Reply. Hugh Gibson.

New York Times. p. 9. S. 25, '43. Excerpts from the proposals of leaders to assure peace after the war ends; statements at New York Times Hall, September 24, 1943.

New York Times Magazine. p. 5. My. 4, '41. Faith of Woodrow Wilson. William Langer.

New York Times Magazine. p. 3+. Jl. 13, '41. If we had joined the League—there might not have been a Hitler. Edwin L. James.

*New York Times Magazine. p. 10+. Jl. 18, '43. America's faith— a call for revival. Robert N. Wilkin.

New York University Law Quarterly Review. 10:58-63. S. '32. Problem of the admission of the United States into the League of Nations. Clyde Eagleton.

New York University Law Quarterly Review. 13:216-43. Ja '36. Interpretation of the Covenant in the Sino-Japanese dispute. Miroslas Gonsiorowski.

Newsweek. 22:88. Jl. 26, '43. Postwar peace machinery. Raymond Moley.

Nineteenth Century. 120:182-92. Ag. '36. Future of the League. Lord Queensborough.

Nineteenth Century. 123:1-10. Ja. '38. Principle of collectivity in international relations. Konstantin Freiherr von Neurath.

People and Freedom (London). no. 49:3. Jl. '43. Reglionalism and the League of Nations. Robert Barton.

Political Quarterly. 8:337-52. Jl. '37. Resurrection of the League. Leonard Woolf.

Political Quarterly. 12:121-33. Ap.-Je. '41. Resurrection of the League; review of A Great Experiment, the autobiography of Viscount Cecil. H. Lauterpacht.

Political Science Quarterly. 47:274-81. Je. '32. Machinery of experiment at Geneva. Charles W. Pipkin.

Political Science Quarterly. 49:544-75. D. '34. Small states in the League of Nations. William E. Rappard.

Predictions of Things to Come. 1, no. 2:49-54. F. '43. Plans for peace; a new League of Nations. Clark M. Eichelberger.

Public Opinion Quarterly. 2:399-412. Jl. '38. League publicity: cause or effect of failure? Pitman B. Potter.

Rotarian. 63:8-10. Ag. '43. Setting the pattern for peace. James T. T. Shotwell.

Round Table (London) 29:447-53. Je. '39. Why the League failed.

Saturday Evening Post. 214:1-11+, 14-15+, 31+. N. 1-15, '41. First American crusade. Herbert Hoover.

Scholastic. 34:18S. My. 6, '39. Two more states desert fading League of Nations; Peru and Hungary.

Scholastic. 35:7-8. D. 11, '39. Russia rejects Finnish peace; boycotts League of Nations.

Scholastic. 41:14-15. O. 5, '42. Forum of the future; coming world order.

Social Forces. 21:265-72. Mr '43. World reconstruction and European regionalism. Nicholas Doman.

Social Research. 10:378-95. S. '43. Problems of international organization; remarks on current literature. Erich Hula.

Social Studies. 34:121-4. Mr. '43. Why did the League of Nations fail? Laurence G. Paquin.

South Atlantic Quarterly. 41:1-17. Ja. '42. War aims and peace proposals. René Albrecht-Carrié.

South Atlantic Quarterly. 42:162-71. Ap. '43. Do not make the Atlantic Charter official. John Earle Uhler.

*Southern Review. 1:120-38. Jl. '35. Covenant of the League of Nations as a pact of peace. Manley O. Hudson.

Spectator (London). 169:119-20. Ag. 7, '42. From charter to what?

Survey Graphic. 28:238-9. Mr. '39. Despite the uproar—the League of Nations. John Palmer Gavit.

Time. 42:105-8. S. 13, '43. Freedom from attack; international police.

Town Meeting (Bulletin of America's Town Meeting of the Air). 7: 1-24. Ap. 20, '42. What are the essentials of a lasting peace? Clark M. Eichelberger, Henry J. Allen and Harry D. Gideonse.

United Empire (London). n.s. 29:143-53. Ap. '38. Crisis of the League. A. Wyatt Tilby.

University of Chicago Round Table. 249:1-26. D. 27, '42. Woodrow Wilson: prophet or visionary; radio discussion. Avery O. Craven, Mrs. Philip La Follette and Quincy Wright.

Virginia Quarterly Review. 18, no. 3:379-88. [Jl.] '42. League of Nations in wartime. Hans Habe.
  *Same* abridged. Congressional Digest. 21:231. O. '42.

Virginia Quarterly Review. 19, no. 4:481-97. [O] '43. Versailles in perspective. Charles Seymour.

Vital Speeches of the Day. 2:695. Ag. 1, '36. Future of the League of Nations. Charles G. Fenwick.

Vital Speeches of the Day. 5:703-4. S. 1, '39. Successes and failures of the League of Nations. Max Habicht.
  *Also separate.* 6p. mim. Institute of Public Affairs. University of Virginia. Charlottesville, Va. Jl. 10, '39.

Vital Speeches of the Day. 8:485-6. Je. 1, '42. Isolation policies and the League of Nations. Wendell Willkie.

Vital Speeches of the day. 9:555-9. Jl. 1, '43. Challenge of the future world. George N. Shuster.

World Affairs. 104:213-17. D. '41. Institute on world organization. Laura Puffer Morgan and Jan Hostie.
  *Also separate.* 7p. American Peace Society. 734 Jackson Pl. Washington, D.C. '41.

World Affairs. 105:240-5. D. '42. What? another League. Joseph F. Thorning.

*World Affairs Interpreter. 12:235-46. O. '41. Coming revival of the League of Nations. J. Eugene Harley.
  *Also separate.* University of Southern California. Los Angeles.

World Affairs Interpreter. 13:246-57. O. '42. Political pattern of the world of tomorrow. J. Eugene Harley.

World Affairs Interpreter. 13:336-52. O. '42. Summary of proposals and efforts for international cooperation and world peace. Eugene J. Harley.
*Also separate.* 26p. Woodrow Wilson Memorial Library. 8 W. 40th St. N.Y.

Yale Review. n.s. 24:274-92. D. '34. States' rights and the League. Nicholas J. Spykman.

## REFERENCES FAVORABLE TO THE LEAGUE

Barton, Robert. Brave new League. 68p. Goose Pubs. 15 Claremont Park, Finchley, London, N.3. '42.

Bassett, Milton Elisha, jr. and Elliott, Arthur Roland, jr. Covenant for the new League of Nations. *In* Six plans for international organization, by Ten Oberlin College Students, p. 10-24. Oberlin College. Oberlin, O. My. '38. o.p.

Bondreau, Frank G. League of Nations in a world at war. 12p. League of Nations Association. 8 W. 40th St. New York. Ap. '40.

Brailsford, Henry N. Towards a new League. 64p. New Statesman and Nation. London. Jl. '36.

Cecil of Chelwood, Edgar Algernon R. Gascoyne-Cecil, 1st Viscount. Great experiment; an autobiography. 390p. Oxford University Press. New York. '41.

Colombat, Francis Henry. Commonwealth of nations. 39p. The Author. 1118 Guinda St. Palo Alto, Calif. '43.

Davies, David Davies, 1st Baron. Problems of the twentieth century; a study in international relationships. 819p. Ernest Benn. London. '34.

Fleming, Denna Frank. United States and world organization, 1920-1933. 569p. Columbia University Press. New York. '38.

Garnett, Maxwell. World unity. 32p. Oxford University Press. New York. '39.

Halifax, Edward Frederick Lindley Wood, 1st Viscount. Speeches on foreign policy. p. 52-9, 68-73. Oxford University Press. New York. '40.

Jacks, L. P. Co-operation or coercion? 153p. E. P. Dutton & Co. New York. '38.

Keen, F. N. Better League of Nations. 160p. George Allen & Unwin. London. '34.

League of Nations Society in Canada. League of Nations and a world police. 8p. The Society. 124 Wellington St. Ottawa, Ont. '43.

League of Nations Union. Reform and development of the League of Nations. The Union. 15 Grosvenor Crescent. London S.W. 1. Jl. '36.

Milbank Memorial Fund. Proceedings, 1942:59-71. Design to keep the peace. Albert G. Milbank.

Mitchell, Theodore G. Formula for 100 years' peace. 144p. Dearborn Publishing Co. Chicago. '42

War aims, peace terms, and the world after the war; a joint declaration by Democratic Socialists of several nationalities. 16p. Rand School Press. New York. '41.

Woolf, Leonard. War for peace. 244p. George Routledge & Sons. London. '40.

## PERIODICALS

Agenda. 1:192-205. Jl. '42. Inevitable League. Gilbert Murray.

Agenda. 2:56-66. F. '43. Reconstruction of the League of Nations. John Fischer Williams.

*American Academy of Arts and Sciences. Proceedings. 75, no. 1:11-13. O. '42. Discussion of Professor Whitehead's paper. Hans Kelsen.

*American Academy of Arts and Sciences. Proceedings. 75, no. 1: 39-53. O. '42. International utopias. Zechariah Chafee, Jr.

*American Bar Association Journal. 27:690-3. N. '41. Challenge of international lawlessness. Robert H. Jackson.
*Same.* International Conciliation. 374:683-91. N. '41.

American Scandinavian Review. 27:66-7. Mr. '39. Adventures in peace; excerpts. C. J. Hambro.

American Scholar. n.s. 11, no. 1:275-91. [Jl.] '42. International utopias. Zechariah Chafee, Jr.

Annals of the American Academy. 175:123-32. S. '34. League of Nations and the promotion of world peace. Cromwell A. Riches.

*Annals of the American Academy. 210:57-65. Jl. '40. Peace through international co-operation. Viscount Cecil of Chelwood.

Annals of the American Academy. 222:60-73. Jl. '42. Organization of peace. Francisco Castillo Najera.

Asiatic Review. n.s. 34:817-20. O. '38. The League of Nations and world peace. H. H. The Aga Khan.

Christian Science Monitor Magazine. p. 5+. F. 27, '43. World league to enforce peace. William Hermanns.

Christian Science Monitor Magazine. p. 2+. S. 11, '43. League that didn't fail. Ruth Cranston.

Congressional Record. 85:Appendix 241-3. O. 10, '39. Police powers for the League of Nations. Harry Frease.
*Also separate.* International peace without war. 7p. Government Printing Office. Washington, D.C. '39.

Contemporary Review. 155:44-51. Ja. '39. Future of the League. Sisley Huddleston.

*Contemporary Review. 163:71-7. F. '43. League of Nations; new League must be formed by the United Nations. Luigi Sturzo.
*Same* revised. Commonweal. 37:488-91. Mr. 5, '43. Coming League; shape of a future federation.

Foreign Affairs. 11:66-80. O. '32. League of Nations: successes and failures. Eduard Beneš.

Foreign Affairs. 15:102-11. O. '36. Alternatives before the League. A. Lawrence Lowell.

Foreign Affairs. 20:243-52. Ja. '42. Danubian reconstruction. Otto of Austria.

Fortnightly. 155 (n.s. 149):313-20. Ap. '41. Poland and the new Europe. Tytus Filipowicz.

Forum and Century. 101:108-10. F. '39. Let the League live. Jan C. Smuts.

Harvard Law Review. 38:903-42. My. '25. Amendment of the covenant of the League of Nations. Manley O. Hudson.

Hibbert Journal. 36:501-8. Jl. '38. What India thinks about the League. C. F. Andrews.

International Conciliation. 298:83-90. Mr. '34. League's defenders make answer. Clarence K. Streit.

Living Age. 358:17-21. Mr. '40. What is left of the League; ready for the new order is a great deal of idle and expensive machinery. J. William Terry.

New York Times. p. 6E. D. 7, '41. League still a factor. Herbert S. Houston.

New York Times. p. 22. Ap. 27, '43. Work of the League defended; exception taken to conclusions of Messrs. Hoover and Gibson. C. J. Hambro.

New York Times Magazine. p. 6+. Je. 27, '43. Needed: one American peace plan. Edwin L. James.

People and Freedom (London). no. 43:1. Ja.; 44:1. F.; 45:1. Mr.; 46:3. Ap.; 37:3. My.; 48:sup. Je.; 49:1. Jl. '43. New League of Nations *now*; with discussion. Luigi Sturzo.

Rotarian. 45:12-13+. S. '34. Evaluating the League of Nations; the choice we face is: it or anarchy. Joseph A. Avenol.

Rotarian. 49:11-13. S. '36. What's ahead for the League? Arthur Sweetser.

Rotarian. 55:22-3+. S. '39. League lives—and labors on. Arthur Sweetser.

*Social Science. 18:68-77. Ap. '43. Essentials of international stability. Dell G. Hitchner.

Spectator (London). 162:522. Mr. 31, '39. What failed at Geneva? H. C. A. Gaunt.

Spectator (London). 167:347-8. O. 10, '41. Post-war League.

Spectator (London). 170:375-6. Ap. 23, '43. Post-war structure. Discussion. Spectator. 170:408, 428. Ap. 23, My. 7, '43.

United States News. 15:28-9. O. 1, '43. And so we resolve. David Lawrence.

Vital Speeches of the Day. 6:208-9. Ja. 15, '40. Towards a new world order. P. J. Noel Baker.

Vital Speeches of the Day. 9:370-3. Ap. 1, '43. Lessons from the League of Nations; faults that must be avoided. Felix Morley.

World Affairs. 105:34-6. Mr. '42. Possible reorganization of the League of Natios. Benjamin Gerig.

## REFERENCES FAVORING ALTERNATIVE PLANS

Bonnet, Henri. Outlines of the future world organization emerging from the war. 128p. World Citizens Association. 84 E. Randolph St. Chicago. '43.

*Bonnet, Henri. United Nations: what they are, what they may become. 100p. World Citizens Association. 84 Randolph St. Chicago. '42.

*Byng, Edward J. Five-year peace plan; a schedule for peace building. 184p. Coward-McCann. New York. '43.

*Culbertson, Ely. Summary of the world federation plan. 64p. Garden City Publishing Co. Garden City, N.Y. '43.

Doman, Nicholas. Coming age of world control. 301p. Harper & Bros. New York. '42.

Greaves, H. R. G. Federal union in practice. 135p. George Allen & Unwin. London. '40.

Jaszi, Oscar. Political organization of the future. *In* Toward international organization; a series of lectures at Oberlin College. p. 190-218. Harper & Bros. New York. '42.

MacIver, R. M. Towards an abiding peace. 195p. Macmillan Co. New York. '43.
    Chapter 10, Framework of an international order.

Straight, Michael. Make this the last war; the future of the United Nations. 417p. Harcourt, Brace & Co. New York. '43.

Streit, Clarence K. Federal union of democracies. *In* Hintz, Howard W. and Gebanier, Bernard D. N. Modern American vistas. p. 192-213. Dryden Press. New York. '40.

Streit, Clarence K. Reform of the Covenant is not enough. *In* Problems of peace. Series 11, p. 213-32. George Allen & Unwin. London. '37.

Streit, Clarence K. Union now; the proposal for inter-democracy federal union. 256p. Harper & Bros. New York. '40.

### PERIODICALS

American Federationist. 50:16-17. Je. '43. American postwar policy. Sumner Welles.

American Mercury. 50:276-84. Jl. '40. End of small nations. H. N. Brailsford.

Barron's. 23:5+. Ag. 30, '43. Inside news from Barron's capital reporter. Edson Blair.

Canadian Forum. 20:46-7. My. '40. League and the British Labor party. J. R. Mallory.

Commercial and Financial Chronicle. 158:9+. Jl. 1, '43. Basis for permanent peace and methods of preventing aggression. Forum. James T. Shotwell and others.

Commercial and Financial Chronicle. 158:1020. S. 9, '43. Canadian blue print calls for post-war world organization embracing all nations.

Congressional Record. 89:A1298-9. Mr. 16, '43. Winning the war and planning for the peace; address, March 11, 1943. Harold E. Stassen.

Congressional Record. 89:A2421. My. 7, '43. United States federal union is proposed as model for world organization. Clarence K. Streit.

Congressional Record. 89·A3599-601. Je. 30, '43. Fulbright resolution. William P. Elmer.

Congressional Record. 89:A3829-30. Jl. 7, '43. Federal union. John Schmidt.

Congressional Record. 89:A3850-2. Jl. 7, '43. Post-war idealism. Paul W. Shafer.

Congressional Record. 89:A4203-4. S. 21, '43. Participation in world peace. Melvin J. Maas.

Congressional Record. 89:7917-19. S. 27, '43. Peace we hope for. Carl Hinshaw.

Congressional Record. 89:A4384. S. 29, '43. Post-war government. W. L. Gleeson.

Congressional Record. 89:A4393-4. S. 30, '43. Post-war foreign policy. Joseph H. Ball.

Debaters' Digest. 17:1-10, 11-24, 25-8, 29-32. Ja.-Ap. '43. Federal world government; briefs. William R. Foulkes, ed.

Foreign Policy Reports. 18:94-108. Jl. 1, '42. Machinery of collaboration between the United Nations. Payson S. Wild, jr.

*Free World. 3:78-82. Je. '42. Power in international government. Egon Ranshofen-Wertheimer.

Free World. 5:297-301. Ap. '43. Some problems of the post-war world. Bertrand Russell.

Frontiers of Democracy. 9:108-11. Ja. 15, '43. Some plans in detail; federal union to win the peace. Brice Toole.

International Conciliation. 386:21-4. Ja. '43. Official Soviet theoretical statement on the League of Nations, Moscow, 1926.

National Review. 119:201-2. S. '42. Cloven hoof peeps out; League of Nations annual report.

New Statesman and Nation. 17:858, 895. Je. 3-10, '39. Federalism of the League. Lancelot Hogben; reply: W. E. Lucas.

New Statesman and Nation. 19:741. Je. 15, '40. Death of the League of Nations.

New York Herald Tribune. Sec. 2. p. 4. S. 12, '43. World ahead: public support is seen for permanent U.S.-British alliance. Emmet Crozier.

New York Times. p. 14. S. 7, '43. Address at Harvard; text. Winston Churchill.
    *Abridged.* Commercial and Financial Chronicle. 158:1015. S. 9, '43. Churchill urges post-war alliance between U.S. and Britain for world peace.

Nineteenth Century. 119:715-21. Je. '36. Ethical case against the League of Nations. Oliver E. Bodington.

Rotarian. 45:14-15+. S. '34. Evaluating the League of Nations; a good forum—but impotent. William R. Castle, jr.

Rotarian. 49:6-10. S. '36. What's ahead for the League? H. G. Wells.

*Rotarian. 60:8-12. Mr. '42. Shall the next peace also fail? Norman Angell.
    *Same slightly condensed.* Case, Leland D., ed. World to live in. p. 57-61. Rotary International. 35 E. Wacker Dr. Chicago.

Saturday Evening Post. 215:20-1+. Ap. 10, '43. Roosevelt's world blueprint. Forrest Davis.

Social Science. 13:208-15. Jl. '38. League of Nations—what it is today. Joseph Slabey Roucek.

United States News. 15:18-19. S. 17, '43. Britain as a partner for U.S.: how postwar union would work.

Vital Speeches of the Day. 9:318-20. Mr. 1, '43. World affairs; proposal for a definite United Nations government. Harold E. Stassen.

Vital Speeches of the Day. 9:720-2. S. 15, '43. Some wrong roads to peace. Norman Thomas.

Yale Review. n.s. 31, no. 3:433-53. [Mr.] '42. Making democracy safe in the world. Carl L. Becker.

# University Debaters' Annuals

## E. M. PHELPS, Ed. *Cloth. Price* $2.25

Series of year books, each a collection of representative intercollegiate debates on important questions of the day. Constructive and rebuttal speeches for both sides. Each debate is accompanied by selected bibliography and briefs.